NATIONS OF THE MODERN WORLD

ENGLAND
The Very Rev. Dr. W. R. Inge, K.C.V.O., F.B.A., D.D.

SCOTLAND
Sir Robert Rait, C.B.E., M.A., LL.D., and George S. Pryde, M.A., Ph.D.
Revised by G. S. Pryde
Reader in Scottish History and Literature, Glasgow University

AUSTRALIA
J. C. Horsfall
First Editor of the AUSTRALIAN FINAN-CIAL REVIEW

FRANCE
P. E. Charvet
Fellow of Corpus Christi College, and Lecturer in French in the University of Cambridge

MODERN INDIA
Sir Percival Griffiths, C.I.E., I.C.S. (Ret.)
Honorary adviser to India, Pakistan and Burma Association

ISRAEL
Norman Bentwich, O.B.E., M.C., LL.D. (Hon.)
Professor of International Relations, Hebrew University of Jerusalem

ITALY
Gerardo Zampaglione
Italian Diplomatic Corps

PORTUGAL
J. B. Trend, Litt.D.,
Fellow of Christ's College, and Emeritus Professor of Spanish in the University of Cambridge

SA'UDI ARABIA   H. St. John Philby, C.I.E., F.R.G.S.
Economic Adviser to the late King Abdul-Aziz II Ib'n Saud

SOUTH AFRICA   J. H. Hofmeyr, B.A., B.Sc.
Revised by J. P. Cope
Editor-in-Chief of THE FORUM

THE SUDAN   Sir Harold MacMichael, K.C.M.G., D.S.O.
One time Civil Secretary to Sudan Government, and Governor-General

SYRIA AND LEBANON   Nicola A. Ziadeh, B.A. (Hons.), Ph.D.
Associate Professor of Modern History, American University, Beirut

TURKEY   Geoffrey Lewis, M.A., D.Phil. (Oxon.)
Senior lecturer in Islamic Studies, Oxford

PORTUGAL

PORTUGAL

By

J. B. TREND, Litt.D.

Fellow of Christ's College, Cambridge

LONDON
ERNEST BENN LIMITED

First published 1957 by Ernest Benn Limited
Bouverie House · Fleet Street · London · EC4
© J. B. Trend 1957
Printed in Great Britain

Contents

Preface   ix

1   Ancient History   13

2   Suevi and Visigoths   23

3   Moslems and Mozárabes   42

4   The Reconquest and the Reconquered   57

5   Farms, Fruit, Fairs and Fish   77

6   Dom Denis and the Pine Forest   98

7   The Revolution of 1383   114

8   Discovery and Pepper   130

9   The Age of Camoens   143

10   The Restoration, Methuen, Pombal   158

11   The Nineteenth Century and the Twentieth   175

12   The Language   196

Index   211

MAP

Portugal   *facing page* 210

FOR
EVELYNE BENOIT CONTREIRAS

Preface

ONE OF the great lessons of Portugal to a battered world is good manners. I may be forgiven, therefore, for not parading in a preface the names of all those whose writings have helped me, or the friends who have lent me books and periodicals from private libraries. Forty years ago the Spanish novelist Pío Baroja complained that in his country there were no facilities for doing anything. Over a large part of the world, that condition has now become general, at least for unofficial persons; but Portugal has been, so far as I am concerned, an exception.

It is an old-fashioned idea of Portuguese history, but one which has not entirely disappeared, to confine it to the praise of famous men and startling events, royal princes and royal mistresses, like a gallery of portraits and battle-pieces in some former royal residence. But there are also such things as medieval institutions: occupation of land and what people did there, how they were spread over the country and tried to make a living, how they developed a collective spirit and an idea of belonging to a particular place; and again how the king tried to prevent them from quarrelling and did rough justice, though what most occupied him was calling them up for military service and collecting taxes to pay for his wars.

Not that one would deny the part which individual creation has played in Portuguese history: how Afonso Henriques carved out a kingdom, and then had trouble to control the blacksmiths and bakers in his mud-hutted capital of Coimbra; how the Master of Avis preserved the country's independence and married Philippa of Lancaster, daughter of John of Gaunt, but only after he had been screwed up to revolt by a gouty ex-chancellor and made to commit murder – a thing which (the chronicler implies) was repugnant to the Master of a religious order, even when done on the Queen-Regent's Spanish lover; what the great sea-captains did with the maps and nautical

instruments provided for them by Henry the Navigator, and
the pepper out of which they and the colonial officials made
their fortunes – when the overloaded ships managed to make
Lisbon without sinking; Albuquerque, who founded, at Goa, a
people of Eurasians still passionately devoted to Portugal; King
Sebastian, who lost his life on a magnificently muddled expedition to Morocco, and the messianically-minded folk who, when
the Spaniards came in with Philip II, refused to believe that
Dom Sebastian was dead and looked for his second coming to
deliver them from the exactions of Olivares. Then there was
Pombal, the great administrator, the one man who kept his
head after the earthquake of 1755 and began to build the new
Lisbon which we see to-day; Serpa Pinto, the much-enduring
explorer who crossed Africa from sea to sea; Mousinho de
Albuquerque, the dashing cavalry-officer who saved Mozambique almost single-handed, by arresting a gigantic African chief
in his own kraal, under the noses of his astonished guards with
their European rifles; Gago Coutinho and Sacadura Cabral,
who, with a new navigating instrument, first flew the South
Atlantic to Brazil. . . .

These are, or should be, in all the books, the fullest and most
modern of which is the *History of Portugal* (1947) by Mr H. V.
Livermore, to whom the Portuguese Government very properly
awarded a prize, and the most recent, the *History of Portugal* by
Professor C. E. Nowell (1953), which has been translated into
several languages. But even Camoens, the University poet and
shipwrecked sailor who made the first half of the story into an
epic, sang of arms and the *men*, not arms and the *man*. So it may
be allowable to write of the anonymous men and women of
Portugal, who, in its grim moments and in its great ones, have
kept the country going; though their portraits were seldom
painted except when they were called in unexpectedly, like the
horny-handed fishermen who brought their net with them to
the family group of the children of Philippa of Lancaster.

The origins of modern Portugal are to be looked for in men
of all conditions. The Portuguese people came of age, and
first expressed themselves as a nation, in the movement which
brought in the Master of Avis. Till then, the country had been
an aggregate of separate regions, towns, classes, with interests
that were isolated, separate and often contradictory. The

change of dynasty was the work of merchants and sailors, with a clever lawyer to get round the dictatorial minorities, and an alert soldier with the wit to try out the new English tactics in a small affair of patrols, before the day came when he threw in all his men and kept them steady, though dismounted, against waves of mounted men-at-arms. The victory of Aljubarrota led on to the period when the whole country seemed to be dominated by the desire to do something overseas – a feeling which, as we saw, Camoens lit up in a flash when he made the hero of his epic the whole nation. There are many more reasons for the existence of Portugal, some of which will be examined in the first chapter; but the most convincing, perhaps, is the least scientific: Portugal exists because the inhabitants want it.

Whenever possible, I have tried to give a Portuguese point of view, rather than a foreign one; and I have quoted Portuguese writers liberally in my efforts to do so. References will be found in the notes.

Chapter 1

Ancient History

1

THE COUNTRY which was afterwards to be known as Portugal was not discovered by the Romans in the way that the coasts of Africa, India and Brazil were discovered by the Portuguese. The pioneers were Phœnicians – and perhaps also Mycenæan Greeks – who had sailed from the back of the Mediterranean out into the Atlantic and up the Portuguese coast, though unlike the later Portuguese in pursuit of pepper they were in search of tin. Portugal was on the way to Galicia, Brittany and Cornwall, the places where tin was found – the tin which was alloyed with copper to make bronze; but the voyages were so long that they led to the idea that Lisbon (Ulyssipona) had originally been founded by wise Ulysses, and for that reason an old Spanish writer could say that the Portuguese, whatever else they were, were never stupid.[1]

2

We may wonder now what geographical reasons could account for the formation of a separate state in the west of the Peninsula. To the Visigoths, the Trastamaras, the Hapsburgs – as to some hot-heads in Madrid in recent times – there seemed no good reason: no cause to justify any political division of the Peninsula at all. That polygonal mass, shaped roughly like a pentagon – so clearly separated from the rest of Europe by the Pyrenees and so narrowly cut off from Africa by the Straits of Gibraltar – seems geologically formed for unity: the intermediary between two seas and two continents.

Considered more closely, this judgement is shown to be superficial. Even a tidy-minded civil servant like Philip II found it unworkable; and when it came to practical administration the Romans were right: Hispania was not one province but several. Only worldly adventurers or unworldly theologians could hope to govern the coastal regions – whether level plains or tumbled

mountains – from the fortress of the central plateau. The population of fishermen and sailors, fruit-growers and foresters, were
too unlike the migratory shepherds up above. It was the old
contest between the Centaurs and the Lapithæ, Cain and Abel;
and in the west at any rate, in Portugal though not in the north
(Biscay) or the east (Catalonia), the sedentary Lapithæ have
won. The Peninsula is slightly tilted towards the west; there is
more room, the slopes are more gradual than they are in the
Basque or Catalan country; and it is Portugal which offers
the greatest number of distinctive characters in relation to the
central plateau and enjoys the greatest contact with the ocean.

Portugal and Spain have been compared to Norway and
Sweden,[2] Norway being distinguished by its sea-fishing and
forest-clad mountains, with something like an arctic desert
separating it from Sweden. The Swedes may be the Castilians
of the north, but Sweden does not compare well with Castille;
with its mines, its forests, its industry and its water-power, it is
more like the Basque Provinces, but gives the impression of
having agreed to differ from its neighbour in mild amusement
rather than actively oppose it. Again, Portugal has little of the
terrifying coast-line of Norway. Like England, it offers distinct
advantages to men of maritime occupations. The sea is shallow;
and the fact that a branch of the Gulf Stream runs along the
coast allows water of different temperatures to mix, and produce
a condition admirably suited to certain kinds of fish, notably
sardines and tunny.

Modern Portugal is about 350 miles long and, on an average,
100 miles wide: the width varies from 136 miles in the north to
70 miles in the south. The frontiers are partly formed by big
rivers: Minho and Douro in the north, Guadiana in the south.
The relief is broken into rough, uneven fragments, and almost
all the topographical features are due to abrupt transitions between plateaux of different altitudes: high, dry land with considerable differences of level. It is a mountainous country in the
north. In the south the vast central Castilian plain drops down
to the sea more gradually. On the east the climate is that of
central Spain, with extremes of heat and cold; while on the
west it is softened by the Atlantic. The coasts have been compared to those of Morocco: massive bluffs, like Cape Espichel
or Cape St Vincent, or else sand dunes; but there are few inlets

except those of the Tagus, the Sado and the *foz* (mouth) of the Douro.

In medieval times the few estuaries were deeper, and there were many others which have since silted up. A greater proportion of the population could live by sea-fishing; and river-fishing, too, would have been more productive. As a rule maritime peoples begin by fishing and exchanging fish; then they take to the coasting trade, and exchange fish and salt for other products with other peoples. This is what happened in Portugal.

But Portugal was in the beginning, and remained to the end of the fifteenth century, one vast forest, broken here and there by small country towns and villages surrounded by strips of cultivation. A little clearing here, and you could pasture sheep or goats; another clearing, and you could grow cereals of some sort: rye, oats or millet, to be ground in hand-mills by women, like the women forever grinding maize in Mexico to make tortillas.

3

After the cave-dwellers of Neolithic times – farmers and herdsmen who cultivated olives as well as cereals [3] – came a time of 'shifting cultivation' based on 'slash and burn'. Small clearings in the continuous forest would have been opened up by fire; and after the fire had burnt itself out, small plots would be cleared and tilled, probably with hoes.

The first settlements in the north were the hill-villages, *citânias* or *castros*; rocky islands in a sea of virgin forest. Scattered everywhere were blocks of granite which served for building huts or loose stone walls, to keep off enemies or wild animals. There were flints to make implements and, later, metals were discovered and mined. A more stable system of farming was gradually introduced, with ploughing. Exhausted fields would be invaded by herbaceous plants and grasses, and become pasture for sheep; their droppings would help to restore the fertility of the soil. Once rotation was established, there was a possibility of permanent settlement. The inhabitants of the hill-villages seem – to an economic historian [4] – to have been reasonably happy. The climate was pleasant, food abundant and the first necessities of life easily procured. The danger, which spoilt everything, was the danger of war. The inhabitants of *castros* had to live together in small groups behind walls; and their settlements had to be on heights so that they could watch the movements of their neighbours, in other *castros*, from a long distance. They took care that their own *castro* was difficult of approach, with steep slopes which were almost inaccessible.

Particular types of archæological finds make it possible to divide *castros* into pre-Roman and Lusitano-Roman. In reality, all were probably of pre-Roman origin, dating from about three centuries before our era, though some would have been abandoned before the Roman occupation, while others have undergone Romanisation to a high degree. Among the latter is Conimbriga, not far from Coimbra, where the Romans left the comforts and refinements of a considerable town: palaces with colonnades, mosaic pavements, baths and heating. At Citânia de Briteiros, however – farther north and about 10 miles from Guimarães – the signs of Roman influence are less evident, and native culture has not been supplanted to anything like the same extent. There are circular stone huts, enclosed within three circuits of ramparts, with a thin veneer of Romanisation which never seems to have been very deep. Both Conimbriga and Citânia de Briteiros probably had the same beginnings in a remote past: though one was better situated, or had richer soil, or came to have closer connexion with the outer world through the Roman roads. But at Castro de Sabroso, a mile or so from Briteiros, there are no signs of Roman culture at all, and it may have been abandoned before the Roman occupation began.

The more ancient *castros* are those where objects of the Neolithic and Bronze Ages have been found. A sure sign of Roman occupation is an inscription in Latin, which gradually came into use instead of the primitive languages. There are earlier inscriptions, in characters which still have not yet been deciphered. Others, of the first and second centuries A.D., are in Roman letters, but include words in an unknown language, like the rock-inscription to be seen near Castro Daire. The letters often have unaccustomed shapes, and the native gods have strange names, like Endovelicus, Bormanicus, Tongoenabigus, Durbedicus, Tameobrigo, Ilurbeda.

South of the Tagus – and indeed south of Vouga (VACUA), the next river below the Douro – right down to the beaches of the Algarve on the south coast, conditions were originally much the same as in the north. The Algarve was covered with trees, but not so well-wooded as the north; the hill-tops were lower and farther apart. The population lived in pleasant conditions, generally established in the open country and easy of access. Before the cattle came on to the plains beyond the Tagus, the Alentejo was wooded too. From the visits of Phœnician and Punic traders the inhabitants had their first lessons in commerce; saw how ships were sailed, how harbours were chosen and built and how precious metals were got out of the earth.

4

The country had first attracted the attention of Roman writers through revolts and brigandage. During the Punic wars and the menace of Hannibal it had been necessary, for military reasons, for the Romans to occupy the Peninsula; and economic reasons were soon added through the richness of the Spanish mines. Portugal, or a great part of what Portugal is to-day, became part of the Roman world, though on the extreme edge of it: those western beaches from which, Strabo said, you could hear the sun sink into the sea with a sizzle; but the military expeditions sent to subdue it and make it safe for trade cost the Romans a great deal of money. The gold which was supposed to lie in the sands of the Tagus found its way into poetry more easily than into the Aerarium, the Treasury of Rome.

When history begins and Portugal enters the modern world, it is with a contrast between the north, inhabited by wild herdsmen from the *castros*, and the south, already to a certain extent acquainted with the town ways and country life of the Mediterranean. The Roman occupation smoothed away some of these differences; but the southern regions show by their archæological remains that at this time they were more civilised than the north.

The northern Lusitanians are mentioned in 194 B.C. as enemies of Rome. They were part of those mainly Celtic and not Iberian peoples who had built the fortified hill-villages, and were descended from those who had arrived in two principal waves of migration [5] and established themselves first between the Tagus and the Guadiana; [6] they lived, it was said, by stealing one another's sheep. Little is known of them beyond their

military exploits, and that they threw criminals down from
the rocks and stoned parricides. The Romans were 'gravely
vexed by the Lusitanians'. The terror of their attacks, creeping
up silently, unobserved, was not less than that of other inhabitants of the Peninsula, and lasted down to the time of Virgil,
towards the end of the next century. Never, he says in the
Georgics, with guards like these (i.e. good sheep-dogs), will you
fear the thief by night or attack by wolves, 'or the unpacified
Iberians creeping up from behind you'.[7]

Viriathus, their great guerrilla leader, is first mentioned in
150 B.C. 'Ouriatthus' Appian spells him in Greek; but in Latin
writers he is Viriathus, the man with the bracelets, as Tor-
quatus is the man with the necklaces or torques. Torques and
bracelets were characteristic of the Celts, and have been frequently found in Lusitania and Galicia, generally of gold or
bronze. Viriathus, according to Livy and the later historian
Orosius, was originally a shepherd; then he became a hunter,
and from a hunter a brigand, infesting the roads, wasting provinces and at last overcoming and putting to flight large armies
commanded by prætors and consuls. His favourite tactical
move was a pretended flight, by which he defeated a prætorian
army of between 10,000 and 15,000 men, and drove the Romans
back to the towns, where they stayed 'wintering' in the height of
summer while Viriathus went on with his depredations. Placed
in command of all their armed bands, he occupied the whole
of Lusitania. Orosius adds details of his appearance: as commander in the field he wore a toga with purple stripes, the
TRABEA, a Roman distinction of high employment. He had the
FASCES carried before him,[8] and Silius Italicus describes his
wedding and the ostentation of his father-in-law, Istolpas.

The Lusitani, in 141–140 B.C., were described as wild men
who went bareheaded with their hair flying in the wind. They
fled when the Romans brought up elephants; but Viriathus,
by one of his feigned retreats, turned the tables and the Romans
lost heavily. Eventually he offered peace – probably from utter
weariness of war. The story goes that, in order to arrange the
terms, Viriathus sent his three best friends; but the Romans
bribed them, and on their return they murdered him in his
sleep. Appian describes the despair of the Lusitanians when they
discovered that their leader was dead; but they gave him a

grand funeral, burning his body and performing military exercises round the pyre.

After the death of Viriathus, the Lusitanians began their raids over again; but the new Roman general, Junius Brutus, was too clever for them. He did not follow them into the hills, but attacked their villages and caught the Lusitanians when they came down to save their possessions. Their women fought too, and died in battle. The Lusitanian herdsmen had been fighting for their independence, and to avenge the perfidy and massacres of the Roman general, Galba; but Viriathus' soldiers were given land, in some places, as soon as they were conquered; for the transformation of herdsmen into cultivators was part of the regular Roman policy of pacification.

The Romans advanced to a river which they called 'Lethe' – probably the Limia – the 'River of Forgetfulness', FLUMEN OBLIVIONIS, Livy calls it – and one which the troops crossed unwillingly. They reached the country of the Braccari, whose name lives on in the modern Braga; and then turned south against the Vaccei and the 'Island of Morona', which may be the modern Almourol (the original name having picked up the Arabic article al-), where there is a charming medieval castle on an island in the Tagus at the junction with the river Zêzere. Their base for supplies, by that time, was down the river at Ulyssipona (Lisbon), and the campaign against the people of the *castros* was as good as over.

The most important source of information for the social development of the population of northern Portugal is an inscription recording the renewal of a pact of hospitality between two clans, the Desonci and the Tridiavi, in A.D. 27.[9] It was probably pre-Roman, but still valid, now that they no longer went on living among their wild rocks and inaccessible heights, and had been persuaded to come down into the plains and submit to the law and discipline of Rome, to give up pillage and become peaceable and law-abiding farmers.

Roman roads connected Lisbon with the north and the south; they were really branches of the great north–south main road, now in Spain, which ran from Astorga through Salamanca, Cáceres and Mérida to Seville. A road ending at the mouth of the Guadiana in the south ran through Alcácer (SALACIA), Beja (PAX JULIA) and Mértola (MYRTILIS) to Castro

Marim (BÆSURIS). The other main road ran northwards to
Braga (BRACCARA AUGUSTA) through Santarém (SCALABIS),
Condeixa-a-Velha (CONIMBRIGA), Coimbra (ÆMINIUM), a van-
ished port near Aveiro (TALABRIGA) and Oporto (PORTUS
CALE). From Braga, roads went northwards again to Tuy
(TUDE) and Lugo (LUCUS) in Galicia, afterwards bending east
in the direction of Astorga (ASTURICA AUGUSTA). In the south,
also, there were roads connecting the coasts and rivers with
Mérida (EMERITA AUGUSTA); a road from Mérida joined the
Tagus at Santarém and followed the right bank to Lisbon,
while a lower road connected Évora, Alcácer do Sal and a point
opposite Lisbon on the south bank. The Roman roads generally
united the river-ports; and it was along the roads, and at the
meeting-places of road and river, that there grew up the towns
of importance in Roman and medieval times.

The creation of Roman provinces completed the plan of the
roads in Iberia. Under Augustus there were three: TARRA-
CONENSIS, BÆTICA and LUSITANIA; and though these were varied
and increased as time went on, their administrative divisions
(CONVENTÛS) remained approximately the same. The western
part of the Peninsula had four, joined by the north–south road:
PACENSIS and SCALABITANUS belonging to the province of Lusitania, and BRACCARENSIS and LUCENSIS to Callæcia. The eastern
boundary of the first three of these corresponded almost exactly
with the present Spanish frontier; it was a natural, geographical
boundary which, in process of time, became a linguistic and
social one. The Christian dioceses of later times followed closely
the divisions of the CONVENTÛS; so that one of the reasons for the
gradual differentiation was due to the territorial, 'conventual'
divisions introduced by the Romans, and the close communication between the four CONVENTÛS maintained by the Roman
roads.

5

Through all that part of the country which the Romans
civilised in the time of Augustus and later, and especially in the
north-west when the road was made from Astorga to Braga,
there were few great natural difficulties to be overcome. The
Romans did not undertake vast works of irrigation, but they
taught the inhabitants a better use of the plough and harrow,

to carry their produce in wooden carts with movable axles, to divide their land with loose stone walls, or hedges, or marked stones; and to grow beans, peas, lentils, chick-peas, flax, vines and olives; pears, plums, walnuts, figs, cherries, quinces, almonds, mulberries; and to make wine and olive oil.[10] That is a long list of good things to be attributed to the Roman occupation; and if the Romans compelled the natives to work in the mines of Aljustrel and to make paved roads, they also built stone houses, aqueducts, temples like the one at Évora, and bridges like the one with sixteen arches at Chaves.[11] Roman imperial administration took mining in hand and issued written regulations to govern it. An inscription found at Aljustrel shows that the Roman customs were not unlike the customs of medieval mining communities in the twelfth and thirteenth centuries, particularly in the division of interests between the landowner and the occupiers of the pits.[12] To the Romans (as we saw) Lusitania began by being one of the outer defences of Hispania Ulterior, 'Further Spain', occupied – not without prolonged resistance – and eventually becoming a Roman province with frontiers on the DURIUS (Douro) in the north and the ANAS (Guadiana) in the south, and in the east on a line drawn roughly from Salamanca to Talavera in modern Spain. Lusitania came to include, in fact, almost all Portugal, with parts of León, Castille and Spanish Estremadura. Its chief town was the Roman colony of EMERITA AUGUSTA (Mérida, now in Spain), built in a waterless desert with three aqueducts of its own, to show what the Roman Empire could do.

In 180 B.C. the Lusitani were once more in revolt against Rome, and sent envoys to Sertorius in North Africa. Sertorius had formerly been Roman proconsul in Spain, but had been deprived of his command by Sulla. His return from Africa was the beginning of an extraordinary adventure in which, for eight years, he repeatedly led the Lusitanians to victory against the legions sent from Rome. But he still considered himself to be the true representative of Rome in the Peninsula and conducted his administration on Roman lines, with his capital probably at Évora, until at last he fell before an assassin in 72. Viriathus is a legend; but Sertorius, with Marius and Sulla, belongs to the history of Rome.

NOTES TO CHAPTER 1

(English books, except where otherwise stated, are published in London, French in Paris and Portuguese in Lisbon.)

[1] Porque jamás se halló portugués necio, en prueba de que fué fundador el sagaz Ulises. Gracián, *El Criticón*, 1ʳᵃ parte, crisi 10, and 3ʳᵃ parte, crisi 8.

[2] J. Brunhes et C. Vallaux, *La géographie et l'histoire* (1921) 291 ff., and, in general for this section, Jaime Cortesão, ch. I of *História do Régimen Republicano em Portugal*, edited by Luís de Montalvor (1930), I, 1–36.

[3] V. Gordon Childe, in *The European Inheritance* (Oxford, 1943), I, v, 56. The geography and history of the peripheral regions in relation to the central plateau are clearly demonstrated by F. Soldevila, *Historia de España*, I (Barcelona, 1952).

[4] E. de Campos, *Problemas fundamentais portugueses* (1946).

[5] See, for instance, P. Bosch Gimpera, *La formación de los pueblos de España*. (Mexico, 1945), 76–82; *El pueblo indígena de Portugal*, and Los Iberos, in *Cuadernos de Historia de España*, IX (Buenos Aires, 1948). He takes the view that the Iberians were African in origin. J. Caro Baroja, however, *Los pueblos de España* (Barcelona, 1946), does not believe them to have been African at all. See the summary in L. Pericot, *L'Espagne avant la conquête romaine*. French translation (1952).

One of the facts that stand out most clearly is the division and subdivision of the various tribes. The first travellers and geographers were impressed by this; see A. Schulten, *Hispania*, Spanish translation of the article in Pauly-Wissowa, *Realencyclopädie der klassischen Altertumswissenschaft* (Barcelona, 1920), 120–121.

[6] Guadiana: Wadi-Anas, a typical Peninsular place-name, half Arabic and half prehistoric.

[7] *Georgics*, III, 408: AUT IMPACATOS A TERGO HORREBIS HIBEROS.

[8] *Fontes Hispaniæ Antiquæ*, ed. A. Schulten (Barcelona, 1935, III, 145 and IV, 98, 1937.

[9] Hübner, *Corpus Inscr. Lat.*, II, 2, 633, p. 366; and Joaquim de Carvalho, 'A cultura castreja: sua interpretação sociológica,' in *Rev. Occidente*, 50 (1956).

[10] A. Arala Pinto, *O Pinhal do Rei* (Alcobaça, 1938), II, 40.

[11] E. J. Wiseman, *Roman Spain . . . and Portugal* (1956), 178. The best preserved Roman bridge in Portugal is at Vila Formosa, where the military road from Mérida to Lisbon crosses the river Sêda on six arches. A recent authority however considers the bridge to be Moslem; Mário Saa, *As grandes vias de Lusitania* (1956), I, 285.

[12] *Cambridge Economic History of Europe*, II, 452.

Chapter 2

Suevi and Visigoths

I

THE THREAT of Germanic invasion, the rumour that the wandering tribes were actually on the way and coming down the Roman road, is nowhere more vividly brought home than on the site of Conimbriga, 10 miles from the University town of Coimbra. That early settlement, with its Celtic name and its Roman remains, had begun to rebuild its walls; But either because the population had declined, or because there was neither time nor labour to build a new wall long enough to enclose the whole town, many villas and other fine buildings had to be left outside, with their marbles, their statues and their tessellated pavements, for the invaders to do with them what they liked.

The invasions began in the fifth century, with the Alans, Vandals, Suevi and Visigoths. Of these, only the last two, the Suevi and the Visigoths, played a part of any importance in the history of Portugal. The Suevi are first heard of in the Commentaries of Julius Cæsar. They were warlike and organised on a war basis, wore few clothes and those mostly skins, washed in rivers and could stand extreme cold. They were good horsemen, but fought dismounted. Pliny describes them as West Germans, though their original home seems to have been the Havel and Spree country near Berlin. At first the Suevi had no private property. All land was 'folk-land' belonging to the community and was let by the community to individuals, for farming. Like the other wandering peoples of Germanic stock, the Suevi lived in temporary houses made of wood, which they took down and packed on carts.

The great trek across Europe began in 405 or 406, more than 400 years after the observations of Julius Cæsar. The Suevi crossed the Elbe, and reached the Main, where they were joined by the Alans and Vandals, with whom they crossed the Rhine while it was frozen over in the winter of 406. By 409 they had passed the Pyrenees. Their appearance in Portugal was described by Hydatius (Idacio), who was an eye-witness.[1] In 411 they made a treaty with the Emperor Honorius, by whom they were regarded legally as allies, FOEDERATI (the origin of our word 'federated') and received grants of land taken from the earlier inhabitants. The wanderings of the Suevi had taken them – probably by chance – to Gallæcia, the province which included, besides the modern Galicia, the Spanish Asturias and León, and the north of Portugal down to the Douro. After passing the Pyrenees by the Roman road through Roncesvalles, they took the turning to the right which led to Asturias. They appeared to Hydatius and other Romans in the Peninsula as they had to Julius Cæsar: a collection of tribes, with no great unity between one tribe and another; and the Roman inhabitants were puzzled to find that, like the Spartans of old, they sometimes seemed to have two 'kings' at the same time. South of the Douro, Lusitania was invaded by tribes of different origin: the Vandals and the Alans. The former seem to have come originally from central Sweden. The latter were an Iranian people from the Caucasus; but it would be as rash to see a survival of their name in the town of Alenquer, as it is to find the name Vandal in (V)Andalucía.

The settlement made with these unwelcome guests was upset by the Visigothic King Wallia, who came in the name of the Roman Emperor to deliver the Peninsula from the other tribes and occupy it for himself; his price was 600,000 bushels of wheat.[2] It was then, probably, that the greatest destruction began: the kind of destruction associated with the Vandals – vandalism – but inevitable in any attempt at reconquest, then or now. There is a record of their retreat from Oporto, Lisbon and Faro in 419 before a Roman army under Count Asterius, after which the surviving Vandals and Alans crossed the Straits of Gibraltar from Tarifa.[3]

The Suevi were left in the north-west of the Peninsula. The expression *tipo suevo*, for a noble and manly type of hidalgo, has become proverbial in Spain, like the phrase *tipo visigodo* for a fair and beautiful woman.[4] Many of them became cattle-men or farmers, or treated their kingdom as a centre for raiding their neighbours, while their women worked on the land. At last the Visigoths retaliated with a raid from the Pyrenees as far west as

Astorga,[5] routed a large force of Suevi, and advanced to their chief town, Braga, where there was a cathedral and where the Suevic king Rechiar had minted coins bearing the image and superscription of the Emperor Honorius. Braga was sacked, and Rechiar fled in the direction of Portus Cale (Oporto), the place from which modern Portugal takes its name. Here he was eventually captured and killed.

Hydatius was particularly shocked by the behaviour of the Visigoths. Like other Hispano-Roman Christians, he was a helpless spectator of the battles of barbarians who were either pagans or heretics; they showed no respect for virgins, who were abducted (though often returned intact), or for the clergy, who were driven out indecently clothed, while churches were converted into stables and pigsties.[6] Yet he was something more than the irate chronicler of barbarian excesses, for he introduced into his history a practical system of chronology, the Spanish Era.

The system usual at the time of the Germanic invasions attempted to determine the date by the year of each Emperor; St Jerome had also reckoned by the years of the Olympiads. The new system dated events by the Era of Augustus, which was considered to have begun thirty-eight years before the birth of Christ, and by the third century the date of the Era appears in inscriptions from Cantabria, and by the end of the fourth it had spread to Lusitania, Bætica and Gallæcia. The date of the Hispanic Era was believed to be the date of the tribute imposed on all countries in the Empire by Augustus. According to the explanation of Isidore of Seville, the word *era* was derived from AES, 'money', pl. AERA, 'tribute'; and the initial year, B.C. 38, was afterwards used in Spain and Portugal in the belief that it was the date of the Roman pacification of the Peninsula, with the submission of the Cantabri and Astures, or with the establishment in Hispania of the government of Augustus. Hydatius, by adopting the *era* as a fixed point, helped to introduce a clearer idea of chronology; but Dionysius Exiguus, in Rome, proposed another fixed point, the birth of Christ, and ANNO DOMINI, 'in the year of the Lord', became general through the work of Bede in England and the chroniclers of the Carolingians, while the era continued in use in Portugal until 1422, when it was changed to A.D. by decree of John I.

The Suevi had at first been pagans and then Arians, heretical Christians like the Visigoths. 'The barbarians', it was said, were 'amazed at the eloquence of the Latin clergy', though they preferred the simpler Arian teaching to the more subtle theology of the Catholics. They were only converted 100 years later by St Martin of Braga, at the time of the Council there, in 561. The apostle of the Suevi was by birth a Pannonian from what is now Hungary; [7] his favourite author was Seneca. His books, *De Officiis* and *De Ira*, are full of Senecan reminiscences, while *De Correctione Rusticorum* [8] is a disarming work in which the pros and cons of Christianity are put before country people in the north-west corner of the Peninsula. 'The heathen gods are the devils who fell with Lucifer: therefore all observances which entail any show of reverence towards them are so many denials of the profession of faith you made at baptism.' He condemned the pagan names for the days of the week; [9] and in Portugal, unlike the rest of Europe except Greece, these views ultimately prevailed. In Portuguese – and modern Greek – you do not talk of Moon day, Mars day, Mercury day and so on, but Second, Third and Fourth, adding the word *feira*, fair or fair-day. St Martin also deplored the pagan celebration of the first of January as New Year's Day; he disliked the observance of 'days of moths and mice', the object of which was to protect clothes and store-rooms from their ravages. He told women that they should not invoke the name of Minerva when they sat down to spin or weave, or light candles by rocks and springs. These are INDICULI SUPERSTITIONUM, indications of the superstitious practices – and incidentally of familiar customs – which are condemned later in the canons of Church councils; while again and again he asks the question: 'Is this consistent with your promise at the font to renounce the devil and all his works?' St Martin of Braga also wrote a pleasant set of Latin elegiac verses for the refectory of his monastery at Dume, a suburb of Braga; they are printed by José Vives in his book of Roman and Christian inscriptions; and it is interesting to find him using a colloquial word, thinly latinised (*gavessas*) for 'plates'. Again, like the Spanish–Roman poet Martial, he spells 'living' and 'drinking' in the same way: *bibas* for VIVAS.

Hydatius remarks that the defeat of the Suevi at Braga meant that their realm was 'destroyed and finished'; but his joy was premature. Some of them had escaped to the mountains of Gallæcia, which the Goths had not yet reached; and his history admits many more raids, one of which reached AQUÆ FLAVIÆ (Chaves), where the historian himself was arrested and put in prison. After three months the Goths, to their great credit, procured his release. Hydatius' history ends in 468, and nothing is heard of the Suevi for seventy years, when a chief called Chararicus became a Catholic in the hope that his son might recover from an illness if he did so. The son recovered, and under the name of Theudemirus (or Ariamirus) became king in 559 and converted his unruly bands to Catholicism. By this time they had probably, most of them, settled down and intermarried with the inhabitants; but there is evidence that they still held themselves to be Sueves rather than Goths. Then, after 176 years of independence, they were formally incorporated into the Visigothic kingdom by Leovigild (585); though the Chronicle of Sebastianus (ninth century) still distinguishes, in the time of King Egica (687–701), the realm of the Goths from that of the Suevi.

Something of the extent of the sixth-century kingdom of the Suevi, and the way it was governed, can be deduced from the list of parishes, the *Parochiale*, now in the Escurial.[10] This shows how the ancient civil divisions were adapted to ecclesiastical purposes. The date is approximately 569, in the reign of the Suevian King Theudemirus; and it brings out once more how valuable the bishops were, with their administrative tradition derived from the Roman Empire.[11] The province of Gallæcia, with its metropolis at Braccara (Braga), included the episcopal sees of Coimbra, Idanha, Viseu and Lamego, all situated south of the Douro. They had originally formed part of Lusitania, with its capital at Mérida; and after being attached to Braga for a century or so when they formed part of the Suevian kingdom, they were returned to Mérida under the Visigothic King Reccesvinth, about 666. In later centuries these territorial and episcopal divisions became a legend: a pious fraud to support the rival claims of different episcopal sees during the Reconquista; but the list of parishes remains, along with the names of those country churches which had no parishes of their own. It must be genuine, for in the twelfth century, when it was a question of determining the extent of a diocese or any other district, no one would have thought of making a list of the parishes and churches which had once been contained in it. By that time, boundaries were defined by the tops of mountains, rivers and the vestiges of ancient camps – *castros* – and monuments.[12] The country including the two dioceses of Coimbra and Idanha formed a triangle; with its base resting on the coast approximately from Nazaré to Gaia (just south of Oporto), and another side following the upper course of the Tagus to the present Spanish country. This had been the country of the Suevi.

The Suevi left few identifiable traces of their language: [13] *britar*, to break stones; *trigar-se* or *atrigar-se*, to be in a hurry; *lobio*, an obsolete word for a vineyard, and *laverca*, lark, a word not far from the Scottish 'laverock'. The proper names and place-names of Germanic origin – something like 2,000 of them – in northern Portugal and Galicia, not counting the rest of the Peninsula, may equally well be Suevian or Visigothic.

Had the Suevi really ruled, or were they merely robber bands, living on the country of others? Their political history would lead to the second supposition. The imposing list of the names of their rulers, the careful collation of ancient authorities made by Pauly-Wissowa and the detailed narratives of Dahn and Ludwig Schmidt, lead in the end to the same conclusion. With all allowance for their Germanic virtues and their traditional good looks, they were never taken seriously by other peoples. The single coin of King Rechiar, the five places in Galicia still called Suevos and the joke about the *tipo suevo* are all that remain of what might have become a great people.

Yet one thing the Suevi did. That was to introduce the heavy, Germanic and Slavonic, quadrangular plough, fitted with wheels, and drawn by one or two yokes of oxen,[14] the plough which the Belgæ had earlier introduced into Britain. Its distribution in Portugal, down to modern times (except for a later extension to the south), almost exactly fits the distribution of the Suevic farmers who had brought it with them right across Europe.

2

The Suevi deserve to be taken more seriously than they have been taken in the past, although history has little to tell of them,

and archæology and linguistics next to nothing. Their successors, the Visigoths, have, if anything, been taken too seriously.
They, too, began as robber-bands, or something very like it;
but after being received into the Imperial armies as FOEDERATI
(332) they seem to have lost many of their Germanic virtues to
become second-rate Romans. Their laws are certainly important; but the fact that they have been elaborately studied by
modern scholars must not blind us to the fact that in some aspects they are among the most intolerant in the world. Further,
the Visigothic policy of making the Peninsula one unit, and
governing it centrally from Toledo, was a less practical form of
administration than the separate, regional Roman provinces,
while its mystique brought countless woes to the later history
of Spain and Portugal.

The Visigoths had an advantage over the Suevi that in the
'wanderings of the peoples' they had wandered further. Originally from Gothland in the south of Sweden, between the great
lakes and the south coast of Skåne, for some time they inhabited
the district between the Danube and the Dnieper; their industrial arts began when they lived in the Ukraine and the
Crimea, and show (in the famous crowns, for instance) Greek
and Sarmatian influences.[15] They invaded the Roman Empire
in 376, driven on by the pressure of the Huns behind them, and
defeated an Imperial force at Adrianople in 378, after which
they were allowed to live within the borders of the Empire.
Something like their language was still reported to be spoken
in the Crimea by a traveller in the sixteenth century.[16]

Their subsequent adventures as Roman allies do not concern
us until their appearance in the Iberian Peninsula, where they
followed the other Germanic tribes; [17] but even then it is difficult to dissect out what concerns Gallæcia and Lusitania, remote country districts which in the north were always Suevic
rather than Visigothic. After the military occupation by Euric
(468–476), the Visigoths began to arrive in numbers; [18] like
the Suevi, they trekked through the Pyrenees, probably by the
Roman road through the pass of Roncesvalles, but also through
Catalonia: a collection of Gothic farmers with a rural aristocracy and an Arian clergy. Land was allowed them according
to Euric's code, which was derived from Roman practice but
was more severe on the original inhabitants. Instead of one

third, they had to hand over two-thirds of their arable land –
the division known as SORTES GOTHICÆ – including cattle, slaves
and COLONI working on the farms. There was no assignment of
land by lot; the term SORTES simply means 'shares' or 'allot-
ments' and was used of divisions of land among the Goths
themselves. This may not have been so hard on the Roman inhabitants as it seems; the Visigothic rulers did not at first
oppress them with the same crushing weight of taxation to
which they had been exposed before the invasions,[19] and it
is possible that only the larger estates were divided in this
way.

The Gothic settlers expelled the Suevi from Lusitania and
confined them to Gallæcia; but the king himself continued to
reside in Septimania – the coastal band joining the Pyrenees to
the lower Rhône. In the sixth century however, he made his
headquarters at Emerita (Mérida), the chief town of Lusitania,
until driven out by dissident Visigothic troops from Bætica (An-
dalucía); the '*pronunciamento*', so familiar a feature in modern
Spain, was practised also by the Visigoths. Then Toledo became
the capital. The monarchy was not hereditary but elective; and
of the thirty-five kings chosen, seventeen were dethroned and
generally assassinated afterwards. The Visigoths generally left
local government alone. Their laws do not tell us how taxes
were assessed or collected, though they appropriated the
amount.[20] Roman municipal organisation, however, appears in
a new form: the old Roman offices, like the names, have disappeared and the towns are in charge of a COMES or a JUDEX,
a count or a judge, a military and civil governor holding an
office which the Visigoths had come to know in Gaul.[21] Round
him stood the Germanic guard, the COMITATUS, the officers of
which were called *gardingos*.

The Visigoths had at first some difficulty in making contact
with the Romanised inhabitants. Being followers of the Arian
heresy, which Cardinal Newman so neatly dismissed as 'an
amateurish piece of theology', they had neither the same
religion nor the same laws, and mixed marriages with the
inhabitants were forbidden. The 'Romans' were now a subject
people, like the Greeks, Jews and Syrians, who lived among them
and did their trading for them.[22] The outlook of the Visigoths
was 'rural rather than municipal'. They were small in numbers,

though sometimes superficially Romanised; and were gradually absorbed by the Romanised native population, especially after the time of King Reccared. Their commerce was largely in foreign hands, and the Byzantine outposts in the south, which favoured Mediterranean trade, were renewed and strengthened between 554 and 629. Greek inscriptions belonging to the sixth and seventh centuries have been found in Portugal: at Lisbon, Mértola and elsewhere.[23]

The solemn, public conversion of King Reccared (587), while it put an end to the Arian heresy in the Peninsula, led to a great increase in the power and influence of the Catholic clergy. They became, indeed, the virtual rulers; exercised civil jurisdiction, were exempt from taxation and ordered all Jews to leave the country. The result of this was seen sixty years later (693), when a widespread conspiracy was discovered, by which the Jews were to deliver the Peninsula into the hands of the Moslems. The Jews were enslaved; and though amnestied by King Witzia (700) they were still liable to the persecution and anti-Semitic discrimination of the Visigothic Code. They saw to it that when the Moslems arrived in the country in 711 most towns opened their gates and were handed over peacefully to the invaders; in some towns, it is said, the garrisons were mainly Jewish.

The chief reason why the Visigoths have a permanent interest for historians of Portugal lies in their law, which was applied to Romans as well as to Germanic peoples;[24] and medieval law, it has been said, is 'the tool to prise open to our view the mind of medieval man'. Laws, the historians tell us, are not made only by legislation; they grow out of custom. For a long time the Visigoths, like other Germanic peoples, had been ruled by their customs; while systematic, written codes of law only came later, under the influence of Rome. Yet Germanic customs reached the Peninsula early, and lasted for a long time – in fact the later *fueros* (in Spain) and the *foros* (in Portugal) are really collections of Germanic 'folk-right' from the north of the Pyrenees. In the Frankish kingdoms of France, from the sixth century, such collections were gradually enriched by new regulations added by the kings and modified or supplemented the original folk-right; and by the end of the ninth century these 'capitularies' become the main sources of information on how people in those times actually lived, for folk-right still continued to be administered in local courts. On the other side there was 'king's law', which supplemented folk-right and often contradicted it. The two outstanding and most influential examples of folk-right are the compilations known as the Salic Law and the Ripuarian Law. In Portugal the Visigothic codes by no means included all the legislation which existed. Apart from a good deal of Roman law, still administered by and for the original inhabitants, there were numerous Germanic customs which had become firmly rooted among the people; and these, after an existence which is still buried in obscurity, came to the surface in the legislation of the customs and charters at the time of the Christian reconquest of Spain and Portugal from the Moslems.

At first the Visigoths left unaltered the laws which they found in their new country. Only fragments remain of the laws of Euric; but a compilation called 'Lex Romana Visigothorum' was promulgated from Toulouse, and the later 'Liber Forum Judicum' (Book of the Law of the Judges) became the law of the land in Portugal. This was translated – or, rather, transformed – into Spanish (FORUM JUDICUM becoming *Fuero Juzgo*) for King Ferdinand III to give as a code to the city of Córdoba, just captured from the Moslems (1236); it was confirmed by his son, Alfonso the Sage, in his encylopædic law-book 'The Seven Divisions' (*Las Siete Partidas*). The *Fuero Juzgo* is a compilation of the judgements of the Visigothic kings. They were trying to act in the spirit of Roman law; but much of the inspiration, as well as the actual drafting, came from the Church, and that accounts for the homiletic tone in which many of the decisions are formulated.

Recent estimates of the value of the 'Forum Judicum' as a code of law are probably too generous. Modern readers may feel that Montesquieu was nearer the mark; for he found them 'stuffed with rhetoric and void of sense, frivolous in substance and bombastic in style'.[25] Again, their homiletic tone has vexed the legal historians in Germany.[26] But when the laws of the Visigoths in Spain and Portugal are compared with laws promulgated by other Germanic princes of the time, especially in Gaul, the comparison turns to their advantage. It was clearly not a law of barbarians, Guizot considered, but one drawn up by learned clerics, and included a number of ideas and theories entirely strange to barbarian customs.

There are still primitive elements in the Visigothic Codes; though not so many as in the Salic and Ripuarian laws, or the ancient customary laws of Spain and Portugal preserved in charters between the ninth and twelfth centuries. It is noticeable, too, that the Visigothic laws rarely use a local country word or one that is not Latin, while the Salic Laws are full of Frankish words, and the Latin version of the Laws of King Alfred has a number of Anglo-Saxon words mixed with the Latin and explained by it.[27] In the same way, the ancient customary law of Portugal contains a number of old words for country objects, half way between Latin and Portuguese – a Latin continually sliding into old Portuguese whenever it is a question of everyday things; for it was important to use the word which everyone understood and used: you had to call a spade a spade.

The men and women who had these customs knew more of country life than the ecclesiastical compilers of the 'Lex Romana Visigothorum' or the 'Forum Judicum'; but in other respects they had learnt little from them save their intolerance. The virulent anti-Semitism of the Visigoths is extended later in the *foros* to cover Moslems as well as Jews; and the primitive, countrified English laws of Ine and Alfred belong, by comparison, to a better and more innocent world. The English lawgivers seem to be explaining the customs of the country to a village gathering of unlettered rustics,[28] while the Visigoths are addressing a King in Council with all the trappings of Byzantine splendour. The former may be rough and ready in their methods, and the later laws of King Athelstan have a 'doom' concerning hot iron and hot water – the ordeals by fire and water known as 'the judgement of God'; but, with the Visigoths, organised persecution has become an affair of state.[29] It is not clear how far the Visigothic Law was in fact applied to the local administration of justice.

The part of Visigothic legislation which most affected ordinary men and women in their daily life was that concerning slaves, particularly runaway slaves who had illegally left their masters. There were also the powers of an outraged father over the seducer of a daughter, and the barbarous treatment of a

B

free woman who married a freedman or slave. The law recognised divorce, however; and under certain conditions allowed a
woman to marry again. The illegitimate children of priests became slaves, but were the property of the Church.

About seventy years ago a theory was proposed to account
for the existence in Spain and Portugal of customs like the
ordeals by hot iron and boiling water, of which the laws of the
Visigoths made no mention.[30] It was that there may have been
some relationship between the customary law of the Peninsula
and that of Norway and Iceland – a relationship which seemed
particularly clear in regard to the legal position of unmarried
parents; but the theory has not stood the test of historical
criticism. Among the West Germanic peoples (including the
Suevi) concubinage was regarded as a perfectly natural relationship, so long as there was no question of force or influence
brought to bear by a third party. The East Germanic peoples,
however, including the Visigoths, refused to give legal recognition to concubinage or any relationship outside the married
state, unless the fact of paternity was definitely established.
Further, it was pointed out that the old Spanish and Portuguese
words for concubinage (*barraganía, barraguice*) were not Germanic in origin, but Arabic; while the word for 'mistress', *man-
ceba*, is the late Latin MANCIPIA. The canon of the Council of
Toledo of the year 400 shows that the Hispanic Church, before
the invasion, allowed a man to live with an unmarried woman,
provided that he lived with only one at a time; and concubinage still existed as a legal relationship after the foundation of
the Visigothic monarchy. The fact that the same was true in
the Scandinavian countries does not necessarily prove any connexion between them and Portugal.

Another argument depended on the ordeals by hot iron or
boiling water, to show whether a man was telling the truth.
Later research has shown, however, that these could not have
come to Portugal from Scandinavia, where they were only introduced after the comparatively late conversion of the northern countries to Christianity. In Spain and Portugal the ordeals
were inflicted especially in cases of disputed paternity; but
again, they are comparatively late, and not earlier than the
ninth century. The fact seems to be that the ordeals were not
introduced into Portugal by the Suevi or the Visigoths, nor yet

from Iceland or Scandinavia, but were borrowed from the Franks after they had become Christians. The 'Judgement of God', in fact, was, as the name implied, a Christian procedure, and the first code in which boiling water is given a certain authority is the Salic Law.[31]

3

The Suevi settled down in the north to their deep ploughing; but the Visigoths, though they may have introduced cattle-breeding into the Alentejo – the 'land beyond the Tagus' – preferred to govern from a distance at Toledo. Some of them were farmers, it is true; but the typical Visigoth was a member of a military caste, administering the affairs of a subject population with different laws and a different religion. A great deal has been written on their laws, and something on their art; but it is difficult to find any specific reference to that part of their dominions which afterwards became Portugal. The Suevi (or at least their women) worked on the land, and so did some of the Visigoths, living side by side with Hispano-Romans; so far as their economic activities went there was no separation between them.[32] For a long time after the division of the arable land at the conquest there was forest land, undivided and unfenced pasture, in common possession and common use by both Goths and Romans. This may be deduced from the Visigothic laws.[33] If a CONSORS – that is, a partner or sharer in the two-thirds division, SORS GOTHICA – made a clearing, his CONSORTES (the other partners) were to be compensated by the grant of a corresponding piece of forest in another place, or else he had to hoe up part of the clearing himself.[34]

The Roman owner still had access to the COMPASCUA, the 'common' or undivided part of the woodland or pasture. The Goth became entitled to this right also, with his share; and the uncultivated land remained undivided for economic reasons. The object of this law was to prevent the partners doing anything to each other's disadvantage. Goths were expected to do farm-work; there was no legal difference between the partners. Communal pasture was permitted only where the individual cultivator had not completely marked out his land.[35] According to the surviving laws of Euric (about A.D. 475), the old boundary-marks, the TERMINI of the Roman properties, were to be taken as a guide. If they had gone, there was an inquiry to which both parties could send representatives. In Euric's law, the technical expressions are still those of Roman surveyors: INSPECTIO, LIMITES. No one was to fix fresh boundaries without the knowledge of his partner, or of the officials in charge: the INSPECTORES.[36]

From the Visigothic laws it is possible to deduce something of the appearance of the Portuguese countryside in Visigothic times: the sown fields, the olive-groves, fig-trees, vegetable plots, orchards, bee-hives. There were penalties for those who damaged these things. The law also tried to protect trees; and though the invariable preliminary to clearing a piece of land was to burn them, one should remember that the cultivators were pioneers dealing with virgin forest, and that virgin forest is not like anything to be seen or imagined now in western Europe. There are masses of trees of all sizes, growing so close together that it is almost impossible to force a way through; while the ground is covered with fallen trunks and branches and heaps of rotting dead leaves. The trees which the Visigoths protected were generally cultivated trees.[37] The heaviest fine was for cutting an olive. After that came the fine for damaging fruit trees, and a little less for oaks and other trees 'which could be used for making many necessary things'. Ships are not mentioned yet, but among the necessary things are hoops for barrels. It may be owing to a Germanic custom that port wine is kept 'in the wood', instead of in earthenware jars smeared with pitch, which had been used by the Romans and are still to be seen in some parts of the south of Portugal to-day – at Mértola on the Guadiana, for instance, the former Roman MYRTILIS. Another piece of typical country legislation in the Visigothic Code concerned the owners of animals straying into vineyards or sown fields; they had to hand over to the injured party a portion of vineyard or cornfield equivalent in value to that which had been trampled down or destroyed, and the plaintiff, after gathering the fruit or harvesting the grain, would then restore the land to the original owner.[38]

From some passages in the Visigothic laws we can see that, in spite of the insecurity of the times, there were in Portugal isolated homesteads and village settlements. When people quarrelled over boundaries or buildings, they were summoned before a jury of their neighbours, to whom also information about strayed cattle had to be reported; the damage was assessed, and if boundary marks had been removed, they had to be replaced.

The country parish was a more or less autonomous group, and the priests who served it were, of course, distinct from those in the towns. In the country, the parish priest ruled a FAMILIA – not a family of his own children but a family of serfs, ADSCRIPTI GLEBAE.[39] A FAMILIA ECCLESIAE, the Leges Visigothorum tell us,[40] meant a number of serfs who cultivated the glebe land. A parish was considered poor if it had only ten ADSCRIPTI. The parish priest was responsible for repairs to his church, whether the job were done by local men or by masons from elsewhere. He was answerable to the bishop, who could suspend him if he seemed unsatisfactory; and the bishop was empowered also to act as civil judge of the serfs of the ecclesiastical family. At the same time the Council (e.g. at Mérida) was strict in its control over the penalties which it permitted the bishop to administer. In the dark ages a form of punishment often employed was mutilation. The Council of Mérida, the ancient capital of Lusitania, forbade it altogether; if a case were reported, action could be taken by the judge from the nearest town. Such ill-treatment seems to have been exceptional: and in fact the texts point to there being a considerable number of instances of slaves being set free altogether. The canon of the Council alludes to the compensation which a prelate owed to his Church when he deprived it of a slave by setting him free; and when no compensation was given, the freed man might ultimately revert to slavery.

The Visigoths left little behind them in Portugal that is still visible to-day: the church of S. Fructuoso at Braga, the parish church of Balsemão near Lamego, the battered edifice of Santo Amaro at Beja and about fifty broken pieces of columns and capitals in the museum there.[41] As usual in Visigothic buildings, the larger columns were taken bodily from an older Roman construction, while the smaller ones were roughly hewn in one piece: base, shaft and capital. Lisbon, reputed to have been founded by Ulysses but more probably by the Carthaginians, has two objects which date from the time of the Visigoths: the old walls (*cêrca velha*) used afterwards by the Moslems for stronger fortifications; and probably also the cathedral, which, if originally Visigothic, was adapted for a mosque and then rebuilt to suit the taste of each succeeding generation. At present it appears in a disguise which might be described as 'neoromanesque'. In their architecture, as in their law, their administration and most other forms of activity, the Visigoths rebuilt, but rebuilt roughly with Roman materials.

NOTES TO CHAPTER 2

[1] *Mon. Germ. Hist. Auct. ant.* IX:
'In the year ccccix when the provinces of Hispania had been overrun by the fullness of violence which we remember, the barbarians were converted by God's mercy to the introduction of peace, and divided the regions into lots so that they might be inhabited. The Vandals occupied Gallaecia, and the Suevi, the western sites on the edge of the open sea.'

[2] F. Newton de Macedo, 'O dominio germânico,' in Damião Peres, *Hist. de Portugal* (Barcelos, 1928), I, 309.

[3] Ludwig Schmidt, *Histoire des Vandales*, 2 ed. (1953), p. 35. For the atrocities committed by the Vandals in Africa, see the contemporary accounts printed by P. Courcelle, *Hist. litt. des grandes invasions germaniques* (Paris, 1948).

[4] 'Tiene el noble y varonil tipo suevo de un hidalgo montañés,' Valle-Inclán, *Romance de Lobos*.

[5] The engagement took place on the Campo Páramo, 12 miles from Astorga, by the River Órbigo.

[6] *Mon. Germ. Hist.*, VI, c. 7; and Fortunato de Almeida, *Hist. da Igreja em Portugal*, I, 43 (1910).

[7] M. R. James, in *The Cambridge Medieval History*, III, 490, gives a charming account of this saint.

[8] Text in *Videnskabs-selskabet i Christiania* (Oslo, 1883).

[9] The names of the days of the week, which in Portugal are on a different system to that of most countries in Europe have been the subject of much controversy of late years, see M. de Paiva Boléo, *Os nomes dos dias da semana em português* (Coimbra, 1941), and Gerhard Rohlfs, 'Les noms des jours de la semaine dans les langues romaines.' *Miscelânia . . .á memoria de F. A. Coelho*, I, 88–94 (1949).

It is curious that one of the few epitaphs known with a Suevic name should give Monday the modern Portuguese form, *Segunda Feira*, proposed by St Martin of Braga, and that the stone should have been found in the Saint's own country:

```
+   HIC   REQVIESCIT   REMISMVERA
IV  KAL  MAIAS  ERA D C  QVINQVAGIS
IV  DIE  SECVNDA FERIA IN  PACE AMEN
```

(Here lies Remismuera, 28 April, A.D. 616, Monday. In Peace. Amen.)
Another probable Suevic name is Thuresmude:

```
+ PROTHEVS   FECIT
THVRESMVDE      VXO
RI  SVE  OBIIT  IPSA
SVB DIE VIIII KL JA
NVAR  ERA  DCLXXII
```

(Protheus made this for Thuresmude his wife. She died 24th December A.D. 634.)

This stone was also found near Braga. J. Vives, *Inscripciones cristianas de la España romana y visigoda* (Barcelona, 1942), Nos. 183 and 502; J. M. Piel, *Estudios, dedicados a Menéndez Pidal*, VI (1956), 111-150.

[10] Pierre David, *Études historiques sur la Galice et le Portugal* (Coimbra, 1947). The MS. is an 8th cent. copy of a 7th cent. original.

[11] This point is well brought out by Delisle Burns, in *The First Europe* (1947).

[12] Pierre David, op. cit., 73.

[13] Gamillscheg, *Romania Germanica*, I, 384-385 (Berlin). There are about thirty place-names formed from the word Goth (Godos, Godin, Godinhos, etc.) but only four Suevos.

[14] Jorge Dias, *Os arados portugueses* (Coimbra, 1948); Oswald Craufurd, *Portugal Old & New* (1882), ch. V: 'Farming and Farm-people'; Adolfo Coelho, 'Alfaia agricola portuguesa', in *Portugalia* 1 (1899-1903), 403-412.

[15] W. Weinhart, 'La tradición Visigoda en el nacimiento de Castilla', *Estudios dedicados a Menéndez Pidal*, I, 535-554 (Madrid, 1950).

[16] A. A. Vasiliev, *The Goths in the Crimea*, Medieval Acad. of America, Mon. No. 11 (Cambridge, Mass., 1936). In 1554, the Flemish noble, Ogier Ghislain de Busbecq, came to Constantinople as ambassador of the Holy Roman Emperor. He was interested in language, collected Greek MSS., founded Turkish studies in Europe, and invited two of the bellicose Gothic villagers to dinner where he noted some of their words. Doubt on the correctness of Busbecq's information has been cast by M. H. Jellinek, *Gesch. der gotischen Sprache* (Berlin-Leipzig, 1926). See also Norman H. Baynes, 'The Goths in South Russia', in *Byzantine Studies and other Essays* (1955).

[17] G. Zeiss, *Die Grabfunde aus dem spanischen Westgotenreich* (Berlin, 1934).

[18] G. Yves, 'Euric roi des Visigothes' (466-485). *Études d'histoire de moyen âge, dédiées a Gabriel Monod* (1896), pp. 11-46. Note that, in Pauly-Wissowa, Euric is spelt 'Evarix'.

[19] Pauly-Wissowa, Suppl. Bd. III, 839-845 (1918-1932), quotes Salvian on the Government of God, V, 5, 21; but this writer had gone over to the Goths, and thought the presence of unwashen barbarians a healthy corrective for Roman luxury. See Dahn *Die Könige der Germanen*, VI, 54; Dopsch, *The Economic and Social Foundations of European Civilization*, English translation (1937), 97, and the brief chapter on the Visigoths in Spain in J. B. Trend, *The Language and History of Spain* (1953).

[20] For Visigothic coinage see, amongst others, Alois Hess, *Déscription générale des monnaies des rois wisigoths d'Espagne* (1872); A. Vives, *La moneda hispánica* (Madrid, 1924), *Atlas*, xci. F. Mateu y Llopis, *La monedas del Museo Arqueológico Nacional* (Madrid, 1936). J. Elias García, 'As moedas visigodas de Lusitânia', in *Revista de Guimarães*, LX, 1950, nos. 1-2, pp. 73-154 (Catalogue and bibliography).

[21] C. Sánchez-Albornoz, *Ruina y extinción del municipio romano en España* (Buenos Aires, 1943).

[22] *Vitae sanctorum patrum emeritensium*. Text and translation with an introduction and commentary by Joseph L. Garvin (Washington, 1946). These lives show landowners in Lusitania with Roman names, bishops coming from the East, Greek merchants going to Mérida to sell their silks and Oriental wares to the bishops and Visigothic kings helping Arians against Catholics. I am grateful to Dr. J. M. Batista i Roca for calling my attention to this book. The language has interesting examples of colloquial Latin.

²³ J. Vives, t.c. The following inscription from Mértola is in the Archæological Museum at Belem:

```
    +  ΕΝΘΑ  ΚΑΤΑ
  ΚΙΤΕ      ΕΥΤΥΧ
  ΕΣ      ΑΝΑΓΝΟΣ
  ΤΕΣ ΛΙΒΙΣΙΝΤΕΟΣ
  ΥΙΟΣ        ΖΟΣΙ
  ΜΟΥ     ΕΙΣΙΔΩΡ
  ΙΤΟΥ     ΕΖΕΣΕΝ
  ΗΤΗ    ΚΑ  ΕΡΑ
  ΦΠΒ            +
```

Here lies Eutyches, reader [in church] at Lisbon, son of Zosimus Isidoritus. He lived 21 years. Era 582.

Isidoritus: cf. the Spanish diminutive, Isidorito. The date is equivalent to A.D. 544. (Vives, No. 524, pp. 173–174.)

²⁴ Fr. W. Rauchhaupt, *Geschichte der spanischen Gesetzesquellen* (Heidelberg, 1923), and the unfinished *Geschichte der Westgotischen Gesetzgebung* (1897–1900), by Karl Zeumer, Spanish translation by Carlos Clavería, *Historia de la Legislación Visigoda* (Barcelona, 1944).

²⁵ Montesquieu's comment is as follows: 'Mais les loiz des Wisigoths, celles de Recessuinde, de Chaindasuinde, et d'Egica, sont puériles, gauches, idiotes; elles n'atteignent point le but: pleines de rhétorique, et vuides de sens, frivoles dans de fond, et gigantesques dans le style'. *De l'esprit des lois*, Livre XXVIII, ch. 1.

²⁶ W. Brunner, *Deutsche Rechtsgeschichte*, 2nd ed., I, 493. A. v. Halben, *Das römische Recht in den germanischen Staaten* (1899).

²⁷ The Laws of King Alfred show a mixture of languages analogous to that which we find later in Portugal, e.g. emendet ipsi ceorlo, id est rustico (25); Si quis folcmot id est populi placitum . . . (38); si quis in ceorlisces mannes flet gefechte, id est in rusticani hominis domus area pugnet (39). Note how the descendants of these Old English words have come to have an entirely different meaning in Modern English: 'churlish man's flat', for 'the house of a ceorl'.

²⁸ But if anyone cut down a tree under which thirty swine may stand, and it be discovered, let him pay sixty shillings (Laws of King Ine, 44). If a man burn or hew another's wood without leave, let him pay for every great tree with five shillings, and afterwards for each, let there be as many of them as may be, with five pence, and thirty (shillings) as 'wite' (King Alfred, 12). The laws have their exact counterparts in Portugal. See also *English Historical Documents*, I (1955).

²⁹ The second title of the twelfth book is described as DE OMNIUM HERETICORUM ADQUE IUDEORUM HERRORIBUS AMPUTANDIS: 'the amputation of the errors of all heretics and Jews'. The Jews in Visigothic lands might not keep the Passover (Tit. 5) or marry according to their law (Tit. 6) or be circumcised (Tit. 7) or cause any Christian servant to be circumcised (Tit. 12). They might not give evidence against Christians (Tit. 10), or persuade their servants to join their sect (Tit. 14). No Christian might show them favour or defend them (Tit. 15). These vexatious regulations were reinforced at the end of the seventh century. See also Norman Baynes, *English Historical Review*, XLVIII, 639–640. It is impossible to accept such favourable judgements as those of Aloysius K. Ziegler, *Church and State in Visigothic Spain* (Washington, 1930).

[30] Julius Ficker, 'Über nähere Verwandschaft zwischen gotisch-spanischem und norwegisch-isländischem Recht', *Mitteil. d. Inst. für österreichische Geschichtsforschung*, II, Ergänzungsband, 455–542 (Vienna, 1888). This was answered by Konrad Maurer, 'Zur nord-germanischen Rechtsgeschichte', *Kritische Vierteljahrsschrift für Gesetzgebung und Rechtswissenschaft*, Bd. 12, Neue Folge, 190–197; Bd. 13 (Leipzig, 1889).

[31] The ordeal of fire was also invoked at Toledo, to decide which of the two service-books with their appropriate and characteristic music, was to be used in the Spanish Church: the Mozarabic or the Roman; though the legendary account is not entirely accepted by the latest authorities—not by Pierre David, for instance. For centuries after the Reconquest, from 1147 down to 1536, Lisbon cathedral sang the 'Use of Sarum', introduced by the first bishop, the Englishman, Gilbert of Hastings. No copies are known in Portugal now, even if they survived the earthquake and fires of 1755; but there is no record of their having undergone any other ordeal by fire. F. de Almeida, *Hist. da Igreja em Portugal*, I, 627 (1910).

[32] E. de Campos, t.c., 6.

[33] Dahn, t.c., VI, 53–55.

[34] Lehes Visigothorum X, i, 9: De silvis.

[35] Dopsch, t.c. 98.

[36] ibid., 148.

[37] Leges, I, i, 14.

[38] Leges, VIII, ii, 2 and 3; VIII, iii, 1.

[39] Pierre David, t.c., and E. Magnin, *L'église wisigothique au VIIe siècle* (1912), 168–169.

[40] Leges, III, iii, 3; V, i, 7.

[41] Virgilio Corrêa, 'Arte Visigótica', in *Hist. de Portugal . . .* dirigida por Damiso Peres (Barcelos, 1928), I, 365–388. Abel Viana, 'Visigótico de Beja', in *Arquivo de Beja*, VI, 1949, 253–291.

Chapter 3

Moslems and Mozárabes

I

IT IS impossible to understand how Portugal became a nation without considering the effects of the civilisation of the Moslems, either directly or through the 'Mozárabic' Christians who lived under their rule.

One of the characteristics which most distinguish the medieval Moslems is that, like the Prophet, they were merchants and, like Sindbad, sailors; and the medieval Moslem merchant was often a cultivated man who brought books to read on the voyage. During the Middle Ages they extended their traffic to the three continents which were then known. Long before the Crusades had brought East and West into contact, the Peninsula had benefited from Moslem trade and traders. From the earliest times of Moslem dominion, relations between the Peninsula and the East had been continuous. Then, as the Christian conquest proceeded, ports formerly open to Moslem trade began quietly to renew or continue their traffic, much as it had been before.

Another aspect of Moslem culture which undoubtedly had an influence in Portugal was the interest in geography,[1] in geographical position, in the taking of bearings which, among Moslems, was not solely in order to determine the direction of Mecca, as the holy men believed – or were led to believe, so that they should not interfere with the progress of scientific inquiry.

The Moslems who arrived at the beginning of the eighth century succeeded in making themselves at home in more than half of Portugal. They were a miscellaneous collection: Arabs, Syrians, Persians, Jews; Copts from Egypt, who were (or had once been) Christians, and Berbers from Morocco, who, being fanatics by nature and the latest converts to Islam, were (with some of the desert Arabs) the only really intolerant members of the invading force. There is evidence that people from the eastern Mediterranean (Syrians, Byzantine Greeks and Jews) had been coming for centuries to the coastal areas of Lusitania; and the Arabs and other Moslems, when they came, were only a continuation of these other Levantines, both in their culture and their economic interests. The difference was that the Moslems brought a new religion, and a new ideal of the equality of all men before God, which seemed more easily attainable than the nebulous inequalities of eighth-century Christianity.

In Roman times, northern Portugal and Galicia had been in close contact – by sea – with western Gaul, trading with Bordeaux; but the contact had been broken by the Germanic invasions, and had only been renewed in the later days of the Visigoths. Now the West had been 'opened up' – that is the literal meaning of the Arabic word for conquest – to the civilising influence of the Near East; and as time went on that influence produced one of the greatest civilisations that the Iberian Peninsula has ever known. To-day there are fewer traces of it in Portugal than in Spain; but there was in those days no distinction between the two countries, and the intellectual capitals were, first, Córdoba, and then Seville and Granada, and in Portugal, Silves. To the Visigoths, governing from Toledo in remote, theocratic splendour, Lusitania was a countrified region of no great importance. To the Moslems in Córdoba and Seville it was no less remote or rustic; but it sometimes excited the curiosity of Arab travellers.

The pompous Visigoths had never been popular enough for anyone to wish to defend their government; and the persecuted, enslaved Jews would have opened the gates of fortified towns to any reasonable newcomers, in Portugal as they had in Spain. But the Moslems held most of the country, and for 500 years 'the great majority of the Hispanic Goths', Herculano says,[2] 'accepted the fact of the Moslem conquest and the shadow of toleration of the Moslem princes. They formed with the conquerors a political society, which, if not compact, was at least united by many bonds, including those of blood. . . . Beliefs were not insuperable barriers.' They settled down to tolerant and productive country life; while in the small towns people from all over the Mediterranean and the Middle East lived in peace and amity with western, 'Sephardic' Jews and Mozárabic Christians – Christians, that is, who, except in religion, had accepted the Moslem way of life and were allowed to worship as they liked. They talked and traded, sang songs and made poetry, in a common Latin patois, which when written down, was written with Hebrew or Arabic characters instead of Roman.

This was the condition from the south coast right up to the river Vouga, which nowadays disappears among the dunes and canals of Aveiro, 45 miles south of Oporto, but is in some ways still recognisable for a former frontier with the Moslems. North of the Vouga, and still further, north of the Douro, was a country where no sensible Moslem would have wished to settle. It was too dangerous, too exposed to the raids of those wild hillmen from Asturias who thought themselves the heirs of the Visigoths. And there was another consideration. The Moslems were mainly people from dry countries, and they settled in places where they could live by irrigation. Some writers have claimed that they learnt this from the Romanised inhabitants of the Peninsula. The way of 'watering with a hoe' was known to Virgil. *Rega a sacho*, the Portuguese call it – letting the water run along one channel and then damming it up to let it run in another direction or back into the main stream. That, at any rate, must be the meaning of the last line of the third Eclogue: CLAUDITE IAM RIVOS, PUERI: SAT PRATA BIBERUNT (stop the streams now, boys; the fields have drunk enough), though here, of course, it is used metaphorically. But it is there already in Homer – in the picture of the man, hoe in hand, leading a stream of water through a field to an orchard (*Iliad*, XXI, 261), and it is remembered in the *Georgics* too (I, 106).[3] The great contribution of the Moslems was to irrigate, not with a hoe but with a water-wheel: that peculiar form of water-wheel with pots fastened to the rim, bringing up water from a cistern and worked by an ox or an ass – the *nora* (*na'ura*) from Mesopotamia – which made the Algarve and other districts occupied by the Moslems the prosperous and productive places they once were and are again to-day. Every farm or every family still has one; and if no longer home-made but industrially produced, they are still used individually.[4]

2

The chronicler known as the pseudo-Isidore, or Isidore of Beja,[5] who was an eye-witness of the Moslem invasion, gives a picture of bitterness, recrimination, discouragement and terror natural to one who had seen the destruction and ruin which an invasion must cause. Yet, as the years went by, friendly relations grew up between the people of all three religions; and the words, customs and institutions which passed from one society to another show that, in spite of opposing beliefs and jealousy over government, the three ways of thinking were modified, and their asperities softened, by living in contact. 'The invasion of the Peninsula by the Moslems (Herculano said) was not a war of extermination. As at all times, the path of the invaders was marked by blood and ruin according to the amount of resistance; but even in places where the resistance had been most tenacious, the Moslems did not follow victory by useless slaughter.' Chroniclers, and more recent writers too, have exaggerated the importance of the handful of men who took refuge in the mountains of Asturias; but the real history of the Hispano-Gothic peoples continued with the Mozárabes. Able (like the Jews) to make public profession of their religion, protected by the authorities, left in enjoyment of their property provided that they paid their taxes, these Hispano-Roman Christians who had submitted to the Moslems were probably better off (and the Jews much better off) than they had ever been under the Visigoths. They were not disposed to sacrifice all these advantages for a vague longing for independence – if indeed they ever had such a feeling – and it is probably romanticising history to credit them with one, as with the rebellion of the Christian 'nationalist' Ibn Hafsún, and the exaggerations of the Christian scribes concerning the barbarities of the infidels. Even the author of the *Chronica Pacensis*, who compares the destruction of the Visigothic kingdom to that of Troy, Babylon and Jerusalem all rolled into one, and the persecution to that of the early Christians in Rome, has yet a good word for the Moslem emirs who protected the defeated inhabitants.

By Moslem (Malekite) law the payment of land-tax and poll-tax left Christians in occupation of the lands they cultivated; occupiers were only deprived of their land if they neglected it. The principles of Malekite law in relation to non-Moslem territory under occupation confirm the mild policy which the Moslems pursued in Spain and Portugal, when the inhabitants submitted to their authority. Before hostilities began, the law required an exhortation to be addressed to the unbelievers to embrace Islam; if they refused, they could still capitulate according to Islamic law. The first part of this recalls nothing so much as the Catholic *Requerimiento*, required in the sixteenth century to be read out by the Spanish Conquistadores to the Indians in Spanish America, before an attack was opened. The alternative was not offered. If the non-Moslem refused, or did not understand – in the case of the Indians, the *Requerimiento* was not read in their own language but in Spanish – he was subdued by force of arms, and could be enslaved; though he could free himself by paying the ransom required by law from conquered unbelievers. This amount (in the case of capitulation) was fixed at a round sum for the whole population, the land remained in possession of its owners, who could dispose of it as they thought fit or bequeath it to members of their own sect. The Moslem law also allowed the building of new churches.[6]

The Hispanised Goths and other Christian inhabitants of the Peninsula had another advantage under the Moslems. Among themselves, they continued to be ruled by their own civil law. The evidence for this comes from Christian writers most hostile to the Moslems.[7] The fanatical Christian, Álvaro de Córdoba, alludes to the Mozárabic counts, and to their judges who were also Mozárabes. They are also referred to by Eulogius. The Mozárabes were allowed to keep not only their ecclesiastical hierarchy but also their titles of nobility. The Moslem rulers may have tolerated the Christians from contempt; but they kept to the letter and spirit of their treaties with them. Wealthy Visigoths kept up their establishments of slaves, and went on with their hunting-parties and banquets. They could serve in the Moslem armies. Indignant Christian writers who complain of the Mozárabes forgetting their Latin sometimes show in their own writings how they were forgetting it too. They are horrified at the increasing practice of circumcision, not thinking that there may have been a hygienic reason as well as a theological one. Churches and monasteries multiplied, decorated in a fantastic oriental style; we hear of churches lately built: ECCLESIAS NUPER STRUCTAS, between 750 and 788.[8]

Moreover, the frequency of mixed marriages prepared the

way to a complete fusion of races, which might have come about (as in Norman England or Portuguese India) if the difference in religion had not been raised by clerical obstinacy into an insuperable barrier. Intolerance on the part of some of the Catholic clergy and the excessive zeal of some ardent souls among the laity led first to hate and then to persecution, which even in the blackest tints of ecclesiastical writers does not seem to have been so violent as they have tried to make out. Moslem judges were obliged to pass sentence on those zealots who spat on mosques or insulted the name of the Prophet. The more reasonable Mozárabes protested; and by the time of Abdu'r-Rahmán III, in the tenth century, the Christians had become much more reasonable. They were never forbidden to use their own laws.

3

Moslem Portugal has little of the interest or importance of Moslem Spain: hardly a poet, a historian or a philosopher; hardly a herbalist, doctor or man of science. Their experiments in architecture for hot countries have perished, with the exception of the use of many-coloured tiles, an art which persisted among the Portuguese down to the Age of Reason, and is still alive to this day. Practically nothing else has descended from them, except carved, 'coffered' ceilings.

Yet under the tenth-century khalifs of Córdoba and the twelfth-century kings of Seville, Silves (Shelb) became one of the intellectual capitals of Al-Andalus. It was inhabited by families tracing their descent to Arabs of Yemen; and the geographer Idrísí praised the purity of their Arabic speech and the beauty of their pronunciation, so different from that of many of the Arabic-speaking inhabitants of Spain (Granada, for instance) who made a curious change – imála, it was called – a change in the colours of the vowels comparable with the vowel-changes in local English dialects to-day. The men and women of Shelb had not been corrupted in their speech by the 'foreign' or 'indistinct' language (al-'ajamíya) spoken by the Christians, the words of which – to an Arab ear – were merely comic. 'Tell me,' the Moslem ruler would remark, 'what do they call that in the outlandish language?' – 'that' being something not often mentioned in polite Moslem society. 'O Prince of Believers, it is called . . .'; and the result is that some of the earliest vernacular words in Spain and Portugal are relegated to the decent obscurity of an appendix. 'Then', the story ends, 'he laughed, did the Prince of Believers, till he rolled on his back-side' – he was, of course, sitting cross-legged on a carpet – 'and ordered it to be written in a book.'

The town of Shelb contained palaces with cool, airy galleries and bazaars full of gold and silver, silks, pottery and spices; it was surrounded by orchards and gardens, and at the same time was strongly fortified, while the river was navigable right down to the sea. Yet in the end it was captured, re-taken again and again: first by Ferdinand I of Castille in 1060, then by the Moslems, and then starved out after a long and waterless siege in the summer of 1189 by a horde of international cut-throats on their way to the Holy Land as crusaders – so brutally treated that even the King of Portugal, Sancho I, protested. Retaken by Moors from Morocco, it finally became Christian again in 1242; but was found to be so ruined and deserted that it had to be rebuilt and re-populated. Meanwhile the river had been silting up, and in the sixteenth century the place was reported to have only 160 miserable inhabitants. Earthquakes – particularly that of 1755 – completed the ruin which fanaticism had begun so many centuries before.

Évora, in spite of its Roman history and its Roman temple, has more the character of a Moslem town in the west: cool courtyards with trickling fountains, coloured tiles, horse-shoe arches,[9] paired twin windows, airy terraces and roof-tops, carved oriental capitals. Idrísí visited it in the twelfth century, and another geographer and traveller, al-Himyárí, in the fifteenth. Yábura (Idrísí calls it) was a large, walled town with a great mosque and a castle; the country round it was of singular fertility, especially for wheat, fruit and vegetables. There was cattle-breeding and a flourishing trade – just as in the Évora of to-day, the truth being that an agricultural and trading centre like Évora will go on, whatever the religion of its rulers. Al-Himyárí devotes a whole chapter to it, and gives the biography of one of its poets: employed at the Treasury in Granada, he was arrested for some irregularity and sent for trial to south Morocco; on the way, however, he stopped at the little walled seaport of Salé, where he was recognised and the recitation of a poem produced someone to go bail for him, and he returned to Granada a free man.

Another Roman town which kept its importance, in Moslem times as well as Visigothic, was Beja. Idrísí does not mention it, though al-Himyárí gives it a whole chapter. Alas, 'the generations which have successively occupied it have apparently tried to blot out all memory of those that came before'.[10] Mértola, one of the least known, least accessible, but most striking places in the whole of Portugal, was captured by the Suevi from the Romans (439), by the Moslems from the Christians (712) and by Sancho II from the Moslems (1238) – that King Sancho who, like the Emperor Henry IV in 1077 at Canossa, had to go on his knees to a Pope (Innocent IV) and then to abdicate in favour of Afonso II, who gave Mértola to the military order of Santiago. Mértola – built, like Cuenca and Toledo, at the junction of two rivers in deep gorges – has a cathedral half fortress and half mosque; five aisles and rows of columns, and Moslem horse-shoe arches which are now being gradually excavated from behind centuries of Christian plaster. There is also a 'saint-house' on a hill, for all the world like a *qubba* in Morocco. The castle, too is Moslem, though built of Roman materials; the bridge is Roman, but re-shaped in Moslem times; and there are ruins of Roman constructions in the river which look as if they too had been employed by Moslems.

The coming of the Moslems was a blessing to Portugal. Their water-wheels enabled great progress to be made in methodical cultivation. These 'Moors', the mixture of Arabic-speaking Moslems from all over the Near and Middle East, proved to be clever in the management of agricultural land, and they profited by everything they had seen on their way to the West. They introduced new ways of doing things, which they had seen in other places: rotation of crops, grafting fruit-trees, systems of irrigation-channels, grinding corn by water-mills, distillation. They brought oranges and lemons; and the English crusader, Osbern, who was present at the capture of Lisbon from the Moslems in 1147 and wrote an account of it preserved in the Library of Corpus Christi College, Cambridge, was particularly impressed by the sight of oranges and lemons grown on the south side of the Tagus, where they are only just beginning to be grown again.

It is possible, however, that the Moslems had something to learn about agriculture from the local inhabitants. Many, if not most, of the country people in Portugal were Romanised Christians – those Mozárabes, whose religion was tolerated by their rulers and whose bishops were recognised by the Government. The position can be summarised by saying that 'the culture of the peoples who had come over from Africa was more tolerant and more advanced than that which existed in the Peninsula at the end of the rule of the Visigoths. On that account . . . there was no reason why those who had submitted to the Moslems should decline in civilisation. The irrigation-canal and the *nora* completed the conquest of the Peninsula by the Moslems'.[11]

No less important than his remarks on Moslem territory are Idrísí's observations on territory which at that time (mid-twelfth century) was already in the power of the Christians. 'A flourishing country, covered with houses; strong places [castles?] with villages next to them.' This shows that already the north presented a contrast in population with the south; one necessitated by natural conditions. South of the Tagus, Idrísí refers to the number of towns, while in the north the population was dispersed. Conditions of insecurity in the north led to the increase of towns which had good possibilities of defence, like Coimbra. There might even have been a return to the hill-villages: the easily-defensible *castros* of pre-Roman times; but this does not explain the sudden appearance of towns at the far ends of estuaries. That was probably due to the invasions of the Vikings, which had begun as far back as the ninth century, causing a retreat of the population from the coast. But the fact that they chose the ends of estuaries and not the hills shows an interest in maritime occupations. Indeed, contrary to what one might have supposed, the Vikings also maintained commercial relations with the people on the coasts. They existed, sometimes for several years, on harvests by the sea; and from this fact their influence on Western maritime civilisation is to be explained. Essential parts of a ship, *barca*; the keel, *quilha*; mast, *mastro*, and perhaps the helm, *leme*, are Germanic words which must have come in with the Northmen; the earlier Germanic invaders were not interested in the sea. *Caravel*, however, is said to be derived from the Arabic; for, like the Northmen, the Moslems extended their commercial activities by sea to the west of the Peninsula; references in Idrísí leave this in no doubt.

The figs of Silves were exported to all countries of the west, Idrísí says. (We remember the fig-trees in the Algarve to-day.) Moslem exports went not only to their own ports, but to places far up the estuaries, no longer navigable: the Sado up to Alcácer, the Tagus up to Santarém, the Mondego to Montemôr-o-Velho, to Soure on the southern tributary of that name, and even up to Coimbra, the Minho up to Tuy, and the river that runs up to Padrón in Galicia, the end of the sea-route to Santiago. During the Galician–Mozárabic period there came into existence not only the beginnings of the future Portuguese language, but also a new distribution of the people who talked it, concentrated on the navigable rivers and estuaries.

4

Portugal has fewer place-names of Arabic origin than Spain.[12] Alcácer, the castle, is ultimately the word *castro*, CASTRUM, in an Arabic disguise; but Alcácer do Sal is derived from a genuine Arabic root, *al-quasil*, meaning barley. Alcaria do Cume and Alcaria de Ruivo are from *al-qarya*, the grange. Alfama, that famous and picturesque quarter of Lisbon, is referred to by Idrísí as *al-ḥamma*, the bath; Almada, on the south bank of the Tagus, he knew as *al-ma'din*, the mine, Arrábida, *ar-rabat*, signifies a fortified hermitage where you might expect to find a marabout – a word derived from the same root. Azeitão, on the way to it, is a place of green olives, *az-zaytuna*. Atafona was named from a bakery, *aṭ-ṭaḥuna*; Azambuja and Zambujeira are places of wild olives, *az-zunbúj*, while Santiago do Cacém recalls in its name the number of times that picturesque hill-town has been taken by the Knights of Santiago and lost again to the Moslems. *Ode-* and *Odi-* in the first part of a place-name are equivalent to river-bed, *wadi-*, which appears as *guad-* in place-names in Spain.

These names were not used only by the Arabic-speaking part of the population, but by the Romance-speaking part as well; and when in later times, during the Berber invasions from Morocco and the Christian reconquest, the Mozárabic Christians were forced to migrate from one part of the country to another and ultimately to the north, they brought the familiar Arabic place-names with them, and re-named, in Arabic, their new homes which till then had had perfectly appropriate names from Latin. Having been administered for some centuries by men of Arabic speech, they kept the Arabic words for officers and institutions – which they had learnt by ear and learnt somewhat incorrectly – long after the Arabic-speaking administrators had gone.[13] They had plants with names which once were Arabic and are still good Portuguese; and these are not fancy names.[14] The words derived from or through Arabic are as intimately Portuguese as the names of the English flowers in Shakespeare. Jasmine is no less English for having a name that was originally Persian.

The Moslems in Portugal grew cotton, *algodão*, and rice, *arroz*; they measured land by the size of a field which could be sown with an *alqueire*, approximately a bushel of seed. When land lay fallow it was called *alqueive*, from the Arabic, though in many parts of the country it is now called *pousio*, connected with the Latin PAUSA. Their houses had *adufas*, shutters; *aldraba*, a latch, and generally an *algeroz*, a gutter or spout. They were, and often still are, beautifully decorated with coloured tiles, *azulejos*, a word which was originally Persian but has reached Spain and Portugal in an Arabic form. Their clothes were, and still are, made by an *alfaiate*, tailor, if not bought ready-made, 'off the peg', from an *algibebe*; the pockets are called *algibeiras*.[15] Their horses and mules have *albardas*, pack-saddles; and the farrier or vet was called *alveitar*, an Arabic word ultimately derived from the Greek for 'horse-doctor'. They measured by the *arrátel*, pound, and the *almude*, gallon: the Latin MODIU(s) in an Arabic disguise: and, unlike the Spanish over the border, who were always inclined to dramatise everything, the Portuguese were more peaceable, and hated anything which could be described by an expressive word which the Mozárabic Christians had picked up from people who spoke Arabic: *azáfama*, a fuss.

When all is said and done, it is the Mozárabes who give permanent interest to the Moslem period in Portugal. In Spain, the Moslems have an interest of their own, apart from what they enabled others – Christians and Jews – to accomplish under their generally tolerant and easy-going government.

But in Portugal the chief Moslem contribution to the future was the policy of live and let live. It enabled the Mozárabes to learn trades and handicrafts, to acquire some notion of administration and government, of which the bellicose reactionaries in the north had little notion. They may have despised the Mozárabes, but they needed them. The tolerance of the Moslems is the more surprising the more we consider it, both for itself and for what came afterwards when dominion passed to the Christians. The monastery of Lorvão, near Coimbra, existed all through the Moslem occupation. A document (admittedly of doubtful authenticity) states that while some monasteries enjoyed their goods in peace by paying the statutory sum of fifty gold pieces, Lorvão paid nothing, because the monks were ready to show visitors round and gave Moslem guests a particularly friendly welcome.[16] Idrísí records the same of the monks of Cape St Vincent.

Perhaps the Moslems were only tolerant because it suited them; but that is a good reason for being so, and shows political wisdom. There were Arabs and Berbers who were not tolerant, even before the bitterness of the last stages of the Reconquista: those accustomed to a nomadic life, with their arms always in their hands, who did not wish to settle down and cultivate the land which had been allotted to them. They left the Mozárabic Christians in possession, provided that four-fifths of the produce was paid or handed over, according to the law. Those who were left to cultivate the fifth part belonging to the State were better off, since they only had to pay a third part of the produce in taxes. These privileged Mozárabic farmers were known to the Moslems by a special name, *al-akhmás* 'those of the fifth'; and their descendants, *Banu'l-akhmás*. Américo Castro brings ingenious and perhaps convincing reasons to show that these may be the origin of the class afterwards known for *hidalgos* in Spain and *fidalgos* in Portugal.[17] When the Moslem King of Seville, Abu'l-Qásim, made a raid into Portugal in 1025, he found at Alafões (north-west of Viseu) some Christians who had already made peace with the original Moslem conqueror, Músá ibn Nusair. They claimed descent from one Jebala ibn Alayham, an Arab convert to Christianity; but the truth was that they were descended from old Christians of the time of the conquest.[18]

A delightful example of Mozárabic customs, and of the friendly feeling and social contact between Mozárabic Christians and Moslems, is the Arabic description of the New Year Festival quoted long after by the seventeenth-century Arabic historian of Spain, al-Maqqarí.[19] A Moslem, visiting a Christian household on that day, found that they had made 'cities of cardboard with fine little figures'. And when, by gazing at the city, it seemed to have pleased him, the Mozárab said: 'Describe it, and take it.' The Moslem improvised the following verses:

> 'A walled city: how startling in its magic!
> It was not built but by the hands of a pure virgin.
> It is a bride paying a visit, all made of bread and flour and sweets;
> And it has no other keys than the ten fingers.'

This is probably the earliest reference in the Peninsula to the Christmas crib, the *presépio* still popular in Portugal, and Spain too; the crib, a little model of which most people still have somewhere in their houses, and which provided such wonderful opportunities to the seventeenth- and eighteenth-century *barristas*, makers of painted clay figures. In every church they put up what looked like a large toy theatre, with an immense, operatic scene filled with the processions of the Three Kings and a crowd of shepherds and shepherdesses, all apparently singing at the tops of their voices in praise of the Christchild born in the grotto somewhere in the middle of the scene.[20]

It throws much light on the condition of the Christians, the Mozárabes, under the Moslem governments in the Peninsula, that so characteristic a way of keeping Christmas and the New Year should have existed among them, and that a record of it should be preserved for us in an Arabic description written by a Moslem.

NOTES TO CHAPTER 3

[1] J. Cortesão, *Histório do regimen Republicano* (Introduction). Ed. J. Montalvor (1930), 37.

[2] Herculano, *Hist.* (8 ed.), tomo VI, Livro vii, 50.

[3] It is curious that neither Luis de León nor most of the Spanish or Portuguese translators or Virgil have seen the point, though often enough they must have seen the thing. Or was it – for Luis de León – that Salamanca was too far from what had been Moslem territory for that way of watering to be

known to him? It was used in Madrid, in the garden of the Residencia de Estudiantes. One would wake in the morning to hear the water under the window, running along the channel just opened for it by Marcelino with his hoe – the sound which Virgil heard in the Georgics and Camoens in the Lusiads:

> O tom das frescas agoas entre os pedras
> Que murmurando lava.

[4] The frontier between the Christian and Moslem states in the Peninsula is still shown by the distribution of the Near-Eastern water-wheel. J. Caro Baroja, 'Norias, azudas y aceñas.' *Rev. de Dialectología y tradiciones populares* (Madrid), X, 1954, 29–160.

[5] Sánchez-Albornoz, San Isidoro, 'Rasis y la Pseudo Isidoriana'. (*Cuadernos de Historia de España*, Buenos Aires (1946).

[6] Gama Barros, *Hist. da Admin. Publ. em Portugal*, 2nd ed. (1945), I, 75–76.

[7] *Chronica Pacensis*: *Neminem nisi per justiciam propriae legis damnat*; cf. Herculano, t.c., p. 26, n. 3.

[8] 'Ecclesias nuper structas et quicquid novo cultu in antiquis basilicis splendebat, fuerat qu(a)e temporibus arabum rudi formatione adjectum.' *Memoriale Sanctorum*. III, c. 3. Morales reads *formationi*.

[9] The horse-shoe 'Moorish' arch was known in the Peninsula – and in Portugal – some centuries before the Moslem invasion. It appears on a tombstone from Mértola (now in the Ethnological Museum at Belém), the date being Era 563, i.e. A.D. 525.

[10] *Guía de Portugal*, vol. 2: Extremadura, Alentejo, Algarve. (Bibl. Nac. de Lisboa, 1927), p. 145.

[11] E. de Campos, *O enquadramento geo-económico da população portuguesa através dos séculos* (1943), p. 30.

[12] David Lopes, 'Toponimia Arabe de Portugal'. *Revue Hispanique*, IX, 1902, 35.

[13] *Açougue* (or *azougue*) market 'souk', *aduana* customs, 'douane', *alcabala* purchase-tax, *alfândega* custom-house, *alfaqueque* an agent for the redemption of slaves or prisoners of war, and so messenger, *aljube* dungeon, *algoz* executioner, *almirante* admiral, *almocreve* carrier or muleteer, *almotacé* clerk of the market (there is an official with this title at Oxford), *almoxarife* tax-collector, *alvará* warrant, *alvazil* councillor.

[14] *Açafrão* crocus, *açafroa* safflower (Carthamus tinctorius), *açufeifa* jujube, *alcachofra* artichoke, *alcaçuz* liquorice, *alcaparra* caper (through the Latin CAPPARIS), *alcar* rock-rose, *alecrim* rosemary, *alface* lettuce, *alfarroba* carob, *alfavaca* pellitory or Portuguese milk-vetch (Astragalus lusitanica), *alfazema* lavender, *alfenheiro* privet, *alforva* a kind of spurge or fenugreek, *almeirão* chicory, *almeiroa* hawk's beard, *alpercheiro* (through the Latin) apricot, sometimes called *damasqueiro* or *albricoqueiro* (from Latin PRAECOX, with the addition of the Arabic definite article), *alquepenge* winter cherry, *alquitira* milk-vetch (Astragalus massiliensis), *anáfega* jujube, lotus, *arroz* rice, *azeitona* olive, *azaroleira* hawthorn, *azevém* English rye-grass, 'reigraz dos ingleses', *azinheira* ilex (through a Latin form like ILICINUM), *azuraque* or *zuraque* convolvulus.

[15] *Algibeira* is an Arabic word which has reached Portugal from Morocco; it is one of those Portugese words in common use which are not used in Spanish, v. *The Legacy of Islam* (Oxford, 1931), 23. It is worth noting that *Dicionário de algibeira* is a dictionary for the pocket, not a dictionary of algebra.

[16] F. J. Simonet, *Historia de los Mozárabes de España* (Madrid, 1897–1903), pp. 65–66:

> habeant sua bona in pace et *pechen* (pectent) praedictos L pesantes (besants?). Monasterium de Montanis qui dicitur Laurbano (Lorvão) non *peche* nullo pesante, quoniam vone (bona) intentione monstrant *mihi* loca de suis venatis et faciunt sarracenis bona *acolhenza*.

[17] A. Castro, *The Structure of Spanish History* (Princeton and Oxford, 1954), 100, 230.

[18] Dozy, *Scriptorum arabum loci de Abbadidis*, II, 7; Simonet, t.c. 654; Menéndez Pidal, *Orígenes del español y estado lingüístico de la Península Ibérica hasta el siglo, XI* (Madrid, 1926), 442.

[19] Al-Maqqarí, t.v., II, 463.

[20] *Presépios* lasted on, in cathedrals and parish churches, until well into the present century (the 1920's) when the clerical government foretold by the Virgin of Fátima (1917) ruthlessly 'dismounted' the *presépios* and swept them away, a few pathetic single figures being saved and exhibited in museums; the art of the *presépios* and the *barristas* did not fit the new ecclesiastical fashion for restoring or rebuilding churches in a style reminiscent of romanesque. The restored cathedral at Lisbon still has its *presépios*, and the Basilica of the Estrêla has one too, though the authorities are not overanxious to show it to foreigners and heretics. The Museum of Fine Arts, besides a few separate figures, has managed to preserve two whole *presépios* complete.

The quotation from Al-Maqqarí shows the custom to be an ancient one, going back to the time of the Mozárabes and the Reconquista – to those very times, in fact, which the modern restorers of Portuguese churches would like to imitate.

Chapter 4

The Reconquest and the Reconquered

I

'THERE WAS no ethnographic reason for the foundation of the Portuguese monarchy,' Oliveira Martins wrote.[1] The phrase was startling in 1882; but by now it is generally, if reluctantly, accepted. Oliveira Martins was not a historian in the modern sense, but a brilliant writer of prose who took history for his subject. Though his sources were secondary and conventional he often understood in a flash of intuition things which the trained historians of his time and the generation after him had missed by working to rule; and his phrases, without being mere fireworks, sometimes soar into the air like a rocket and illuminate the whole landscape with a burst of stars. On this occasion he knew that the northern part of modern Portugal, at first as far south as the Douro and then as far as the Mondego, had been 'reconquered' (or, rather, devastated) by Alfonso III of Castille towards the end of the ninth century, and colonised by Christians from Galicia and Asturias who came down to populate the border marches on the orders of their king. They were joined by Mozárabes coming up from the south; and thus it was with both northerners and southerners that the Portugal of the future may be said to begin.

To talk of 're'-conquest is begging the question. The various Christian kingdoms in the north of the Peninsula had arisen as points of resistance against the Moslems, and the frontiers changed frequently owing to the punitive expeditions sent up from Córdoba, the seat of the Caliph. The only territory with some degree of stability seemed to be that of Galicia, the southern frontier of which was then on the Mondego. The name *Portucale* appears from early times for a town on the right bank of the Douro, near its mouth; then, from the ninth century, it was applied to the territory between Douro and Minho. This was separated from Galicia in the tenth century, and then enlarged so as to include Coimbra (1064) on the Mondego, and granted as a fief to Count Henry of Burgundy, who had married Teresa ('Tareja' was the local pronunciation), an illegitimate daughter of Alfonso VI of Castille and León. Count Henry (d. 1112) and his widow (who in 1115 assumed the title of Queen) carried the boundaries of the family property east to Zamora in León and north to Tuy and Orense in Galicia. These she was unable to hold, and the boundaries returned to their present position as the frontiers of northern Portugal; but in the south things went better. Afonso Henriques,[2] their son, found the duties of vassalage to León a hindrance and broke them, declaring himself a vassal of the Pope. He then (for he was a bold and dashing commander) expanded his southern boundary to the Tagus, including Santarém, Cintra, Lisbon (1147), and across the river to Almada and Palmela. To capture Lisbon he had the help of a number of crusaders on the way to the Holy Land from Cologne, Flanders, and not least from England, one of whom (Osbern) left a vivid account of the siege, not forgetting the unedifying squabbles over the loot (even before it was taken), and implying the familiar types of English private soldier, sitting out all night in a machine like a wooden tower, and then appearing at dawn on the walls at a point where the exhausted garrison had never expected them. The crusaders, it must be admitted, behaved very badly. They cut down the Mozárabic Christian bishop, who appeared in his vestments to protect his church plate, and committed atrocities on people of their own religion, whom they had not expected to find there and thought to be only pretending. The saying that civilisation has to be built on a foundation of slaughter and slavery is no less true of the conquest of Lisbon than of other conquests. The crusaders were robber bands like the Northmen, though organised on a larger scale.

Afonso Henriques, like Count Henrique before him, was a Burgundian, at that time the most dynamic and energetic people in Europe. Having no powerful relations among the hidalgos of León,[3] he surrounded himself with horse and foot who were Burgundians too. The influence therefore of this Frankish influx on the population of the Portuguese provinces was important, and increased by the fact that the newly arrived men-at-arms and retainers belonged mainly to the more popular levels of society and fraternised with the original inhabitants.

They had none of the exclusive pride of the would-be Goths from León. In the west they found men of other stocks: Mozárabes, Moslems and Jews; the first likely to be land-workers, the second hard-working and adaptable, exercising all trades and professions, and the third, manual workers and craftsmen, and all more skilled than their conquerors. Only external events, then, made an independent state of Portugal, and created little by little in her inhabitants the sense of being a separate people. We know, of course, that 'Out of a fabulous story We fashion a nation's glory'; but it is well to be reminded of more sober history.[4] 'It does not make sense to explain the separation of Portugal as the consequence of certain hidden peculiarities of its region, when this region is next to Galicia which did not aspire to separation from Spain. Without the Burgundian counts and their will to be independent Portugal would never have become a nation.'[5]

2

It is difficult not to think the Mozárabic Christians happier under the freedom and toleration they had once enjoyed from the Moslems in the south, than under the dictatorial knights and violent churchmen who 'reconquered' them from the north. But often they had no choice. Conditions in the south had changed since the invasions of the fanatical Almorávides and Almohades from Morocco; and the exacerbation of religious feeling caused by the Christian victories over the Moslems made every Mozárabic Christian an enemy or perhaps a spy, so long as he remained in Moslem territory. Their life during the reconquest was not a happy one, and they often ended it worse off than before. Yet these Christian outcasts had a great love for Arabic things. We have already seen their liking for Arabic place-names in the way they brought them with them when they moved to another part of the country; and they went on calling institutions and officials by the Arabic titles they had always used, though by this time the original Arabic words had become something new and strange which would have horrified the correct, Yemenite speakers of Silves, if they had been alive to hear it. For the language that the Mozárabic Christians talked, and sang, among themselves was—we have seen—not Arabic but Romance: a countrified

Latin turning into Portuguese, which we can almost hear in some of their documents.

Another curious thing about the Mozárabes is their fondness for having their names written in an Arabic form, with *ibn* or *ben* before the name of their father, even though they themselves had always been stout Christians. Since most of them could neither read nor write it was not the look of the name that mattered, but the sound; they had grown so accustomed to telling Moslem officials that their names were 'X ibn Y', that they could not think of their names in any other way. Some historians have suggested that the names of this kind found in documents of the tenth and eleventh centuries are the names of Moslems, or of recent converts; but they cannot be explained away in this fashion, for they are witnessing Christian ecclesiastical documents. Again, Moslems are not easily converted; and when they are, it is generally *en masse*, on orders from above —not from conviction. They are as stout in their beliefs as the present-day Syrian Christians are in theirs.

These Mozárabes who are buying and selling land, making donations to churches or building new churches for themselves, are most frequently called in to witness the signatures – or crosses – of others. Their names are curious and characteristic. They may be joined by the Arabic *ibn* (son of), or the patronymic may have the Latin (or Gothic-Latin) genitive in *-is*, *-es*, *-iz* or *-ez*; but one of the names is always – or almost always – Latin or Germanic. One obvious exception is that of the two Mozárabs, Muzara and Zamora – it is not clear whether they were men or women – who had built a church to St Michael in Lauridosa, in 882.[6] Most names of Mozárabic donors or witnesses are of the mixed pattern: Gundemiro iben Dauti (937), Dulcidio iben Almundar (968), Melic iben Flores, Randulfo iven Spidio, Romano iben Froila, Omar iben Lucido and Amatorem iben Vassallo (976). A donation of Natalia and her daughter Palmella to the monastery of Vaccarica, in 1036, which includes various named country houses and possessions to be sold for the building of a church, is witnessed, amongst others, by Zacoi iben Belliti, Iubel ibn Abdela Argeriquiz and Zacoi iben Zacoi. In 1088 Zuleiman, presbyter, signed a deed of conveyance of a vineyard, written in appropriately rustic Latin.[7]

The few early wills which have been preserved give an idea of personal belongings of the time, and the words that were used for them. In 907 Odario Daviz (son of David) made a deed of gift to his sister, Trudillo, of a villa with its water-supply, AQUAS AQUARUM, three female slaves – Mariamen, Sahema and Zafara (clearly Moslems) – a silver cup and two sheets. In 1087 two Mozárabes, Didacus Fredariz and his wife Eugenia Maruaniz, left all they possessed, including their clothing of silk, linen or wool, to their brother Cidi, with the stipulation that he should give something towards the redemption of prisoners of war. Between 1153 and 1162 Petrus Salvatoris left his bed to the Cathedral of Coimbra, and his second-best bed to the Confraternity of Stonemasons, with an *almofala* (originally a Moslem prayer-mat) and a *plumoso* (feather-bed). To his sister, Maria Domna, he bequeathed his gown, *garnacha*; to her daughters, the sheets and blankets, and to Maria Salvatoris, another well-made bed, UNUM LECTUM BENE PRAEPARATUM, a cauldron, four large bowls, two table-services and two table-cloths. About the same time Archdeacon Dominicus bequeathed his large chest and two presses to his two nieces, and a bed with a feather mattress and a counterpane. He also left them his gown, which the scribe has here latinised into GARNACHIAM. Elvira de Sidi, who sounds like a Mozárab or the widow of a Mozárab, left (in 1107) a blanket to Mariam Mozaraba; to her granddaughter, her feather bed, *plumazo*. To the woman who looked after her she left four 'hands', MANUS, of linen or flax and a head-cloth, *tauca* (the modern *touca*, a word probably Celtic), and a pair of shoes, for which she used the same word that she would have used to-day – *çapatos*.[8]

A document of 1026 shows what sort of possessions were expected to be handed over in return for releasing persons who had been captured by Norse Vikings during one of their numerous raids on the Portuguese coast. A lady called Meitilli gave to a certain Octicio who had performed this service for her: the fourth part of two properties she possessed, together with a wolf-skin rug, a sword, a shirt, three sheets, a cow and three measures of salt 'because you have ransomed from captivity myself, Meitilli, with my daughter Guncina, and rescued us from the ships of the *Laudomanes* (Northmen) and gave for us . . .' the goods mentioned above.[9]

3

It may be true that, when the storm of the Reconquista was over, those villagers who had managed to escape in the confusion came back to the trampled fields they had known and the ruined hovels they had lived in. But the fact of being involved in the war of liberation made a great difference to the life of everyone who was left. Among the Christians who had been there before the fighting began, few were better off now that, instead of being subject to a Moslem, they were living under a successful crusader. The man who, under a Moslem lord, had enjoyed personal freedom and the right to own property, now probably found himself deprived of all his possessions by his new fellow-Christian and reduced to slavery by the man who had come to set him free.[10]

Sometimes, on his raids into enemy territory, after villages had been razed to the ground and crops and houses entirely destroyed, the conquering king would carry off all the inhabitants he could catch, Christian or Moslem, all equally prisoners of war and all equally destined for slavery . . . under Christian masters. Had they not been delivered from slavery under the infidel: INFIDELIUM SERVITUTE? [11] On one occasion, after an expedition south of the Tagus, the first King of Portugal and founder of Portuguese independence, Afonso Henriques, brought into Coimbra nearly a thousand Mozárabes; and it was only at the urgent request of the Bishop, Theotonio, that these Christians were not made slaves like the Moslems. The life of St Theotonio – for he was afterwards canonised – gives an idea of what the existence of these transported Mozárabes was like, even when they were not sold into slavery: a considerable number were kept alive only through the charity of the monastery of Santa Cruz.

After such reports of what was in store for them, it is no wonder that Mozárabic Christians sometimes fought against those of their own faith, and stood side by side with their Moslem neighbours; that was the only way to defend their position and their liberty.

Though captured Moslems were at first enslaved, by the end of the eleventh century the charter of Santarém (1093) shows Moslems living there under the protection of their own officials.

The same was true of Valencia when the Cid took it in 1094. This exemplary leniency was due to Alfonso VI of Castille, the 'Emperor of the two religions'; and at first, while the reconquest moved southwards through Portugal, many Moslems went on living in relative freedom. Their lives and goods were respected, with their religion and their liberty; and they were obviously assisted by the old Mozárabic Christian families. But with the Moslems definitely expelled from a conquered district, the sedentary Christian did not find himself any better off than his ancestors 700 years before, when the Peninsula was first invaded by the Germanic tribes. The Visigoths had left the owners with one third of their land, while confiscating the other two-thirds; now, when the land returned to Christian dominion once more, the conquerors took everything: land, livestock, implements and the farm-hands as well. The people became serfs; ADSCRIPTI GLEBAE, inseparable from the land and legally a part of it. On passing from subjection to a Moslem ruler to the lordship of a Christian king, the land was appropriated, in the king's name, for the benefit of a sovereign who could divide it among his companions in arms or keep it for himself.

The original owners, and the free farm-workers who had managed not to be carried off in the previous invasions as prisoners of war, now found themselves reduced to penury. They had nothing left; their deliverers had taken everything, and they had no alternative but to become serfs. The only free men were those who had come with the conquerors. They were permitted, in certain circumstances, to leave the land allotted to them; but the serf, the ADSCRIPTUS, could not do so. He was perpetually chained to the land, and his only compensation was that he could not be expelled from it, and his right of occupation was inherited by his children. When the owner changed, and the land was conveyed to another person, the serfs who cultivated it were conveyed too. 'The serf (Gama Barros says) had not only to do farmwork and act as shepherd, cowman and groom. He was found in domestic service and became cook, baker, fisherman or builder's labourer, as his lord directed. He was smith, saddler, shoemaker or tiler; working in his own hut or in the lord's more spacious abode. There was no other way of maintaining the economic unity of castle, lordship or monastery.' Every settlement had to be self-supporting. But there was one rung of the ladder lower still, one man who was worse off than the serf. That was the Moslem prisoner of war, who was generally a slave in every sense of the word.

These were the conditions in the northern part of the country. In the south the happier state of life had changed too. In the Algarve, and even more in the Alentejo, the perpetual raids had turned agriculture into something that was annual, transitory, as if it were the agriculture of nomads and people always on the move. Even so, the whole year's efforts of a man and his family often came to nothing: documents, particularly from towns and villages near the border, show that expeditions to rob or destroy enemy property, and particularly to burn his harvest, were events which happened nearly every year.

The result was that country-people could not live – as they do to-day in the Algarve and north of the Tagus – in scattered farms and houses. The conditions were more like those of central and southern Spain or southern Italy and Sicily, where people lived, and still live, in walled towns and fortified villages (or at any rate, live together, for mutual protection in a settlement) and cultivate such land as they can reach in a day's journey, backwards and forwards, on a mule. Land that was too far away went out of cultivation; and in some places cultivation was possible only round walled towns defended by a castle. The need for that ended, however, in 1249, when Afonso III captured Faro, the chief town of the Algarve; and from 1268 the kings of Portugal styled themselves 'Rei de Portugal e do Algarve'. The old look of the countryside began to return; isolated houses and farms gradually reappeared, which were (in the north, at any rate) descendants of the original hill-villages, *castros* or *citânias*; while the new population, in spite of everything that had happened – with the invasions of Romans, Barbarians, Orientals and Crusaders – were in a way the descendants of the original inhabitants of the country.

Personal slavery was not a condition peculiar to captured Moslems; the names in the documents are not always Arabic. Indeed, slaves by birth often had high-sounding Germanic names like their masters: 'Our men-slaves and women-slaves, Lovesendo and Animia, Froilo with her daughter Eilo, and

Fernando' are named in a document of 1073. A hundred years earlier (981), Fernando Sandiniz and his wife gave to the monastery of Lorvão a third of their villa of Recardanes, with a freed slave and his wife and twenty measures of salt. The freedman is called Teodemiro Alvitis and his wife Ermesinda. The Christian slaves were valued more highly than the Moslems; they were not mere merchandise like the 'Moor priced at 40 shillings' whom Gotierre Suariz sold to Gundisalvo Nuniz in 1090. The Moor was probably a groom or muleteer; for he went with 'a mule with its saddle and bridle worth 200 shillings and 100 shillings'. In 961, Aldreto Olidiz, bailiff of Domna Elduara, sold Iquila iben Nezeron, his wife and children, 'all for the price of one Christian captive'.[12]

For a time, then, the Reconquest ruined what had been, in most places, a stable and happy civilisation. A population widely dispersed, in the manner of Mesopotamia or Valencia,[13] between the River Lis in the north and the Guadiana in the south, became a people which could be administered by no government for long because it was perpetually subject to invasion from one side or the other. It is usual to speak of a *despoblado* – an uninhabited desert – lying between them; but this is inaccurate. It was not uninhabited – in Portugal, at any rate – because, though often devastated, something could always be found to grow there. So far was the land from being uncultivated, that we find vineyards and orchards which could only have belonged to a sedentary, agricultural population, after living there for a considerable time. When Alfonso I appeared and imagined that he had killed off all the Moslems and carried off all the Christians, the disappearance of the population was likely to have been only temporary. When the King had gone and the danger seemed to have passed, they came out of their hiding-places and set to work to repair the damage. It is impossible to believe [14] that all the inhabitants, from Lugo south to Viseu, had been forced to follow the King back to Asturias. Some may have been carried off; some may have followed him of their own free will; but there must always have been some who stayed where they were, hiding when the troops came, whether they were friends or enemies, and thus making the country look deserted because there was no one to be seen.[15] The documents published by Gama Barros show

C

clearly that, in Portugal at any rate, the land never really became a desert.

Other documents show that the parishes went on existing all through the Moslem occupation. The continued existence of a parish can be proved from the name of its patron saints.[16] In the tenth and eleventh centuries, the older churches, and those which had been rebuilt, were still named after saints who were already in the calendar in Visigothic times. There had been no break in continuity; the religious tradition had never been interrupted, even under the Moslems. It is commonly believed in Spain, however, that it was the Christian refugees in the mountains of Asturias who began the reconquest, coming (their chroniclers claim) as the conscious, legal heirs and racial successors of the Visigoths; if that were so, we may wonder that any of the original inhabitants managed to survive, since reconquest is always more destructive than conquest in the first instance.

4

In any case, the men of the reconquest had acquired a country 'devastated by wars of religion and embittered by racial hatred'.[17] Many villages were heaps of ruins, and even the cathedral city of Braga had not escaped altogether. The first task of the new monarchy was to rebuild the older settlements from their ashes and create new ones; that is to say, to attract men and families who would build new villages and cultivate the land. With this object, charters were granted: *forais* (sing. *foral*), not to be confused with the *foros* (sing. *foro*) referred to in Chapter II, which were the usages derived from ancient customary law. The charter or *foral* was, therefore, a document creating a municipal council, a *conselho*. It regulated the rights and duties of the inhabitants of a town or village. But the word was not always used in the strict sense; it was sometimes taken to mean the code of law given to a municipality which had no customary law of its own; or again, it was used in the sense of a hereditary lease, given collectively to a number of individuals, whose rent was confusingly called the *foro*. But the principal and most important type of *foral* was the charter for founding or refounding a town or village; to attract a population by the offer of advantageous terms.[18]

The genuine *foral*, the charter of a commune, which brought a municipal council into existence, came from the King. In the preamble, the territory is referred to by the words MEAM HEREDITATEM, 'my property'; and if the King did not actually promulgate the *foral* himself, the officer who did so was acting as the King's representative. The *forais* generally refer to an overlord SENIOR TERRAE or *senhor da terra*; but the institutions of the municipality did not need such an office, for the new council had often been established in waste land or in an old settlement which had been destroyed to its very foundations and which the new inhabitants had to rebuild and cultivate, and had no overlord but the King who founded it. The charter foresaw this and provided for the duties of the inhabitants, not only towards the donor of the charter but also to his representative, the SENIOR TERRAE.

The reason for this came principally from the state of war between Moslems and Christians, one of sudden attacks and raids, *arrancadas* and *algaras*; and that involved the existence of a fortified castle into which women and movable property could be put for safety, and which was governed and defended by a royal representative bearing the Arabic or Mozárabic title of *alcaide*. The personal services laid down in the charter included work on the fortifications (called by a Mozárabic name *anuduba*), service with the expeditionary force (*hoste* or *fossado*) which went out on the annual raids to burn the enemy's harvest, and a 'call-up' (*apellido*) for home defence. There were also guard duties described by the Germanic word *guardias* or the Mozárabic *atalaias*. They were not the same; *atalaia* was rather to be understood as duty in an observation post.

It is incorrect to speak of 'feudal' times or conditions in Portugal. Afonso Henriques, by a calculation which proved expensive to his successors, had transferred his feudal allegiance from the King of León to the Pope; and though some fashions from feudal countries crept in, feudal organisation never came completely. The permanent ownership of the land vested in the *feudatorio* and his successors, and the obligation of military service with the overlord, had some faint shadow of the hierarchies of feudalism. But that was all, for these conditions of military service and perpetuity of succession did not always apply; they were not found on domains of the nobles.

The reconquest meant that what had hitherto been a land without a stable government was now administered by Afonso Henriques. From being the great guerilla leader of his time, the first King of Portugal became the cautious legislator, and within a few years of his accession (1145) we find him inconspicuously adding his name to a municipal document in Coimbra, a document chiefly concerned with fixing prices.[19] Its great interest is that it deals with common objects in the life of the time: the things which people used every day and the words which they used for them. The King is most concerned that no one should sell iron except to a smith, and at a fixed price. A ploughshare should weigh six pounds and cost 18 'pence' (*denarii*); other agricultural implements have their weights and prices. Boots and shoes are controlled. Vineyards must be carefully protected, especially from small boys, who were to be beaten till the blood came if they were caught trespassing or stealing. Men were not to go rabbiting in the vineyards, with dogs. Bakers were controlled, and so were fishmongers. Those who complain of the number of controls in a modern state should study the legislation of the first Kings of Portugal.

This document is definitely in Latin, and shows few signs of melting into Romance, though it is bespattered with Mozárabic words: objects are called by the names by which everyone knows them. Again, when Évora was occupied (1166), its first charter (*foral*) is in Latin. There is a fair sprinkling of vernacular words; yet they are not usually of Arabic or Mozárabic origin, but introduced into the lawyer's Latin as if for greater clearness, and to leave no doubt in the minds of all whom it might concern what was actually meant.[20] The King and Queen, wishing to restore and populate 'Elbora which we have taken from the Saracens', give it FORUM ET COSTUME DE AVILA: the *foral* (charter) and the *foros* (customary law) of the type which had been given to Ávila in Old Castille. (There were three main types: Salamanca, Ávila and Santarém.) The first thing was the armed forces; Évora was still a frontier station. The fine for not answering the call-up was ten *solidos* (shillings) for *cavaleiros* and five for foot-soldiers. Every man who had a house, a yoke of oxen, forty sheep, an ass and two beds was obliged to keep a horse and turn out with it for military service. When there was a brawl among the villagers at home, wounds were taxed, and those who caused them fined according to a definite tariff. Then there follow the penalties usual in customary law: in this instance 100 *solidos* for homicide, 300 for rape.

Reconquest was not the most important thing for people in general, however large it loomed in the vision of a king. Most Alentejanos, like the population of Évora, were interested in cattle and sheep; and the customs of cattle-men and shepherds have a special vocabulary of their own,[21] already noticeable in the *forais* of Afonso Henriques, and still more pronounced under Dom Denis, when the customs of Évora were passed on to another town in 1280. The head-shepherd generally bore the Arabic name of *rabadam* and lived with the gentlemen; he was responsible (and is so to-day) for paying and clothing each assistant, *zagal* or *azagal*, the shepherd's boy who sometimes had no wages and served only for his keep. The swineherd, *conhecedor dos porcos*, the man who 'knew about pigs', was termed *alfreyreyro* or *alfeireiro*. *Alfeire*, originally the 'fold', came to be used of a flock of sheep, and then for a ewe. *Amece* was a word for the unappetising cheese which the authorities now say could be so easily improved by more careful preparation.

The King, the Queen and their three sons confirmed the charter of Évora, but made crosses instead of appending their signatures. They could not read or write. It is noteworthy that the fines are to be paid AD PALACIUM, a phrase of Oriental origin, explained by Américo Castro.[22] Afonso Henriques, now styled *Rey dos Portugueses*, King of the Portuguese, gave a charter to the town of Santarém (Saint Irene) after he had captured the castle from the Moslems in 1179 'by the labour of myself and of my body, and the vigilant subtlety both of myself and of my men'.[23] The charter, which is preserved in Portuguese – in a crabbed style and uncertain spelling – removes the land-tax but renews the royal duty on wine; it lays down what crops should be cultivated, how much the labourers should be paid, and deals once more with such things as rabbits and their skins (for furs) and strayed cattle. The life of medieval people in Portugal was very carefully regulated for them in Santarém, as it was in Coimbra. The king also confirmed the customary law (*foros*) of the city, supporting the authority of the municipal officers – who still have their Mozarabic names: *alcayde*, *alvizÿs*, *almoxarife* – in their efforts to ensure that damage done in corn-fields should be set right by March 1, and that if anyone cut down, uprooted or broke a tree, he should plant another one instead.

At Santarém[23] there were also customs dealing with lost or strayed cattle, and a recommendation that owners should protect their land by fencing. We learn that wine used to come up to Santarém in boats on the Tagus. The wine-duty (*relego*) was an important part of the royal revenue. There was a certain time of year (from January 1 to April 1, as a rule) during which all wine sold was the property of the king, with absolute prohibition on any other person from selling wine of the same quality. Later, the *relego* became a tax, and then the word came to mean the place where the tax was paid; but the charters and customs, *forais* and *foros*, show that it was a royal prerogative, jealously guarded.

5

These examples show the new king of the Portuguese engaged in the administration of his newly reconquered territories, and the kind of life which was lived in them. Comparing them with the documents from the north, the first thing that strikes us is the language. The language of administration in the south is almost from the first Portuguese, with a sprinkling of Mozárabic words for the officials whose offices had been taken over from the Moslems. In the north, the language of administration is Latin; but it is a Latin continually sliding into a primitive Romance language – now Portuguese, now Spanish – whenever it is a question of everyday things, for it is important to use the word which everyone understands.

The Latin *foral* de Melgaço of 1181 [24] is a case in point. Melgaço is on the Minho, in the far north of the country and facing Spain; and once more we cannot help being surprised by the way that the smallest details of life are regulated. We have information about the price of clothing which could be bought either at the fair or from a wandering pedlar: *manto* and *saia* and *capa galega*; sheepskin, goatskin or even ox-hide (probably to keep out the rain), though that was distinctly expensive. The goods and prices can be compared with those in a document from the same district of seventy years later. From

goatskin and ox-hide, the inhabitants have now a choice of the
best stuffs of English (*engres*) or Flemish (*framenga*) make; *Gam*
(Ghent), *Ruans* (Rouen), *Ipli* or *Ipri* Ypres, *Trinquintaine* (St
Quentin?), *Abonvilla* (Abbeville), *Lila* (Lille), *Stanforte* (Stam-
ford, or more probably the Stanfort family at Arras), St
Omer, *Caam* (Caen), Bruges, Chartres, Arras, Valenciennes,
Tournay, and from Palencia and Segovia in Spain.[25] In Melgaço there were still fines for assault and battery. To hit a man
'above the beard' cost twice as much as to hit him below the
beard or below the belt; but if the man were killed, the aggres-
sor was liable to a heavy fine, equivalent to the fine for rape.
The officers of justice, accompanied by the sheriff, the representative of the King (VICARIUS), came to the door with an
application for bail, paid by a friend; and the criminal had to
surrender in nine days and pay the amount of the damage. If he
absconded, the fine was levied against his house and property,
though no one might hurt him except his personal enemies.

The most interesting Portuguese *foros* are a group from four
small villages in the north. Two of them, Alfaiates and Castel
Rodrigo, became Portuguese in a raid by King Denis in 1291;
but the others, Castel Bom and Castel Melhor, seem to have
been included in the territory of León until a later date. The
foros of Alfaiates are the most primitive, both in spirit and in
the peculiarly barbarous form of clerical Latin in which they
are drafted, full of local words and clumsy Latinisations, and
date from 1188 to 1230. Those of Castel Bom are also in *Latim
bárbaro*; but in the versions which are definitely in the vernacular, that of Castel Rodrigo (1209) is predominantly in Portuguese, while the later version of Castel Melhor is distinctly
Castilian: their *foros* are clearly derived from the primitive version of Alfaiates. Taken together, the four groups form an extraordinary demonstration of country customs in the twelfth and
thirteenth centuries; and again of country Latin turning, under
our very eyes or while we actually listen, to archaic Portuguese
and Spanish.

First there was the danger of fire, not only from accidental
fires, but from those who deliberately started fires by burning
their stubble, in the Virgilian manner, as a preparation for
the next sowing. There was a fine if someone deliberately burnt
his neighbour's *treznales* or *gavelas* – sheaves or stooks of rye,

barley or oats – in the next field, or, earlier in the year, had set
fire to his hay crop. The fines were usually reckoned in *morabitinos* – *maravedís* in Spain – the small gold coins of the Al-
moravid dynasty from Morocco; but if the fine for a stubble fire
spreading was three, the fine for a more disastrous fire was ten,
or – at Alfaiates – as much as the owner claimed. This included
damage to vineyards, kitchen-gardens, cornfields, bee-hives and
watermills. Deliberate arson, or the destruction of a vineyard,
house or garden 'knowingly committed', would incur the same
fine as that for murder.

Like Coimbra, Alfaiates and the other villages had special
but puzzling regulations for blacksmiths. They might make or
keep ploughshares from one St Cyprian's day (12 October) to
the next; but if they had managed to make as many as fifteen
and have them in stock, they were relieved from two taxes
(*posia* and *fazendeira*) and from being called up for military service on a raid (*fossado*) or for home defence (*apelido*). They were
also expected to keep tools sharp for the whole community.
Shoeing smiths had to use shoes and nails approved by the
Council. A man who left an animal loose, without a head-rope,
was fined a *maravedí*; but if the animal could be proved to have
eaten the rope, the owner had to provide another.

Customs regarding the preservation of trees had existed,
we saw, from Visigothic times and varied from one place to another. The *foral* of Évora (1166) already has an injunction
against indiscriminate cutting. Alfaiates must have had few
trees and fewer vines, and did its best to protect them by *foro*.
The fine for tearing up a tree by the roots or cutting it down (if
it stood on common land belonging to the Council) was five
times what it was in the other villages, and these mention vines
and fruit-trees as coming within the prohibition and incurring a
heavier fine. The Visigothic laws had been careful to distinguish, in the original Latin codices, resinous trees and fruit-
trees; but the Castilian translation, of the FORUM JUDICUM, coming from a country which even then may have been relatively
treeless, compared with Portugal, merely says 'trees of what kind
you will'. Alfaiates, however, is more definite about trees than
any of the other villages. Oaks were protected. Every man who
cuts an oak, *Toto homine qui robre cortar*, is liable to a fine of one
(gold) *maravedí*. But the *foros* are even more severe on damage

to resinous trees. 'Whoso shall strip the bark from a pine-tree or cut a sapling shall pay four *maravedís*, half to him who speaks of it (reports it) and half to the castle.' [26] More decisive still is 'Whoso shall cut down a pine, let them hang him: *Qui pino taiare, inforquen-lo*'.

Running water, *toto fonte perenal*, was protected; but if a spring on a man's land was large enough, other householders might use it. A man who dug a well on his own land was not bound to share it, however. The working of watermills, like windmills, was regulated; the *foros* lay down when the millers shall grind, and when not. Water should not be diverted from other people's gardens. For every mill which might take water from a garden, the owner of the mill pays one *maravedí* towards damage to the garden.[27]

If a man did not duly cultivate his land he was liable to be turned off, and the Council would let it to another. An old and important *foro*—Alfaiates had two versions of it—prohibited flour from being exported to Moslem territory. The prohibition also covers arms and horses, cheese and honey. The penalty was that the culprit should lose all that he had, and that summary justice should be done upon him. The oldest version says bluntly: 'Let them hang him'. The prohibition was repeated and reinforced in the 'Ordinances of Alfonso', the *Ordenações Alfonsinas* of 1273.

Alfaiates and Castel Bom have another *foro* about bread and wine, butcher's meat, dried fish and cheese, which (as Aristophanes said of a statute of Pericles) is 'worded like a drinking-catch':

> Pan de panadera
> et uino de tauernera,
> et carne de carnicero
> et pescado seco de zacatera,
> aut de kesera,
> que habuerit dineros
> a dar de los a tercero die.

> Bread from the baker's lass,
> and wine from the tavern miss,
> and meat from the butcher,
> and stockfish from the fishmonger
> or else from the cheesemonger;
> for him who shall have money then
> to give three days from now to them.

There must be an old Spanish rhymed proverb at the back of this. Alfaiates and Castel Bom also share a *foro* which can only be described as the story of what happened to the man who took his dog for a walk in a vineyard. 'Whosoever has a dog in a village where there are vines, and the dog goes to the vines, and the lord of the vineyard sees him there and catches him, the dog's master shall pay 5 solidos (5 shillings). But if he put the dog into the hands of the lord of the vineyard, and (if) the dog's master were saying: "My dog did not go into your vineyard", let him swear alone that he caught it in his vineyard, and let him pay the fine. But if he puts the dog into the hands of the plaintiff at the time of ripe grapes, and if the dog has (broken) a branch five palms in length and two (one) in width, the dog's master shall pay with a skin of wine, if there be two witnesses, without the branch, according to the *foro*.'

NOTES TO CHAPTER 4

¹ Oliveira Martins, *Hist. de Portugal* (1882).

² Tomas da Fonseca, *Don Afonso Henriques e a fundação da nacionalidade portuguesa*. (Coimbra, 1949).

³ A. Sérgio, *Considerações histórico-pedagógicos* (1915), 9–12.

⁴ These views have been expressed most recently by Américo Castro, t.c. They are also to be found in António Sérgio, passim, and (so long ago as 1901) in the chapter in Gröbers *Grundriss*, II, ii, 129, by Carolina Michaelis de Vasconcellos.

⁵ Castro, t.c., 173, n. 84.

⁶ The examples are taken from *Port. Mon. Hist.*, from Gama Barros, 2nd ed., IV, 44 and Appendix ix and from Rocha Madahil, *Documentos para o estudo da cidade de Coimbra na Idade-Média*, I (Coimbra, 1933). The detailed study of Visigothic names by J. M. Piel, 'Sobre a formação dos nomes de mulher medievais hispano-visigodos', appeared after this chapter was written (*Estudios dedicados a Menéndez Pidal*, VI, 1956, 111–150).

⁷ His Latin is typical; one can almost hear him dictating: Mea uinea qui est in illa uarzena trans flumine mondega. *Várzea*, a cultivated field, is a word confined to Hispanic Latin, and probably of Iberian origin. It occurs in many Portuguese place-names.

⁸ Another twelfth-century document from Coimbra mentions a fur coat (*alphanbaram pelliciam*) and a bed with its Arabic-named bed-clothes: *alifaffe et tapete et almuzala*. P. de Azevedo, in *O Arqueólogo Português*, VI, 1901, 202–204.

The Coimbra documents give the earliest Portuguese word for 'privy': *tristega* (1126, 1145, 1170, 1190). TRISTECA, the original late Latin form. occurs in 1148, and is defined in 1170: CUM VESTRA TRISTECA ID EST LATRINA, For royalty, however (Afonso I), they were described as PRIVATAS DOMOS SUAS SIVE LATRINAS (1172).

⁹ *Port. Mon. Hist.*, *Dipl. et Ch.* I, 161. The term 'Laudomanes' for Northmen is explained by Sousa Viterbo, *Elucidario*.

For Viking raids on Portugal see A. K. Fabricius, *La connaissance de la péninsule espagnole par les hommes du Nord*, and *La première invasion des Normands dans l'Espagne mussulmane en 844*; apud Saavedra Machado, 'Los ingleses em Portugal' (Coimbra, *Biblos*, VIII, 1932, nos. 9–12; IX, 1933, 1–4, etc.).

[10] J. Lúcio de Azevedo, *História de Portugal*, II, 395: 'Organização económica'.

[11] The following examples are taken from Herculano, *Hist.*, 8 ed., VI, liv. vii, p. 54, etc. Two of these men happened to be monks, still wearing their monastic habit: men who had grown old in the service of their religion under an alien ruler; for they had come from 'the Church of S. Vicente, situated on the Cape of the Arabs', i.e. Cape St Vincent. Yet this was described as 'infidelium servitute'.

[12] *P.M.H.*, *Dipl. et Chart.*, nos. 507, 1333, 744, 85.

[13] The comparison is that of E. de Campos.

[14] Sampaio, t.c. I, 54.

[15] Pierre David, t.c., 167 ff.

[16] Pierre David, 'L'hagiotoponymie comme science auxiliare de l'histoire', t.c., 243 ff., and P. Miguel de Oliveira, *As Paróquias Rurais Portuguesas* (1950).

[17] Herculano, 'Apontamentos para a História dos Bens da Coroa e dos Forais'. *Opúsculos*, VI, 205.

[18] Herculano, Hist., VII, 83. The Spanish *fuero* was wider; it included both the Portuguese *foro* and *foral*, and a corpus of laws as well, cf. Alfonso X, *Las siete partidas*, Pt. I, tit. 2, 1.4: Costumbre es derecho o fuero que no es escripto.

[19] *P.M.H.*, Liv. I, fas. 4–6, p. 743. Gomes Ramalho, 'A legislação agricola' (*Bol. da Direcção Geral da Agricultura*, VIII, Anno. No. 4, p. 8). 'Posturas municipaes de Coimbra', 1145.

These municipal regulations have puzzled students of Portuguese Latinity; and well they might, from the number of words which the Mozárabic population had learnt from the Moslems: e.g. *Eisada* ET FERRUM DE ARATRO QUOD PESAVERIT VIes *arráteles* PRO DECEM ET OCTO DENARIIS UNUMQUODQUE ILLORUM; a heavy hoe (*enxada*) and ploughshare weighing six pounds, for eighteen 'pence' each. *Arrátel* was an Arabic or Mozárabic weight of rather less than half a kilo, still used in country places and markets.

Sacjio DE DUOBUS *arratalis* PRO III DENARIOS: *sacho*, from a late Latin SARCULUM is the small hoe.

Azeca ET *seca* DE *uesadoiro* III DENARIOS *arratel*.

Alfabezeiras NEC ALIQUIS FACIAT *alkeires* NISI PER MANUM DE *almutazeb*, ET SIT *alkeir* DE VI *arrateles* ET MEDIUM. *Alfabezeiras* are bakers (*al-khabbâz*); *alkeair* (*alqueire*) is an ancient measure of capacity (*al-kail* or *al-qûîl*), say a bushel. *Almutazeb* (*almotacé*), the clerk of the market, *almuqtasih*.

[20] *P.M.H.*, 'Foralia', p. 392; Gabriel Pereira, *Documentos históricos da cidade de Évora* (Évora, 1887), I. The Portuguese version (Rivara, *Documentos do Archivo Municipal Eborense*, I, and a. Gomes Ramalho, t.c., I, 8–9) should be the oldest document in Portuguese; but it is preserved in a fourteenth century copy in a MS. Livro de Posturas at Évora. The earliest genuine surviving specimen of Portuguese dates from 1192.

[21] Studied by the Conde da Ficalho, 'O elemento árabe na linguagem dos pastores alentejanos' (five articles in *A Tradição*, Lisbon, 1900, vol. 1) and by M. L. Wagner, 'Sobre alguns arabismos do português', *Biblos*, X, 1934, 427 ff. There are characteristic words for cattle, flocks, clothes and utensils; but the number really derived from Arabic is small. 'It is not only, however, in these words that the ancient influence of the 'Moors' (Moiros)

is revealed. In the whole system of cattle-breeding can be discovered the influence of a people of Semitic race, of nomad instincts; a people for whom cattle have been for a long time a chief source of wealth.'

[22] Américo Castro, t.c.

[23] *Foros de Santarém* (1179). A. Gomes Ramalho, t.c., 9–10; from *Ineditos de História Portuguesa*, IV, 531.

[24] *Foral de Melgaço* (1181). A Gomes Ramalho, I, 14–16; from *P.M.M.*, vol. I, fasc. 1, 2 & 3, fol. 422.

[25] Prices in the province of Minho (1252), from J. P. Ribeiro, *Dissertações Chronologicas*, III, 59; and Gomes Ramalho, t.c. I, 88–94:

Cobitus (CUBITUS, yard) of

escarlata englesa meliori	70 solidos
melior escarlata framenga	3 libras
Ingres tinto in grano	405 solidos
meliori panno tinto de Gam aut de Ruans aut de Ipli	400 solidos
meliori engres	1 libram
meliori trinquintane	18 solidos
meliori Grisay	1 libram
bono panno de Abonvilla	1 libram
meliori viado de Lila aut de Ipli, esforciato	1 libram
meiori Brugia faldrada, aut de meliori Stanforte de Brugiis	15 solidos
aliis Brugiis	14 solidos
Sancto Omer	13 solidos
ssargia	13 solidos
Pruis	13 solidos
prumas de Normandia et de Roan, et de Chartes, et de Rocete	13 solidos
Arraiz	11 solidos
Valencina	9 solidos
Stamforte de Caam	9 solidos
Tornay	10 solidos
Stamforte viadu de Ipri	11 solidos
pannis viadis, det planis de Larantona	11 solidos
frisa	8 solidos
barragam	8 solidos
Chartes	10 solidos
piquote Palentiano	5 solidos
Sagobiano	4 solidos
meliori sargia cardada castellana	4 solidos
alia sargia	3 solidos
armarfega	2 solidos
vara de burello	2 solidos

Cf. C. Verlinden, 'Draperie flamande dans la Peninsule Ibérique au XIIIe siècle' (*Revue du Nord*, Lille, XXII, 1936, no. 85, p. 20). The writer identifies the places, but does not mention this document.

[26] Qui pino descortezar aut pimpolo taiare pectet IV morabitinos, medios ad qui lo falaret et medios al castello.

Falaret is an attempt of the scribe to latinise the Portuguese *falar*, to speak, when the real Latin (though he did not know it) was FABULARE.

[27] Toto molino qui aqua toliere ad ortos . . . pectet 1 M. domnus de molino ad dampnum de orto.

Chapter 5

Farms, fruit, fairs and fish

I

THE RECONQUEST advanced slowly southwards. How slow it was becomes clear when we remember that the Moslems took only a year or two to occupy practically the whole country, while the Christians took several centuries. It was 450 years before they got to Lisbon (1147), and 550 years before they had completely occupied the Algarve (1250). In Spain, where the difficulties were greater, there were parts of the country under Moslem government from 711 to 1492—780 years.

One reason for the slowness of the reconquest was that the 'new Goths' found it difficult to adapt themselves to the southern half of the country.[1] The dry summers of Alentejo – and, above all, the Spanish Meseta – proved too much for them at first. That is hardly to be wondered at. Their fathers and forefathers had come from the damp forests of north-eastern Europe. Again, they came of warlike stock; their main idea was to reap and profit where others had sown. It took centuries before some of them could adapt themselves to cultivation and trade; and in Spain the *caballero* – the man on a horse – was by instinct a cattle-man, a migratory shepherd, who looked down on the sedentary cultivator and merchant. In Portugal, expansion towards the south into the territory of the 'infidel' offered a convenient escape from the pressure of the Spaniards in the north, and a livelihood which did not need industry of their own. In northern Portugal, people were living (as we saw) in small groups surrounded by fields, or in clearings in woods. Further south there were the newly acquired lands where more labour was needed than the conquered Mozárabes (Christian) or Mudéjares (Moslem) were able to supply. The only way to persuade others to join them was to give the settlers the land and make them relatively free.

Property abandoned, or without effective ownership, came

to the king by right of conquest; though much of it was afterwards given away in reward for services rendered during the
wars. Yet there still seemed to be land available for those who
cared to take it; and in the ninth and tenth centuries, if not
later, many Crown lands were disposed of in this way. The process had a legal name, *presúria*,[2] and the occupation was conducted in due legal form: a freeman, in the presence of one or
two witnesses, with a trumpeter and a flag, would go out and
mark in the king's name the boundaries of the land he intended
to occupy. The trouble came later, when the owners, or their
descendants, had to justify their title. On 30 April 870, a man
called Cartemiro and his wife Astrilli defended their claim
against a counterclaim by the Church declaring that they held
their land and its boundaries *de presúria*, because they had
taken it first CUM CORNU ET CUM ALUENDE DE REGE, with the
sound of the horn and the standard of the king. In the same
year Flomarico, his sister Gundila and his wife Astragundia
occupied land in the same way, though with less certain Latin
(CUM CORNAM ET ALBENDE).[3] The boundary was marked with a
plough; in the thirteenth century an owner declared: 'This
land . . . our father Roy Periz took with his plough, and I
with him, for ours.'[4] The justification and legal reasoning for
allowing land to be taken in this way – which was not exclusively Portuguese [5] – was that the owner earned his right to the
property by cultivating it: cultivation gave a title to possession.

The first question was to mark out the boundaries. How that
was done is easier to follow in the records of lands that belonged
to village councils than in those owned by individuals. In the
days before maps, landmarks were things like a peculiar rock, a
solitary oak, an old Moorish track, a big stone distinguishable
by its colour, a torrent or stream, the place where a river ran
between thick bushes, or the old ruined farm, the name of
which no one now remembered.[6] Many owners found that they
had marked out more land than they could manage, and they
let smaller parcels to families who would cultivate them. The
king, the great lords, spiritual and temporal, did the same. The
officers who made the division, generally members of the village
council, were called *sesmeiros*,[7] and the *sesmo* was the piece of
land of a size that one family could be expected to cultivate.
Cultivation was a condition of holding land, or soon became

so; and there are records of land being taken away from owners
who neglected their holdings. The earliest example is that of
a college: the Prior and *beneficiados* (Fellows) of the Colegiada
de S. Bartolomeu in Coimbra. The College had an olive-grove
on the other side of the river, opposite the town, and for three
years they left it uncultivated. Perhaps the Prior had read the
Georgics, and had taken Virgil too literally when he says that
olive-trees, once they have taken root, need no further cultivation.[8] That might have been all right for southern Italy or
with wild olives; but it was not the practice in Portugal, where
olive-trees require, and receive, a good deal of attention.[9] The
neglected piece of College property attracted the notice of a
man called João Eanes, who reported it to the king; and after
a lengthy inquiry the sovereign decided that the College should
lose the olive-grove and give it to João Eanes to cultivate.[10]

King Denis had to cope with this difficulty too. He issued
various orders prohibiting religious corporations from mort-
main, from buying land or inheriting it from their members;
but these orders had not much effect. In the fourteenth century
the procurators of municipal councils who sat in the Côrtes
often insisted that owners must be compelled to work their
land; but the power and wealth of the clergy made them
immune. In 1352, again, the *Homens Bons* of the councils lifted
up their voices against bishops, clerics, masters, priors and
abbots who had let their houses in towns and villages go to ruin;
while so much of their land was uncultivated that whole districts 'were without bread and wine – a thing that should not
be'. Within a short time, they added, all the land in the kingdom would belong to the Church, because the greater number
who passed out of this world left it most of what they possessed.[11]
They petitioned the king to prohibit such practices; the Church
had so many estates that it could not use them. They reverted
to a wilderness and then became woodland; how much better
it would be if they could be divided and given to cultivators by
the *sesmeiros*, so that some people might profit by them!

In one province, Trás-os-Montes, the development of cultivation under the first kings rested on a basis of collective ownership (*aforamento*), the opposite to that which obtained in the
neighbouring province of Minho, where individual ownership
was the rule.[12] This ancient form of communal ownership still

occupies a considerable area in Trás-os-Montes in the north-east; between the Támega valley and that of the Cávado, there are communal societies for grazing. The system is due largely to difficulties of transport, sparseness of population and the need for grazing all the year round, the alternation of pasturing in the hills in summer and in the valleys in winter. These communal aspects of village and family life are natural results of the mountainous situation. The summer pastures on the heights are far from any dwelling, and this leads to watch over the flocks being kept by a shepherd employed jointly by all the sheep-owners. The whole mountain district is divided into *baldíos* (commons), the property of various villages. In spring the larger cattle are collected into a single herd, which goes off in charge of a single shepherd, though he may (and often does) have a boy with him. In the autumn the herd comes down again, to avoid the snow.

In a way characteristic of the life of those parts, all the business of the village is still settled at meetings of neighbours, like the medieval councils; while disputes are settled by six men of the highest repute: *homens do acôrdo* 'men of agreement'. This agrarian collectivism is occasionally extended to crops, and is indispensable, owing to the small production of each farm. The lands in individual ownership are insufficient to produce the quantity of cereals required, and it is necessary to appropriate from the common land an area to compensate for it. For that purpose the inhabitants meet in November to discuss which land to choose for crops for the next year; and thus, in spite of the small degree of fertility of the district, the rotation is assured. When the place has been decided by the meeting, the inhabitants proceed to mark out the lot which should fall to each cultivator. This survival of medieval procedure, closely related to the difficulty of attracting farmers to Trás-os-Montes, was described in action by the traveller Rosmithal in 1465.

2

The Church is abused for being a bad landlord; but in one place it was the perfect landlord, the best landlord in Portugal: Alcobaça. Chroniclers and historians exaggerate both the Christian virtues of the monks and their laxity and depravity. They forget their immense contribution to agriculture; even

Beckford's half-regretful, half-amused account – published
when the monastery was dissolved in 1834, but written after
his visit forty years before – hardly gives an idea of what a good
landlord the house had been in the first centuries of its existence
and the last.[13]

The abbot was one of the greatest personages in Portugal.
He had a collection of fantastic titles, including that of 'Lord
of winds and waters' (*Senhor de águas e ventos*), from the number
of windmills and watermills on his estates; he was 'Lord of the
coverts' (*Senhor dos coutos*) and lord also of thirteen villages and
three seaports, in which he held the right to dispense criminal
and civil justice.

The kitchen of the monastery Beckford called 'the most distinguished temple of gluttony in Europe'.[14] Everything, like
everybody, was inclined to fat: the monks, the statues of angels
and the *putti*; even the devil himself showed signs of good living.
Yet for the first 200 years the monks had done a great deal of
heavy land work; and in this time, from the twelfth to the fourteenth century, agriculture, from being a despised occupation
fit only for slaves, became a dignified, not to say a sublime
calling. Through the labour of the monks themselves, and their
knowledge of how to set about it, the bushes and briars and
undergrowth, where you could easily find bears, wolves and
wild boars, were transformed into orchards and vineyards.
What had formerly been a 'blasted heath' became a cornfield;
bog and fen were reclaimed and became useful land; lines of
olive-trees appeared on the hillsides. In improvised smithies,
swords and any pieces of old iron that could be found were
beaten into ploughshares and other agricultural implements.
The waste land which Afonso Henriques had made over to the
monks became, and still is, one of the most fertile areas in the
whole of Portugal.

What was the country round Alcobaça like when the monks
first came in 1153? We are faced once more with the question
whether the conquering kings from Asturias ever really made
the land a desert, as their chroniclers claim. In later centuries
the historians of Alcobaça were divided in opinion: Bernardo
de Brito and Fr. Fortunato accepted the statements of the
chroniclers at their face value; António Brandão believed that
there were scattered groups of inhabitants still left. Even after

the monks had come, there were frequent raids from the south: fire, sack and ruin, followed by famine and pestilence. About thirty years later there was an invasion led by 'Miramolin' in person – 'Miramolin' being the *Amir al-mu'minín*, the 'Commander of the Faithful', or 'Prince of Believers', no longer a caliph, but an important Berber chief from South Morocco. He reached Alcobaça, cut the throats of all the monks he could catch and sacked the monastery. Agriculture was reduced once more to a few fields round the castles where the remains of the population had taken refuge.

The monks began again. Some ploughed; others started to rebuild the church. Some were kept on a war footing, to defend their property from the rapacity of both Christians and Moslems. Forty years later they had cleared about three miles round the monastery; and by clearing the land and creating farms they were among the real builders of modern Portugal. The Cistercians and Benedictines scattered over Europe treated agriculture as a science. Every monastery was an agricultural college, where all the knowledge of the time was collected and put into practice; and Alcobaça is proof that knowledge and practical experience were combined to a high degree. They knew the value of traditional practices; but they tactfully showed how the traditional way of doing a thing might be improved, without frightening the labourers away. For though the monks worked in the fields and vineyards themselves, land-workers gradually collected round them; and it is one of the great contributions of the Alcobaça estates that they redeemed the land-workers from serfdom and slavery. In the monastery itself, the librarian collected MSS. of all the classical treatises on agriculture he could find, not excluding those in Arabic; while monks who went to Rome or travelled in other places were told to keep their eyes open to see how things were done in other countries, and to bring back (if they could) seeds and plants.

The task the monks had set before them was greater and more difficult than might be imagined. 'They had to populate the immense estate which had been given them, by attracting labourers and keeping them; and then farm, carefully and intensively, something like 100,000 acres; and this, in backward, unquiet times, with a scanty population, most of whom would rather have been nomad shepherds than sedentary cultivators.

It demanded unremitting labour on the land, involving complex questions of rotation of crops and fertilisation; a knowledge of the soil, the climate, the needs of the plants grown, and the employment of a varied flora to help feed men and animals.

Most difficult of all, perhaps, they had to make the farm-labourer stay at work. The remark just quoted, that in the beginning most of them would rather have been shepherds, means that there was always a tendency to drift away, however difficult the laws of the time made it for a man to leave his employer or change his employment. The tenants were no longer serfs. They were granted land on the condition of cultivating it, and they became the owners after working on it for a certain number of years – ten, six or sometimes only three. In the deed, however, there was always a phrase about farming the land BENE ET FIDELITER, 'well and truly'. Sometimes the monks handed over to the tenants land which they had already cultivated themselves: the deeds mention olives, vines, orchards and vegetable-plots 'already made'. Otherwise the tenant is required 'to plough up what has to be ploughed up, each one according to his possessions'. The monks advised the tenants on the choice of crops; told them what the soil was good for, the rotations which would be most likely to secure a good harvest. They worked out schemes of drainage and irrigation, taught men to prune and graft. As time went on, they built up model farms which became schools of agriculture, where monks lived and worked and gave instruction. The monks had to see to all this; and they also had to provide implements and buildings, presses for wine and oil; to open up ways of communication and deal with streams which overflowed their banks in winter.

The tenants paid taxes, which were complicated and were assessed differently on different parts of the estate; but the taxes in kind were not considered to be oppressive, and this goes to explain the rapid rise in the population on the Alcobaça estates; 'agriculture had not yet become the laborious and difficult art of impoverishing oneself through hard work'. The tenants were exempt from the obligation to bear arms, and Dom Denis excused from the land-tax (*jugada*) all those who had brought new land under cultivation, though that privilege was confirmed by only one of his successors.

Sr Vieira Natividade has called attention to the simplicity and intimacy of the wording of some of the leases: 'And they shall preserve the said olive-yard, and plant what has to be planted with any graft, and sow and till well and truly, and surround the said olive-yard with a fence or wall which cannot be damaged or destroyed by cattle; and if they do not do this, he that is found guilty and negligent shall lose the share which he had of it . . .' 'In time of reaping or harvest, they shall with their men and with their families well and truly harvest the grain for bread. . . .' 'And you should, after ten years, thrive on the said hereditament, dwelling on it continually with your women, digging in it and making it bring forth fruit and planting vines and olives and orchards, and ploughing well and truly each of one the fields which have been assigned to you. . . .' Neglect, failure to fulfil the conditions or vagrancy meant that the farm would revert to the monastery. The monks discouraged large holdings; and would not let their farms to priests, monks of other orders, Moslems or Jews. A tenant could not make over his land to any of these, nor to a 'page at arms' or a soldier.

After the middle of the thirteenth century, the monks themselves ceased to do farm work, and devoted themselves more to teaching; their school (1269) was the first in Portugal. But mundane and tyrannical abbots, combined with royal interference, led to decadence; until in the eighteenth century the agricultural work of the monastery (which had always gone steadily on) suddenly revived in a burst of activity. An eighteenth-century abbot who was a cousin of Pombal (see Chapter 10) drained a large area of new land and applied all the accumulated experience of the monastery to cultivating it. Great new olive-groves were planted on the slopes of the Serra dos Candieiros; oranges, limes, lemons were grown as never before, while a new apiary produced the clearest honey in Portugal. When the Prior of Avis, in 1794, asked the farmers and fruit-growers in the district who had taught them to cultivate with such care, to manure with such discernment and to spare their cattle from excessive labour, the answer (Beckford says) was always the same: 'Our indulgent landlords and kind friends, the monks.'

One must draw a veil over the dissolution of 1834, Alcobaça

was the one monastery, among all others in Portugal, which deserved separate consideration and better treatment; but it had to suffer, with the rest, from centuries of suppressed anticlerical feeling. Yet the fine tradition of the Cistercian cultivators remains; the fruit of Alcobaça is still of the finest quality.

3

Portuguese merchants, soon after the achievement of national independence, were enterprising enough to reach the North Sea. They appeared at the fair at Lille in the middle of the twelfth century; by the fourteenth century they were established at Arras. Theirs was not a land trade; the Portuguese harbours were ports of call between the Mediterranean and northern Europe. But although Portuguese trading was largely maritime, the fairs [15] arose, as in Spain and Flanders, generally in inland centres of traffic. Then, as communications became easier and more frequent, and conditions of safety improved, the importance of the fair was sometimes greater than that of the place at which it was established. In Portugal there were fairs in inhabited places of all kinds: castles, villages, large settlements and fortified posts (burgos). Some were deliberately off the main roads, or separated from the main distributing centres; it was an advantage, in times of trouble, for a fair to be somewhat inaccessible. For the fairs were not merely big centres of traffic in merchandise: it was in them that the complicated machinery of credit developed with commercial operations on a large scale, and eventually (though this was more the work of the goldsmiths) banking.

At first, fairs in Portugal were held within the walls of a castle or town, or in the big square. Guimarães Fair, which began in 1258, was held in the castle; Beja (1308) in an open space where bulls were also run, the *Chão da corredoira*; Coimbra (1377), Miranda (1404), Lamego (1459), within the walls; Vouzela (1392) in the *rossio* – and the word means the same in Lisbon: the place where travellers tied up their horses. After the fourteenth century, fairs tended to be held in the suburbs.

In Portugal, the foundation of a fair was a royal prerogative. Ponte do Lima (1125), the oldest, began twenty-two years before there was a Portuguese king; it existed under a charter of

Dona Teresa, Countess of Burgundy. It is interesting to find that the document, although in Latin, spells the word 'fair' – to which men from all lands might come – in the Portuguese way: ET HOMINES QUI DE CUNCTIS TERRIS VENERINT AD *FEIRAM*; and there was a heavy fine of 60 *solidos* (shillings) for harming those who came and went. The next fair in date was at Melgaço, far up the river Minho and facing Spain; it had a fair in 1181 with a document from King Afonso Henriques, by which merchants from 'foreign parts' paid a duty of 30 *solidos*. At Vila Mendo (1229), the document issued by Sancho II still spells it MEAM *FEYRAM*; and those who came were exempt from civil or criminal liability for twenty-four days. At Guarda (1255) the period of immunity was extended to thirty days. The customary laws (*costumes*) of Guarda give an idea of the kind of products and merchandise which came into the town during the fair: wine, wheat, barley, rye, nuts, chestnuts, pigeons, hens and capons; cattle, sheep, goats, pigs, cows; horses, mules and donkeys; linseed, iron.

Guimarães (1258) could provide red cloth (Flanders or England?) and cloth from Segovia in Spain, as well as the coarse qualities called *picote* and *burel*; Galician plaid (*manta galega*), linen cloth, household linen, felt, cloaks (either of red cloth or white *zorame*, worn by the Moors in Morocco) and various articles of female attire, including *saios* and *guarnachas*; rabbits' fur, by the piece or made-up; sheepskins, goatskins; assorted feathers, black or white; leather of various qualities and colours, green and red. There were also pepper and salt, horseshoes, pieces of old iron; sardines, dried congers, other fish fresh and dried; oxen, cows, pigs, horses of various descriptions, and mares, mules – and last of all – Moorish slaves. Besides these, there were 'buffoons who put up their tents', for which privilege they paid a fee of three shillings.

In Portugal, as in Spain, we find in medieval fairs and markets the Jewish or Mozárabic middleman establishing contact indirectly between east and west. There were Moslems of Granada who brought spices to the fair at Lamego. Protection was granted by some charters (e.g. Évora) to Jewish and Moslem merchants and travellers, as to Christians: MERCATORES VEL VIATORES CHRISTIANOS, JUDEOS SIVE MAUROS, and the fine for molesting them was put at 60 shillings.

4

What has been said of farms, fruit and forests might lead to the idea that medieval Portugal under the first line of kings (1140–1383) was purely 'an agrarian monarchy.' [16] This description forgets the sea; for it was in fact the sea fisheries and salt which were most important in the first centuries of Portuguese independent existence. Already in the Middle Ages there was a Portugal which was maritime and not only agrarian; and in the passage from the first to the second epoch there was a continuous evolution rather than a sudden mutation and a rapid change of character. Portugal was not alone in this, Sérgio remarks, as one coming from a naval family: 'One and the same impetus towards nautical activity was noticeable from Flanders to the Tagus, from the ports of the Levant to Lisbon ... and it eventually extended from Calicut to Malacca and was spread over three centuries.' What gave the Portuguese a chance of taking their place in the world was not agriculture, but the sea: salt, fishing and sea-borne commerce.[17] The panel showing the fishermen and their nets – even down to the technical detail of the cork floats – in the great picture by Nuno Gonçalves in the Lisbon National Gallery, is a symbol of this view of Portuguese history. 'Navigation', Oliveira Martins said,[18] 'is a trade which is essentially Portuguese, and the merchant navy arose with national independence.'

'Once the reaction against the Moslem states had ceased – that reaction which led to the foundation of the neo-Gothic states in the Peninsula, and among them the western state of León from which Portugal had seceded – it may be assumed that there were regular sailings by Moslems from Morocco to the Atlantic coast of the Peninsula, just as when it had belonged to the Moslems themselves.' This assumption seems now, in view of our knowledge of the continual trade with Morocco, more firmly based than when its author made it; the intertional importance of the western ports—Vigo, Oporto, Lisbon – could only be apparent when conditions permitted the reestablishment of trade between the North Sea and the Mediterranean. It was commerce rather than crusades which opened the seas once more; and we may remember a saying attributed to St Bernard, that the real object of crusading was the love of gold and silver and the enjoyment of fair women; AMOR AURI ET ARGENTI ET PULCHERRIMARUM FEMINARUM VOLUPTAS.

In the conventional view of Portuguese origins too much consideration is given to Portugal as an exclusively Christian state, discounting the influence on the life of the nation of those of the inhabitants who had inherited Moslem civilisation – perhaps more than half the population. The state of war in medieval times was never 'total'; it never completely prevented commercial dealings between Christians and Moslems (in spite of modern claims to the contrary), and until the time of Sancho I (1185–1211), and in Castille until 1172, the coins most in current use were *morabitinos* or *maravedís* – the gold coinage of the Moroccan Almorávides.

Trade with the infidel had been going on all the time, and not least in the sea and river ports of the new Christian Portuguese monarchy. The charters of 1179 given to Santarém and Lisbon grant important privileges to sea-captains. From the Algarve, after its capture later, the greater part of the fruit went, as before, to 'Moorish lands', from which came in return a large number of gold *dobras* (later called 'doubloons') – the *valedíes* of Tunis.[19] In fact, the long-standing overseas trade with the Moslems seems not to have been greatly interrupted by the Christian conquest and was soon restored. It is a mere assumption of modern propagandist historians that, first overseas trade and then the voyages of discovery were due to the Crusades. The Crusades merely put temporary difficulties in the way of a trade which had been going on for generations. We should not deny the importance of the crusaders' conquest of Lisbon; but it may be pointed out (with Cortesão) that the impulse existed already, in a latent form, and had been in evidence even before Lisbon was conquered. The capture of Lisbon in 1147 was prepared by a commercial treaty with the crusaders, or at least an agreement to share the loot.

The basis of Portuguese seafaring was fishing. From the twelfth century to the sixteenth, fisheries increased. Fishing not only bred generations of seamen, but provided crews to man the tiny trading vessels which first ventured round Cape Finisterre, along the Biscay coasts and up the English Channel to Flanders. As early as 1095 the Charter of Santarém (before the foundation of the kingdom of Portugal) allowed for the sending

of 'anything' into other countries, particularly France or Castille.[20] But the *Posturas municipais* of Coimbra (1145) have a
special section devoted to fishermen, and show that boats laden
with fish could come right up to the city. Fish could be sold
from the boat by the municipal official whose name they mis-
prounced *almutazeb*.[21] The charter of Coimbra (1179) gives the
amount of duty payable on fish. Some came up in boats; other
loads were brought by 'men from outside', HOMINES DE *FORA*,
or on pack animals.[22] Boats as well as pack-loads of fish were
brought to Almada, opposite Lisbon (1190), and to Leiria
(1195). In 1194 a Portuguese ship was expected in Bruges with
molasses, oil and timber. It was wrecked and never reached its
destination.[23]

In 1211 there is a law prohibiting customs officers, landowners and other persons from taking possession of ships, 'both
great and small' (*naves e navios*), from the kingdom of Portugal
or other countries with their cargoes if they were wrecked on
the coast, 'for everything in them will belong to their respective
owners'. Wrecking was an illegal occupation. The charter of
Ericeira (1229) pays special attention to fishermen. Boys and
men who were learning their trade paid no duty; the *foral* did not
apply to them for four years. Some went deep-sea fishing. There
was no duty on bait, or netfuls of small fry, and they could take
tunny or dolphin without restriction; if they caught a conger
they might eat it, but if they landed a whale they had to surrender a twentieth part.[24] There was always the possibility that
fishermen in those days might catch a whale.[25] Whales had not
been forced up into the Arctic or down into the Antarctic, and
could be hunted off the coast of Portugal. This is clear from the
charters of Vila Nova de Gaya (1293 and 1395), and the contract between Ferdinand I of Castille and the Order of Santiago
contains the stipulation: 'And if peradventure any whale or
whale-calf or mermaid be taken . . .'[26] As early as 1254 the
monastery of Alcobaça was concerned, in the ports which it
controlled, with collecting the profits derived from whale-oil.

Setúbal (1249) excused fishermen from military service by
land and sea, except to help their neighbours in emergency.[27]
A privilege of an unusual kind was granted to Pena Jóia to construct a canal on the Douro at a place called Aguda, under condition of building it and keeping it in good repair at their own

cost, and of not levying the toll[28] on boats which passed by on the river. By 1254 there are regulations on which ships should disembark at Oporto; and particular reference is made to all ships, great and small, which came 'from France or from Rupella' (La Rochelle), or even from other places with cloth or wood or iron.

By this time many other things were carried besides fish. In 1287 Queen Isabel ('*a Raynha dona helisabeth*') was allowed the customs duties on goods that entered by the port (now silted up) of Selir[29] except the following – and the exceptions are notable – which were reserved for King Denis: scarlet cloth, small arms, gold and silver, pepper, saffron, as well as wrought iron, steel, lead, tin and copper.[30] There were already Portuguese merchants resident in Harfleur under letters patent of Philippe le Bel (1290); and in 1293 it was laid down by Dom Denis that all ships of more than 100 tons burden loaded in ports of Portugal for Flanders, England, Normandy, Brittany and 'Arrochela' (La Rochelle) should pay 20 shillings sterling on the amount of the freight; those of less than 100 tons, 10 shillings, but ships loaded for Portuguese merchants for 'overseas', Seville or other parts, the terms already in force.

5

Turning now to salt,[31] the earliest maritime activity of Portugal, we find that although before 1500 the salt-pans of France were probably more important than the Portuguese, yet Portugal, with its extensive coast-line, strong hot winds, high and constant summer temperature, became a producer of salt of the finest quality. The purest came from Setúbal and Alcácer do Sal, south of the Tagus. Its purity was due to the presence of a curious, minute seaweed (*Microcoleus coleum*), known to the Portuguese salt-workers by various local names. This clears the water, and frees the salt from impurities in it by retaining them in its filaments, and so isolates the salt which is deposited. The weed is peculiar to the basins of the Sado and the Tagus, hardly exists in the salt-pans of the Algarve and is not found at all in those in the north, where chemical aids have now to be employed. The northern salt-pans were profitably worked in the tenth century; the earliest document is from the year 929.[32]

The antiquity of the Setúbal salt-pans is always taken for

granted, and there is archæological evidence. But it is curious
that the Arab geographers do not mention salt at Alcácer,
though they enlarge upon the amount of shipping and the fertility of the soil. Perhaps the salt industry was only reorganised
later. It was working again in the tenth century; and the salt-
trade is a measure of the growth of the population and revival
in the territories reconquered. This is confirmed by the town-
charters; Oporto (1123, before an independent Portugal existed), Coimbra, Santarém, Lisbon (all in 1179). Salt was subject to a tax, and placed generally on the same level as wheat.

Dried or salt fish was always the basis of medieval Portuguese
food, and the salt-trade is prominent in documents from the
thirteenth century onwards. The Prior of Alcobaça instructs the
monks of a smaller house to promote the construction of salt-
pans in a basin near Alfeizerão, now silted up, and also near
Óbidos (1265). In 1422 Alcobaça issued a charter (*carta de foral*)
to the new inhabitants settled at Alfeizerão, stipulating that
they should plant vines and orchards, and construct salt-pans,
paying every year a fifth of the fruit and a quarter of the salt.

Salt, of course, had been indispensable from the earliest times.
It was carried in their ships by the Phœnicians, and used in the
mummification of Pharaohs by the Egyptians. Its vocabulary
is mainly Latin. With the advent of Christianity and the fasts
decreed by the Church, the trade increased, for salt fish became an article of food habitually consumed by all classes in
Europe. Abstinence probably had an economic reason as well
as an ecclesiastical one. But geography and climate divided the
Christian world into two groups: consumers and producers –
northern Europe and the West, including the Mediterranean
and the salt-mines on the Continent. In the sixteenth century religious changes altered the direction of the trade. The northern,
herring-fishing countries, buyers of salt, passed in general to the
Reformation, while the salt-producing countries continued to
be dominated by the 'old religion'. A distinction was established between Rabelais' *terres des Andouilles* and *de Carême pre-
nant*. It was from Protestant fishermen that Catholic fasters had
to buy their fish, salted with the salt which they themselves had
sold to the heretic.[33]

The Hundred Years' War gave Portugal the chance of pro-
viding England with goods which usually came from France:

including salt, wine, oil, fruit, dried fish, honey, wax, hides, furs, cork.[34] The types of medieval cargo have great interest. The *Santa Maria*, for instance (master, Estêvão Domingues, 1383) brought to Southampton 3,000 baskets of fruit, with forty tons of 'bastard' wine from the Algarve, one pipe of grain and two quintals of wax. Portugal needed from the North wheat, timber, metal, naval equipment, hemp, flax and tow, cloth and textiles, rigging and war material. After the accession of Edward III of England, the merchants of Oporto and Lisbon began to receive favoured treatment and protection. The reason was not only the state of war with France, but the knowledge of how important for England Portuguese trade was likely to be.[35]

The Hundred Years' War was not the first time that sailors from Portugal had sailed to the North. The law of Afonso III (1253), giving prices of various merchandise, shows the importance there of produce from Spain, France, England and Flanders.[36] To balance this, there must have been a considerable export trade in the other direction. In 1381 a document refers to an order to the Mayor of Fowey and the Sergeant at Arms to arrest certain persons, at the request of 'John Pynell', merchant of Lisbon 'coming for trade at sea' but attacked 'by the island of Jernesey and crossing towards the town of Middleburg . . . and his ship laden with salt and other merchandise'.[37]

The last phase of the Hundred Years' War, the struggle in the North Sea and Baltic between the Hanseatic League and the Netherlanders, and the improvement in fishing and salting herring, all led to the extension of Portuguese trade. In the sixteenth century there are a number of bills of lading for voyages between Setúbal and Baltic ports, bringing back wheat and other commodities. A ship-master, Cornelis Petterson, was registered in the Sound as arrived from Setúbal on 20 June 1595, and returning from Stockholm on 8 September. At Stockholm the same shipmaster is registered on 4 July with an import cargo of salt shared by two owners; and then on 15 August with an export cargo of 136 ship-pounds of copper and iron, about 36 lasts of tar, and some small parcels of wheat, tallow and timber belonging to six different owners, Dutch and Swedish and a merchant of Elsinore.[38] The shippers cease to be Portuguese after the discovery of India and Brazil, and the Portuguese salt-trade was finally ruined by the vexatious Spanish taxation of Philip III and IV.

6

The conditions which were really decisive in the formation of the Portuguese State were those to be found on the coasts and up the estuaries; they produced a continual drift to the sea, and the desire to make a living from it. The population occupied all the coast that could be used; and down to 1383 we find a rapid development of sea-borne trade, and at the same time the first beginnings of overseas expansion.

Yet the outline of the coasts differed in detail from what it is to-day. Historians refer incidentally to changes in the coast-line – the disappearance of some of the ports, the silting up of some of the estuaries – but it was Cortesão who first emphasised the fact that there were *more* ports at the beginning of Portuguese history, and deeper estuaries, than there were later. There is the evidence of early maps, *portulanos*. In western Europe the coasts were more indented than they are to-day. The wide mouths of certain rivers which used to serve as ports have disappeared entirely; bays and creeks have become completely closed; islands off the coast have been joined to the mainland. There was, for instance, a deep inlet between the mouth of the Douro and Cape Carvoeiro, far more prominent than it is now. The early map-makers were not wrong. They give the names of ports, many of which have disappeared or are difficult to identify, though their names are sometimes found in medieval documents.

Idrísí says that the Minho was navigable up to Tuy, in Galicia, opposite the Portuguese town of Valença do Minho, and that ships stopped at various places on its course. Caminha, near the mouth of the Minho and at the junction with its tributary the Coura, was a port of commercial importance; while Valença in the mid-fifteenth century was a port of call for foreign ships, and had ships of its own trading with other ports in Portugal and abroad. Viana do Castelo, further down the coast, but a little way from the mouth of the Lima, was sending its own ships to France and the Levant as early as the thirteenth century. The river was navigable up to Ponte do Lima, which, as late as the mid-fifteenth century, had caravels trading in

Ireland and the Mediterranean. Vila do Conde, now a bathing beach near Oporto, was still a seaport in the sixteenth century.

Oporto has no documents proving maritime activity before the reign of Sancho I; but then it progressed so quickly that by the middle of the fourteenth century it had a more numerous trading fleet than any port in Portugal, and when Ceuta was taken about half the seventy ships present had sailed from the mouth of the Douro. In the eleventh and twelfth centuries the river Vouga had an open bar; and Idrísí says that many ships crossed it and sailed up the river. In the twelfth century, however, sandbanks began to grow up on the shore to form the present lagoon of Aveiro. In the twelfth century the coastline passed close to Ovar, Estarreja, Lagos and Mira – as far inland as the railway north of Aveiro and the road south of it. Further south still, in the district of Leiria, is the river Lis and the port of Paredes, to which Dom Denis gave a charter in 1282. It was a town and active seaport until the time of Don Manuel I (1495–1521), when it disappeared, buried in the sand.

The list of vanished ports is long; one can mention only a few of particular importance. Just south of Nazaré was a small gulf, at the bottom of which was the port of Pederneira. This was connected with the monastery of Alcobaça, which also owned the ports of Paredes, San Martinho, Alfeizerão and Selir. But since Pederneira was nearest to the monastery, it probably dated from the twelfth century. It was a port for fishing and shipbuilding; but in the seventeenth century the gulf silted up. The present land-locked *concha* of San Martinho was wider than it is now, and though documents of the time of Dom Denis speak of San Martinho, the most important in the wide basin was Alfeizerão, which had (an Italian traveller observed) an intense ship-building industry. In the time of Dom Manuel I it owned eighty ships, but during the seventeenth century it all silted up. Selir disappeared about the same period. Lastly it is almost certain that in Roman days the Lake of Óbidos reached the town walls; while in the thirteenth century the coast-line went direct from the lake to Atouguia and Lourinhã. Peniche was a little island: Osbern and the crusaders stopped there on the way to Lisbon in 1147 and described the INSULA PHENICIS as being eighty paces from the mainland and populated by rabbits.

Before 1122 trading vessels came up the Mondego. This is known from the legal evidence collected to settle a dispute, in the later years of Afonso Henriques, between his daughter the Infanta Dona Teresa, the 'Dame' of Montemôr-o-Velho (from which pilgrims' ships used to sail to Santiago) and the convent of Santa Cruz at Coimbra. They could not agree on the harbour-dues payable by ships entering the river – dues which went back to the time when Portugal was only a 'county'. Some of the fishermen of Montemôr were exempt from taxation. So were the merchant *alfaqueques*, who arranged for the release of prisoners of war and also brought merchandise from the land of the Saracens. Being intermediaries between men of the rival religions, these men were probably Christian Mozárabes who had lived under Moslem government and spoke Arabic, or they may have been Jews. The fact that the municipal *postures* (by-laws) of Coimbra tax pepper as early as 1145, shows that trade relations must have been active with the Moslems, since at that time Moslems were the only people in a position to supply Eastern spices. From the charter of Coimbra (1179) it appears that pepper was still at that time a thing usual in the Portuguese market.[39] Indeed, it was sometimes shipped to the north before the discovery of the direct route to India by Vasco da Gama. In 1198 a Portuguese ship was wrecked on the Flemish coast on the way to Bruges; and in the bill of lading, which has been preserved, were first of all sugar and spice – both extremely rare, and only to be imported from Moslem lands. This is one more indication of the continuity of traffic between two peoples of different religions.[40]

Coimbra was then the most important place in Portugal, and the first trading port until Oporto was opened in the second half of the twelfth century. There is thus evidence of the importance of Mozárabes and Moslems in the maritime origins of Portugal, and it is only common sense to see that the commercial civilisation of the Moslems was not entirely lost in the sea and river ports such as Lisbon, Santarém and Alcácer; the new owners had the greatest interest in preserving it.[41]

NOTES TO CHAPTER 5

[1] Ezequiel dos Campos, *Problemas fundamentais portugueses* (1945), p. 14. A pathetic reminder that the Visigoths sometimes felt the heat is the epitaph preserved by Isidore of Seville that the soul of the departed might be in a cool place: ANIMA EIUS IN REFRIGERIO ERIT (*Fontes*, IX, 139). But the word meant 'rest' as well as 'coolness' (Cumont, *Oriental religions in Roman paganism*, Ch. V, n. 91).

[2] Gama Barros, *História da Administração pública en Portugal*. 2nd ed. IV (1947), 29–31.
Virginia Rau, *Sesmarias medievais portugueses* (1946), pp. 16 ff.

[3] Port. Mon. Hist., Dipl. et Ch., pp. 3, 4. Ribeira explains 'cornam et albende' by the words *buzina e bandeira*: trumpet and flag. *Dissert. Chron.* IV, pt. 2, pp. 110, 118.

[4] Este herdamento . . . nosso padre Roy Periz o apres cum seu arado e eu cum ele por nosso. V. Rau, t.c., p. 21.

[5] It was under this form that Charlemagne and his successors had given land to 'Hispanos' in Septimania. Gama Barros, t.c., II, 11.

[6] E. dos Campos, t.c., p. 15.

[7] *Sesmo*, a sixth part, from country Latin SEXIMUS (for SEXTUS) formed on the analogy of SEPTIMUS.

[8] *Georgics*, II, 420–425.

[9] Ruy Mayer, *As Georgicas de Vergilio, versão . . . e comentarios de um agrónomo* (1948), pp. 324–326.

[10] V. Rau, t.c., pp. 53–54.

[11] A. Gomes Ramalho, 'Legislação agrícola', I. *Boletim da Direcção Geral da Agricultura*, VIII, 1905, No. 4, pp. 109–114.

[12] A. Sérgio, *História de Portugal: Introducção geográfica* (1941), 85; J. Cortesão, *O sentido da cultura em Portugal no século*, XIV (1935), 6–17.

[13] J. Vieira Natividade, *Os monges agrónomos do Mosteiro de Alcobaça* (1942).

[14] Beckford, and see also the diverting study by Rose Macaulay, in *They went to Portugal* (1946), 108–142.

[15] Virgínia Rau, *Subsídios para o estudo das feiras medievais portuguesas* (1943).

[16] A. Sérgio, *Em tórno da designação de Monarquia Agrária dada à primeira época da nossa história* (1941). The phrase was coined by the economic historian J. Lúcio de Azevedo, on the supposition that 'the profits from land under cultivation were the most certain source of the royal rents'.

[17] A. Sérgio, *História de Portugal: Introducção geográfica* (1941), 73.

[18] Oliveira Martins, *Portugal nos mares* (1899), 2.

[19] J. Cortesão, t.c. Here, and in ch. VII, I am greatly indebted to this valuable essay.

[20] João Martims da Silva Marques, *Descobrimentos portugueses*. Vol. I e suplemento ao vol. I (1944), 234.

[21] Ibid., 236.

[22] Ibid., 241.

[23] E. Van Den Bussche, *Flandre et Portugal* (Bruges, 1874), 47.

[24] J. Martims de Silva Marques, ibid., Doc. 4.

[25] Ibid., 267.

[26] Oliveira Martins, t.c.

[27] J. Martims da Silva Marques, ibid. 270.

[28] QUOD NON TOLLANT PASSAGINEM.

[29] Since silted up. See p. 130.

[30] Panos de Cóór e armas miudas e Ouro e prata e pimenta e (a)çafra.

[31] Virgínia Rau, *A exploração e o comércio do sal de Setúbal* (1951); A. Sérgio, t.c., 147 ff.; and cf. A. R. Bridbury, *England and the Salt Trade* (Oxford, 1955).

[32] Gama Barros, 2 ed. IV (1947), 235.

[33] Hauser, in *Les origines historiques des problèmes économiques* (1930).

[34] E. M. Carus Wilson, *Studies in English Trade in the Fifteenth Century* (1951).

[35] V. M. Shillington and A. B. W. Chapman, *The Commercial Relations of England and Portugal* (1907).

[36] Ch. IV, note 22.

[37] P. E. Russell, *English and French Intervention in Spain and Portugal in the time of Edward III and Richard II* (Oxford, 1955). Professor Russell explains the circumstances.

[38] A. E. Christensen, *Dutch trade in the Baltic*, and A. Strindberg, 'Rélations de la Suède avec l'Espagne et le Portugal . . . 16ᵉ siècle' (Madrid: *Bol. de la R. Acad. de la Historia*, XVII (1890), 330–333).

[39] *P.M.H. Leges*, 743–744 and 416.

[40] E. Van Den Bussche, 47–48; Sampaio, t.c., ? 365; Cortesão, t.c., 53.

[41] Teresa afterwards married Philip of Alsace, Count of Flanders; and when he was killed on a crusade in 1191, she put her name to the Charter of Ghent demanded by the citizens after a disastrous fire: REGINA ET DOMINA FLANDRIAE. In Flanders she was known as Mathildis de Portugal. See L. A. Warnkoenig and A. E. Gheldolf, *Hist. de la Flandre* (Brussels, 1846), III, i, no. 6, pp. 226 ff. The charter is printed in App. vi of Warnkoenig, *Flandrische Staats- und Rechtsgeschichte*, II (1835).

D

Chapter 6

Dom Denis and the Pine Forest

I

F ROM THE early Middle Ages some of the monks had been
farming a great deal better than the Military Orders, the
barons or the other great landlords. The Crown lands
(*reguengos*) in the centre and south of the country were not nearly
so well managed as certain monastic lands in the north. 'On
Crown property,' it has been said, 'it was agriculture without
sense or conscience. On the ashes of a burnt field seed was scattered, on land impoverished by a damaging form of cultivation
and by growing nothing but cereals. Flocks pastured on desert
heaths; impenetrable bush extended for leagues around. Wild
animals were protected for the amusement of the nobles, while
the serf of the glebe lived in entire dependence upon his lord,
according to the most primitive forms of serfdom in the
country.' [1]

Yet in all this mismanagement there was one great exception.
On the coast of Portugal, about half way between Oporto and
Lisbon, there is a 'new forest' – new in the sense that the New
Forest in Hampshire is new, or New College, Oxford, or the
Pont Neuf in Paris; they were new once, but have been going
on now for a very long time. In the Portuguese 'new forest', the
King's Pine Wood (*O Pinhal do Rei*), one afternoon in August
1947, the wife of one of the forest guards, with a black handker-
chief tied round her head, brought an apronful of pine-seed
and presented it, shyly and solemnly, to a wandering scholar
who was a guest of the 'Ranger'. That was not only Portuguese
courtesy: it was practical philology, a demonstration of the
meaning of the old Portuguese word *arregaçada*, an apronful;
for popular history relates that one day about 1300 'an apronful of pine seed brought from France' was scattered on the sand
by the sainted Queen Isabel, wife of Dom Denis. [2]

Medieval monarchs are reflexions of the state of local feeling:
their public characters are summaries and symbols of the social

conditions of their reigns.[3] D. Denis is an example, and the practical, peace-loving woman who came from Barcelona in 1282 to be his queen; she was called a saint long before anything was said in Rome, because people in Portugal had found that she behaved like one. Isabel was accessible and helpful; a good fairy but also a good administrator, with the practical sense of people from Barcelona. She collected the rents, but concealed her charities from her husband. On one occasion the money she had with her for distribution was miraculously changed – in his eyes – to roses. King Denis, from 1279 to 1325, looked after the land he had inherited like an improving landlord, and is known to tradition as 'the king land-worker', *O Rei Lavrador*. Besides planting trees and draining swamps, he wrote excellent poetry, much of it in a style that any countryman could enjoy and many countrymen must have sung, and he founded the Studium Generale, which afterwards became the University of Coimbra.

King Denis was not the first of the primitive Portuguese poets. In fact, he was about the last. He came at the end of an epoch, not at the beginning. One of the first poets in Portugal had been his great-grandfather, Sancho I (1158–1211), whose song, put on the lips of the beauteous Maria Pais Ribeiro, singing about a friend, has hardly a word which is not still immediately intelligible. Even earlier was Soares de Taveirós, who also sang the praises of 'La Ribeirinha'. They had, both of them, a beautiful, natural language, far from the clumsy prose of the lawyers and the careful efforts to tell the story of King Lear or the Holy Grail; though it is fair to add that that prose, when we puzzle over it now, has generally been rewritten – and respelt – by later scribes. The poems of King Denis which still make him a living voice are those in which he seems to be hearing and idealising the words of people singing and dancing out of doors; and he made exquisite poems in the same style himself, using a device for singers who were also dancers: parallel stanzas and a refrain. He often puts the words into the mouth of a young girl singing about her *amigo* or *amado*, away at the wars or out at sea, or running after another girl . . . and then she tries to put a magic on him and bring him back.

Dom Denis, therefore, was not merely a king who made verses. One of the later popular rhymes about him explains why he was able to accomplish so much: he finished what he began.

> Esta fiz D. Denis
> Que acabou tudo o que quis;
> E quem dinheiro tiver
> Fará tudo o que quiser.

> Dom Denis he made this,
> And finished all that he could wish,
> For he who has money in hand
> Will do all things that he planned.[4]

He finished not only his castles – Serpa, Moura, Sabugal – and his waterworks, but his agricultural legislation as well: the use of the land for crops or timber instead of coverts for knights and abbots to preserve their game; the planting and protection of trees, and the detailed 'Doomsday' inquiries or *Inquirições* which he continued from his father Afonso III.

2

These *Inquirições* were inquiries carried out by royal commissions to examine the legal position of various properties, with regard to tenure, seignorial rights and patronage of churches and monasteries. Their chief object was to restore to the Crown those rights which individuals had usurped: by making a property into an *honra*, for instance – a piece of land which was 'honorary' because it paid no taxes to the Crown and where rich men had farms or substantial houses and held jurisdiction over their neighbours, vassals and agricultural labourers. These *honras* had often been illegally come by, in early or even Visigothic times, or were founded on a title which was not valid; and it was necessary to prepare a survey of everything in every parish which could be considered Crown land, and also to secure all the information it was possible to collect concerning offenders who had been dealt with summarily on lands acquired illegally.

The first *Inquirições* were held by Afonso II, beyond the Douro, in 1220. The most detailed were those in the Archbishopric of Braga, though this was perhaps due to the unpopularity of Archbishop Soares, who had incurred the royal displeasure. There was considerable resistance from the higher clergy and nobility, stimulated by the intervention of the Pope, and the attempted inquiry was largely frustrated. Those held by Afonso III (1248–1278) failed in their purpose also; and it was only in the reign of Dom Denis that the *Inquirições* had any appreciable result. The royal commissioners summoned in every parish the oldest inhabitants and those best acquainted with the situation and history of the different estates; and inquired under oath what traditions there were on the origin, tenure and conditions of each estate. In this way they obtained information on properties which were really part of the royal patrimony; and on private sales or violent acts of intrusion. Above all, they were able to clear up the amounts due to the Crown, imposing taxes or ordering the reversion to the Crown of *honras* (whether occupied by nobles or the Church) which had been acquired by extortion or deception.

The inquiries were often unfair; the owners were generally not heard, and the existence of the title-deeds was not inquired into. The revelations of the first *Inquirições* of 1284 in Beira Baixa and Entre-Douro-e-Minho, and the sovereign's rigorous inspection, considerably prejudiced private interests; in 1283, prelates and nobles complained to the Côrtes of Lisbon of the disregard of their immunity in places exempt from inspection. The second *Inquirições* of D. Denis aroused further opposition; judgement was only given in 1290, and it was more than a hundred years later, under John I, before the royal power could be imposed. The documents are difficult to read, and show Portuguese spelling at one of its wildest moments; but they give a wonderful insight into how country people of the time really lived.[5]

Once again popular imagination has been quick to seize the important point. D. Denis is *O Rei Lavrador*, the king who was a worker; who in days when most men were in turn farmer, forester, fisherman and shepherd, could himself be the first two and understand the difficulties of the others; and when he sat in council or dictated letters he showed a practical farmer's or forester's knowledge and sent out instructions which, besides being royal orders, were helpful to those for whom they were intended. Take him in the council chamber. In 1309 there had been disputes in the market at Évora, in which Jews and Moslems had been involved, and had of course received all the blame. D. Denis was firm and definite. In the case of market

offences, Jews and Moslems must answer before the Clerk of the
Market – probably a Christian, but holding an office copied
from the Moslems, with a name which, however mispro-
nounced, was still Arabic. In the case of offences among Jews
or Moslems, the Jews should answer before the properly con-
stituted judge of their own community – the *rabino, rabby* or
arraby – and the Moslems before their own *alcaide*.[6]

3

D. Denis wrote several letters to kings of England in his
time: Edward I and Edward II.[7] There was already an important sea-borne trade between the two countries; and in January
1295 Denis writes complaining that hostilities between the
vassals of Edward and those of the King of Castille caused
serious damage to inoffensive merchants: he requested the
King of England to use his influence towards a speedy peace.
Another letter requests the intervention of King Edward on behalf of Portuguese merchants forced by the English authorities
to sell their goods in English ports, though the merchandise had
been consigned to ports in Flanders. D. Denis demanded that
his vassals should be recognised as having the right to pass
freely in England, and undertook that the subjects of Edward
should enjoy equal guarantees in Portugal. Denis had, on one
occasion, taken charge of an English ship saved by his subjects
from an attack by pirates. In 1308 D. Denis wrote a long letter
to Edward II, calling his attention to the friendly relations between their two countries. He was about to renew letters of safe
conduct.

The king showed his superior intelligence and administrative
ability in the question of the Order of the Knights Templar. In
France the Order had been extinguished and the Knights badly
treated; but in Portugal it merely changed its name and became the Order of Christ. When Henry the Navigator became
Master, the Order was extremely rich, and invested large sums
in the voyages he directed, and the Cross – its badge – was em-
blazoned on the sails of the discoverers' ships. D. Denis may
also have been responsible for the introduction of the name and
rank of 'admiral' into Portugal. There is mention of Nuno
Fernandes Cogominho, who was *muy boo cavalleiro*, and was
made an admiral by D. Denis; but it was quickly seen in Por-

tugal (though not in Spain) that the command of a fleet could
only be exercised by a sailor, and there is documentary evidence for the appointment (1 February 1322) of Manuel
Peçanha, who belonged to a nautical family of Genoa. The
post was to be hereditary, and the admiral was not required to
put to sea unless he had at least three galleys under his command.

The galley, as Professor P. E. Russell has lately pointed out,
was the main naval weapon of the thirteenth and fourteenth
centuries. 'Castille was already a first-class naval power. She
possessed a fleet of galleys permanently maintained by the
Crown and based on a dockyard organisation at Seville,[8] and
Portugal too had developed the galley as the main naval
weapon. 'In the last resort it is, no doubt, to their professional
status and technical skill that those who manned the royal
galleys of Castille owed their success.' They were not slaves, but
picked volunteers with a high professional naval tradition.
Captains, pilots, petty officers (comitres), rowers, bow-men and
men-at-arms were 'experienced specialists, proud of their job
and thoroughly at home in it'. Two generations after D. Denis,
during the Hundred Years' War between France and England,
a Portuguese galley or two would sometimes be drafted to support the Castilians in their raids on the English coast.

The reign of D. Denis saw the introduction of a primitive
form of marine insurance. In 1293 the Portuguese merchants
established by mutual agreement that in Flanders, Portugal
and some other countries they should always have a sum of 100
marks in silver (or the equivalent value) to ensure against total
loss. The capital was formed by the payment of a certain percentage of their freights by ships which loaded at Portuguese
ports for Flanders, England, Normandy, Brittany, La Rochelle,
Seville and ports in North Africa. King Denis confirmed this in
a letter of 10 May 1293. But it was not until the time of King
Ferdinand, ninety years later, that there came a series of measures which had as their principal object a real system of marine
insurance. The monarch, who was a shipowner himself,[8] instituted funds in Lisbon and Oporto, the capital of which was
calculated as a percentage on the freights of all ships over 50
tons; and the owners formed a kind of insurance company to
provide mutual assistance against loss by shipwreck or any other

accident. To regularise the administration of these funds, the
King set up a marine register, and at the same time instituted a
technical inspection of vessels, to avoid any kind of carelessness
of the agents. To arrive at a formula for an insurance premium
a long evolution was necessary: the idea of a certain regularity
of risk could only be acquired through solid experience. This,
we know, went back to King Denis, who ratified the practice
which Portuguese merchants had begun in Lisbon, Oporto and
Flanders.[9]

4

Dom Denis was troubled by the claims of the clergy – not
their spiritual claims, but their right to occupy land unpro-
ductively, and other privileges inherited from the founder of
the dynasty, Afonso Henriques, the price of ecclesiastical support for his conquests. With tact and patience Denis was able
to come to an agreement without giving too much away, to
compromise without surrender; and his rulings seem to be
soundly based on earlier legal decisions. They are found in a
series of 'Letters' issued between 1286 and 1308.[10] But he has
gone down to posterity as the planter of the King's Pine Wood;
and whether he was or not, nothing else that he did is more like
him, or better expresses the life and work of a medieval man in
Portugal.

There are other old pine woods in the country, particularly
in the district south of the Douro and south-west of Coimbra
near the Atlantic coast. There are also some south of the Tagus,
and magnificent stone pines on the road to Sines, the birth-
place of Vasco da Gama, while much active and intelligent re-
afforestation has been undertaken in recent years. The principal northern forest lies in the sandy region between the
sea and Leiria, a town with a huge castle on a high hill, a royal
residence which became the Queen's property through deed
of gift from Dom Denis, with all the land and the pine woods
which went with it.

To say that the planting of that sandy district was entirely
due to Dom Denis would be rash, unless all the woods and
forests of Portugal are to be attributed to medieval kings. The
probability is that Dom Denis replanted it and cared for it, and
tried to make sure that the trees were not destroyed by charcoal-

burners and cultivators, or set on fire by shepherds. We know that he cared for trees: amongst other evidence for this is a letter he wrote on 13 June 1310 informing his foresters and keepers (*montaraces*) that no trees were to be cut on the battle-field of Ourique. Where that celebrated engagement took place is not quite certain. The resounding defeat of a Moslem force by Afonso Henriques, with the help of angels (as at Mons in 1914) is so far a legend that authorities are divided as to whether it happened at the Ourique near Leiria, at the one near San-tarém or at another Ourique in Alentejo. This is a treeless wheat-country nowadays, far to the south; and the great battle may have been a brilliant, Smuts-like raid behind the enemy's lines with the object of burning his harvest. But the pine wood at Leiria is a great deal older than the first Portuguese dynasty; there is evidence that it was there in prehistoric times. Under land now covered by the forest, brown coal (lignite) exists; trees in the coal can be identified and prove to have been stone pine with an undergrowth of arbutus.

The stone pine is the umbrella-shaped tree (*Pinus pinea*), with thick, spreading branches and a solid patch of shade: the tree which gave King Denis the idea – and the rhymes – for one of his most attractive and memorable poems.

> Oh flores, oh flores do verde pino
> Oh flower of all trees, the green, green pine

It is a south European tree growing from Portugal to Greece and Asia Minor. The famous pine forest at Ravenna, where Byron used to ride by the shore of the Adriatic, consists mainly of stone pines; and there are other large forests of it, including the mixed pine forest on the other side of Italy, of which Shelley was thinking in his 'Recollection (To Jane)'. Besides its shape, the soft needles, the deep, glass-green colour and the amount of shade it gives, the beauty of the stone pine is increased by the deep grooves in the trunk, producing a rich play of light and shadow which must have been particularly vivid when the girls in King Denis's poems came out to dance in the slanting rays of the setting sun. The seeds in the cones are large and edible, and the husks have even been found in the refuse-heaps of Roman encampments in Britain, sent over for the Roman army of occupation.[11]

Unfortunately – for the traveller, at any rate – the stone pine, and its ally the Aleppo pine, are not so often seen in Portugal now as the cluster pine, or the maritime pine (*Pinus pinaster*), which came in later. This is a taller tree than the others, and grows far better in Portugal than in Britain; but it gives next to no shade. It has a rugged, dark trunk; the pine-needles are stiff and coarse, and the cones longer than those of the stone pine, while the small seeds are not worth eating. It is a native of many countries, particularly the French coast of the Bay of Biscay, the Landes and Gironde; and it may well have been from there that some of King Denis's sailors brought the cones to the sainted Queen. 'This is a new fircone we found beyond the sea, but the seeds are no good to eat.' 'Never mind! We'll plant them in the sand and see whether they'll grow.' Hence the vision of the Queen scattering an apronful of the pale brown, winged seeds in a sandy clearing of the pine wood. It was not an accident that they were sown in sand; medieval people knew these things, and had discovered the power of pine trees to stop drifting sand and improve the soil. Sown by the Queen or not, the trees found in the sand blown in from the shore conditions which suited them; and to-day the tall, bare trunks with a cluster of branches at the top have almost driven out the stone pine which had been there from the beginning.

5

The cluster pine has the advantage of growing quickly – something like two feet a year – and it often grows as tall as 100 feet. The wood is better for ship-building than the stone pine, which had formerly built fishing-boats. The stone pine still came in useful for certain parts of a boat – the ribs and curved pieces – but it was gradually replaced by the other pine, and ceased to be grown in the King's Pine Wood.

Then the voyages of discovery began, and stouter timber was required. Manuel I wrote to the monks of Alcobaça for 'the wood we need for decking and other things'.[12] The later, larger vessels which sailed round the Cape of Good Hope to India and the China Sea, and crossed the Atlantic to Brazil, needed something stronger for the keel, preferably oak. There was plenty of that, too, at first, in spite of the deliberate destruction and disastrous fires against which King Denis, his forebears and

successors tried vainly to legislate. Individuals who had cut
down trees had to plant others – so Afonso Henriques had commanded in 1179; and when this had no effect, and heavy fines
proved equally useless, the drastic order went out, which has
already been quoted: 'Whoso shall cut a pine tree, let them hang
him'. Even to-day, in spite of fire-towers and telephones, shepherds and small farmers will sometimes start fires; for afforesta-
of the bare hillsides has pushed their fields and pastures farther
up the hills and farther away from their homes.[13] There are still
a few large oaks growing in the severe and sombre landscape
of the mountain districts of the north-east; but these are generally lonely trees, growing in the middle of more humble vegetation. There was once a native Lusitanian oak; but it is becoming rare, though a traveller occasionally comes across small
woods of it.

In most places the thickly-wooded country of medieval times
has given way to bare mountain-side, the 'bald, dry slopes, desert and naked at the side of the road' of Guerra Junqueiro's
poem *Lágrima*.[14] Man's first idea in bringing land under cultivation was to burn the trees – even the resinous ones; although
the resin was, and still is, a most valuable product. It was important in Portuguese history for producing pitch. Without
that, the little caravels would never have been able to keep
afloat, or even to put to sea; and the resin is still important for
a number of industries, and worth collecting. Pine trees are
regularly cupped for resin. A long gash is made in the trunk
and a small earthenware pot – like a flower-pot with no hole
at the bottom – is fastened to the lower end of the gash, to collect the thick, white resin which oozes out.

It is sometimes asked whether there are still any trees in the
King's Pine Wood which go back to the time of Dom Denis and
Queen Isabel. No, the foresters reply, though there are three or
four which may be great-granchildren; of the rest the oldest
are not much more than 100 years old. The cluster pine is not
a long-lived tree, and has a large number of natural enemies.
Yet there are still two trees in Portugal which were alive when
Denis was king. One is a large oak, by the superbly situated
little town of Castro Daire, in the hill-country between Viseu
and Lamego: a place which, from time immemorial, has seen
the migratory flocks of sheep pass up and down from the

mountains in spring and autumn. The big oak, the 'oak of the Presépio' (the Christmas Stable), is over 40 feet round and may be anything from 600 to 1,000 years old. Another old oak, 24 feet round, is at Trancoso, a walled town and castle, 3,000 feet up in the Serra da Estrêla, where Dom Denis first met the Queen to whom he had been married by proxy at Barcelona.

The pine wood at Leiria is not a national park, like the one at Buçaco. That is a piece of the original Lusitanian forest which, from the seventeenth century onwards, has been tidied and preserved, while many new and exotic trees have been added during the last 150 years. With its oaks and cedars, its cypresses and mimosas, it is regarded by Portuguese authorities with legitimate pride: an example of how Nature can be protected. Another example is the park of the Villa Monserrate at Sintra, now the property of the State. The forest at Leiria is a very different thing. The trees have always been grown for profit, like any other kind of crop; and their use has affected the economic life and social history of the whole region. A by-product was the glass-factory, started in the eighteenth century by two Englishmen and bequeathed to the Portuguese Government. It still exists and flourishes, with its housing scheme, welfare centre and theatre, and the formal garden, laid out and planted by the two brothers.

Strictly speaking, the King's Pine Wood is only one of the numerous pine woods in the district, some private but most managed by the Government. It is about 12 miles long by 5 miles wide, running along the coast from the river Lis to a stream called 'Woodwater'; Agua de Madeiros. There are broad avenues (*aceiros*) running down to the sea, and narrower ones (*arrifes*) parallel with the shore, their chief object being to lessen the danger of fire. An English forester would call them 'rides' and 'rackways'. It is run on severely practical lines; some parts of it are regularly cut; some are set apart for nurseries, where the tall, isolated 'seed-pines' look like the conventional, stylised trees painted by the primitives. Other parts of the forest are experimental, for growing different varieties of trees or for studying the chemistry of the soil. The two lines of experiment run together. One of the greatest dangers for the future, one which in 200 or 300 years may reduce the whole pine forest to a desert, is the acidity of the soil. The rotting humus which collects under the trees is strongly acid; and this, with the iron salts present in the soil, forms a solid, impermeable layer, a 'pan' through which roots can no longer penetrate.

6

Yet the main problem, the main reason why the pine woods have been kept up all through the centuries – more important even than timber and resin and fuel – is this: if there were no trees to fix the soil, the whole land would be invaded by sand blowing in from the shore; and this, combined with the sand brought down by the rivers, would, not so many years hence, reduce the most fertile part of a most fertile country to a sandy waste. The problem is nothing less than the existence of Portugal, and the solution is the one found for it by King Denis and his sainted Queen. He seems to have been told by people on the spot that the best way of preventing the encroaching sand was to plant trees; and a few years after the Queen had scattered her traditional apronful of pine-seed, it was plain for all to see that the new trees, sprung from the seed which came from France, were growing more quickly than the old ones. The light, winged seeds, blown inland or deliberately planted along the shore, extended the new pine tree down the coast north of the Tagus; and it has penetrated inland to such an extent that some botanists believe the cluster pine to be native to Portugal, after all. The 'Ranger', however, is convinced that the tree was introduced from the Landes of Bordeaux according to the tradition; while the 'green, green pine' – the *verde pino* of King Denis's poetry – was the shadier and more beautiful stone pine, which had been there all along.

This tends to be confirmed by what has been happening farther up the coast. The dunes of Mira, near Figueira da Foz, were once covered by a forest of stone pines; but they suffered severely during the Napoleonic invasion of 1808. Masséna, in fact, during his short occupation, proved a more dangerous enemy than the Moors; for he burnt most of the trees which formed the natural defence, not against him but against a more persistent enemy; the encroaching sand. The defences gone, the sand made rapid advances in the nineteenth century, and most of the trees to be seen there now are cluster pines which have been planted lately.

Without pine trees, the sand moves inland irresistibly, destroying all the arable land it reaches. The dunes are not a defence against the sea, as they are in Holland, but the advancing enemy itself. Compared with the fertile country inland, they are a terrifying sight, even under a blue sky on an August afternoon. In winter or early spring, under leaden clouds, the sand swirls in the wind, and pours over the pine trees as if it would smother them. Sometimes a whole sand dune topples over and blots out all the vegetation within reach; and the struggle of the trees to resist suffocation from the salt breath of a westerly gale can be seen in their twisted shapes. Trees often show the direction of the prevailing wind; the pines on the dunes turn away from the blown sand. It would have needed a Van Gogh to paint them, and a poet to describe them. Poets have done so. Like Shelley's Italian pines at Viareggio, 'Tortured by storms to shapes as rude As serpents interlaced', these are 'convulsed, contorted, ruined; present astonishing forms, terrifying shapes. The storms of a thousand winters have given them tortured bodies and afflicted souls.'

That was the impression of Afonso Lopes Vieira, the poet who lived among them at San Pedro de Moel, with the pine forest on three sides and the Atlantic on the fourth. On a calm day they are 'a green, whispering cathedral, where the light caresses and then vanishes':

> Catedral verde e sussurrante, aonde
> a luz se ameiga e se esconde;

– and where the echoing song of the ocean is prolonged along the coast . . . in lines which have caught, marvellously, the dull roar of Atlantic rollers

> E aonde ecoando a cantar
> se alonge e se prolonge
> a longa voz de mar.

But the pine trees, he says in another poem, must be sailors, too, in rough weather; sailors, still, when ship-wrecked and cast away on the dunes: 'Christs that are nailed in sand that holds you fast, crucified also for us.'[12]

Outside the line of dunes is the place 'wherein the land has an end, and the sea a beginning'. Camoens put it in a line of which the business sense can be conveyed in a prose translation, and something of the rhythm in English verse; but not the soft, rustling fall of the little waves breaking on the beach, which a sensitive Portuguese ear can detect in the e's and a's, the two s's, the s and the ç:

>Onde a terra se acaba e o mar começa

Camoens is always doing that, and escaping the notice of the translators in doing so. There may not be much to meet the eye in

>O nocturno silencio repousado,

but there is everything for the ear in the muted notes of that cadence; while in

>Move-se brandamente o arvoredo

– a movement, ever so gentle, among the trees – the slight noises only make the hush more vivid in the ceaseless, muffled stirring of all the branches. That is what Portuguese poetry can do, expects to do and is still doing. So Lopes Vieira could give 'the white sand, gleaming, tattooed with patterned lines of dry scrub'; and fix the place where the pine-seed was sown with the humble, low-growing plants, which grip the dry, shifting soil and eventually hold it. These are the 'sown dunes'. Behind them, stretching for miles north of the King's Pine Forest, are the 'virgin dunes': extraordinary shapes, astral landscape, an idea of the first hour of Genesis. And the Arch-enemy, present from that first hour, was sand.

Problems like these have formed the subject of conversation, scrambling over the dunes; but more particularly they did so on that August afternoon with the 'Ranger', cruising through the King's Pine Forest on the toy railway with the wood-burning engine, the cool carriage with no sides and no doors, and the engine-driver ready to stop in an instant when any of the three passengers wished. The history of the forest seemed to be the history of Portugal; and its problems, the fundamental problems of the country in medieval times and our own.

NOTES TO CHAPTER 6

[1] A. da Costa Lobo, *Hist. da Sociedade em Portugal no século XV* (1903), cap. II.

[2] 'Uma arregaçada de penisco vindo de França.' The great authority on the pine forest is the present 'Ranger' – to give him the English equivalent

of his title – chief of the whole 'circumscription' of forests in that part of the country, Eng° Silvicultor Sr. A. Arala Pinto, whose book, *O pinhal do Rei*, 2 vols., Alcobaça, 1938, is the foundation of all our knowledge.

³ Sir George Young, *Portugal*, Oxford, 1917, p. 6.

⁴ Other popular rhymes about Dom Denis refer to his building castles and saving money:

> Dizia Dom Denis:
> 'Serpa e Moura fiz;
> E mais fizera se quisera,
> Que quem dinheiro tiver
> Faré o que quiser.'

> King Denis said:
> 'Serpa and Moura I made;
> And more I could have if I would have;
> For he who has money in hand
> Will do all that he planned.'

> Eu El-rei Dom Denis
> Castelo, ponte e fonte fiz.
> Não mais fiz, porque não quis;
> E quem dinheiro tiver
> Fará o que bem quiser.

> King Denis said:
> 'I castle, bridge and fountain made.
> No more I made, because I stayed;
> For he who has money in hand
> Will do all that he planned.'

> Eu, Dom Denis,
> Este castelo fiz.
> Quem depois de mim vier,
> Se dinheiro tiver,
> Fará o que quiser.

> 'I', Denis said,
> 'This castle made;
> And he who comes when I am dead,
> If he has money in hand
> Will do all that he planned.'

⁵ Herculano, *Hist. IV*, 137–146; V, 154–160; VI, 331–343 (Note V).

⁶ Gabriel Pereira, *Documentos históricos da cidade de Evora* (1887), I, 50–51.

⁷ V. M. Shillington and A. B. W. Chapman, t.c.

⁸ King Ferdinand owned twelve merchant ships which loaded wine and other goods in foreign ports. The merchant state was presided over by a merchant king. J. Cortesão, *O sentido da cultura em Portugal no século XIV* (1956).

⁹ *História da Marinha Portuguesa*, I (1940); K. Reatz, *Geschichte des europäischen Seeversicherungsrechts*, I (Leipzig, 1870), 14; A. Goris, *Etude sur les colonies marchandes méridionales . . . à Anvers de 1488 à 1567* (Louvain, 1925), 178–179, and Cortesão, t.c.

¹⁰ A. Gomes Ramalho, l.c. 109–114.

¹¹ W. K. Bean, *Trees and Shrubs hardy in the British Isles*, vol. 2.

[12] A. Arala Pinto, t.c.; *Ciclo de conferências agrónomicas e florestais* (1948–1949), III, and *Duas Dívidas: D. Denis e o nacionalismo de Afonso Lopes Vieira* (Leiria, 1952).

[13] Ferreira de Castro, *A lã e a neve*, cg. III.

[14]   . . . Uma encosta escalvada
              Seca, deserta e nua, a beira de uma estrada.

Chapter 7

The Revolution of 1383

I

IN THE Middle Ages the men who were exempt from manual labour and not so intelligent as Dom Denis had no other way of taking exercise than hunting or fighting. 'Hunting was no rare or chance recreation, but a necessary daily expenditure of excess of physical energy which had no mental application to balance it'; [1] and for hunting wild animals the virgin forest was a paradise. The Crown lands, lands belonging to the nobility, and the enclosures of the monasteries always had a large preserve or covert (*couto*) of wild, natural forest which often came right up to the primitive, comfortless dwelling-house. Even the monastery of Alcobaça was surrounded at one time by thick woods in which game was preserved, and the same could be said of other monasteries as well. This went on until the end of the Middle Ages; Afonso V (*d.* 1487) and John II (*d.* 1495), the last of the race of royal hunters, were in that sense the last Portuguese representatives of medieval kingship.

There had always been a tendency for workers to drift away from the land; and that immediately caused a rise in the price of food, though the Government did what little it could to prevent it. Ever since 1253, by a law of Afonso III, the population which received wages had been subject to rigorous orders to work,[2] and a distinction had been drawn between the man who worked on his own and the man who received a salary. There had been periodical outbreaks of plague all through the Middle Ages, and famine had always followed. But when the Black Death reached Portugal in 1348, something like a third of the rural population died; the famine which came afterwards was worse than any which had gone before, and many of the survivors fled or crowded into the towns. The further effects were summarised by the King to the Côrtes of 1377: 'Some who used to be labourers and keepers of cattle have sold what they had and made themselves merchants or hucksters, and ceased to work or to make anything. And since this is damaging to the country, we pray that it may be in the King's pleasure that we command every man to make use of his trade in the manner which was commanded by the [late] King our Father (whom God pardon!), for they understand that it was to our service and profit from the land.' [2]

Lisbon, according to the chronicler Fernão Lopes, was full of people of all kinds, gambling and spending lavishly; and there were still innumerable beggars disguised as monks or hermits, in spite of the vigorous measures against them which had been passed in 1349. In the country, labour was difficult to find, and wages so high that landowners either gave up or turned their land over to grazing; though they still preserved their woodlands for game and even enclosed more, making the seasonal movements of cattle more difficult than before, and increasing the traditional hostility between farm-labourers and shepherds. There, the King was firm with them; for the kings of Portugal had always protected cattle-breeding; but unlike (or more successfully than) the kings of Spain, they tried to balance the interests of large and small holders, of village councils and cattle-breeders.

At last, after a number of plans for compelling workers to return to the land had been drawn up and rejected, the astute minds of lawyers invented a complicated scheme in which all possible consequences of the crisis were foreseen and a remedy attempted for everything. They had gone back to certain ancient statutes, forgotten laws and local customs, and stirred the whole mixture in such a way that it became in the end one of the first real agrarian laws in Europe.[3] They remembered those men whom the municipal and village councils used to employ for marking boundaries and dividing up the land into parcels which a single family could cultivate: the *sesmeiros*; and from the old name the new legislation became known as the *Lei das sesmarías*. 'Considering', the preamble begins, 'that in all parts of the kingdom there is a shortage of wheat and barley, that prices have greatly risen, that labour is insufficient, that lands and estates which once were cultivated and sown and are good for bread and for other products to maintain the population, are now waste and desolate; all owners shall be constrained to work them and sow them, either for themselves or for another, so that all lands capable of bearing wheat, barley or millet shall be used.⁴ Actually, the new law had only one point in common with the ancient practice, though that point was the most important: the obligation to cultivate the land as a condition of holding it, and expropriation for the owner who left his portion uncultivated.

In Spain, the State seems almost to have lost interest in agricultural problems, or to have given them up as a bad job, except cattle-breeding. In England, however, which suffered even more than Portugal from shortage of labour after the Black Death, Parliament met the situation with a 'Statute of Labourers' (1351), comparable with the Portuguese *Lei das Sesmarías*, not only in the evils it sought to remedy but also in a limitation on the power of the land-workers to seek more remunerative occupations. What Trevelyan says of England is equally applicable to Portugal: 'These Parliamentary laws in restraint of wages mark the gradual change from a society based on local customs of personal services to a money-economy that is nation-wide. . . . The avowed purpose of the Statute of Labourers is to prevent the rise of wages, and to a lesser degree of prices also.' ⁵

After describing the strikes, riots, formation of local unions, persecution and imprisonment, he goes on – and it is true also for Portugal: 'On the whole, the victory lay with the wage-earner, because of the shortage of labour caused by the great pestilence and by its continual local recurrence. Prices indeed rose, but wages rose faster still.' But, as he notes in his earlier *History of England*, the Statute subjected the labour of the rural worker to the oscillation of supply and demand, undermining the right of preference of the lord in relation to the labourer.

Portugal, like England, stood at the beginning of a new age, and both countries were to face it in much the same way: by commercial and maritime adventure, by discovery and colonisation. Portugal, however, was first off the mark; and while England was fighting at Agincourt, Portugal was occupying Ceuta.

2

The English Alliance, signed at Guimarães on 10 July 1372,⁶ and the subsequent Treaty of Windsor (1386) have been

studied by a number of writers in England and Portugal; but
no one has made a more thorough examination of the documentary evidence for the diplomatic events leading up to it
than Professor P. E. Russell, of Oxford.[7] It was preceded by a
treaty on trade and fishing rights, between Edward III and the
'gents, merchants, mariners et comunaltés de la marisme, des
cités et villes de Ulixbon et du Port du Portugal'.[8] The first
commercial treaty is signed by a burgess of Oporto, on behalf
of the burgesses, artisans (mesteirais) of the sea-ports of Portugal.
Oporto appears now, with Lisbon, as the social metropolis of
the Portuguese nation. The relationship between England and
Portugal was economic; trade between the two countries
developed considerably during the fourteenth century and
could not be interrupted by occasional acts of war and piracy.
The English mercantile colony in Lisbon was already so large
that Ferdinand I granted it the privilege of bringing commercial disputes between its members and the Portuguese
before a special judge.

Portugal rapidly assumed the character of a popular monarchy, an alliance between Crown and people against clergy
and nobility.[9] The Church, through its highest representatives,
and with the pretension of placing the kingdom under clerical
guidance, put obstacles in the way of unifying the State. The
excommunication of private citizens, classes, towns, the King
or the whole kingdom, provoked, as Rodrigues Lapa has
shown,[10] the heretical spirit of the medieval lyrics. The popular
revolt in Lisbon was led by a tailor, when the populace rose
against Ferdinand's marriage to Leonor Teles, already married
to someone else – to one of his vassals. There was a new class of
lawyers (letrados and legistas), sprung from the bourgeoisie. One
of them, Alvaro Pais, born at the end of the reign of Dom
Denis, and twice Chancellor, was to prepare the coming of the
Master of Avis.

3

Though the revolution of 1383–1385 was fundamentally
social and economic, it had a dynastic side which seemed the
more obvious and important in its time, and still takes up much
space in the text-books. In Spain, the Trastamaras were in the
ascendant. Since the murder of Peter the Cruel in 1369, Henry

of Trastamara, supported by France, was almost invariably successful. He was efficient and unscrupulous, and the Trastamaras' plans of annexation through matrimonial alliances soon came to include Portugal, where the possibility of union of the two crowns was an old problem. This culminated in 1383–1385, when resistance to the claims of Castille coincided with the revolt of the new middle class of overseas traders, from which arose a new society and a new dynasty.

First, however, there was the piteous episode of Inez de Castro, which has left so deep a mark on the literature of Portugal and is known to every Portuguese, while in Spain, it was the subject of a fine seventeenth-century play. The Infante D. Pedro, eldest son of Afonso IV, married Doña Constanza of Castille. In her suite was a lady-in-waiting, Inez de Castro, for whom the Infante immediately fell. Doña Constanza (who is the heroine of another play by the symbolist poet Eugénio de Castro) could not help being aware of what was going on; and, to prevent the infatuation from going any further, arranged for Inez to be godmother to one of her children, so that the spiritual relationship, at any rate, should raise an insurmountable obstacle between them. It was too late. Doña Constanza died; D. Pedro refused to marry again, afterwards claiming that he had been secretly married to Inez. Versions of the story vary. According to the one generally accepted, some Castilian knights wished to dethrone their own king and replace him by a Portuguese prince, in which conspiracy Inez and her brothers were implicated. This alarmed all those Portuguese who were zealous for national independence. Inez was condemned by an *ad hoc* Council of State and put out of the way by three patriotic murderers who forthwith fled to Castille. D. Pedro rebelled against his father, and on succeeding to the throne two years later, had the murderers extradited from Castille, in exchange for others, and done to death under his windows while he was at dinner.

D. Pedro, according to the chronicler Fernão Lopes, was a man of plebeian manners, fond of rough, practical joking, violent in anger, and with a mania, not exactly for justice but for making the punishment fit the crime. Yet a modern historian [11] can see that he had precious gifts as an administrator, and he legislated well for agriculture and overseas trade. By his marriage with Doña Constanza he had his son and successor, D. Fernando; by Inez de Castro, two sons who played considerable parts later in the English intervention. Another son, by his mistress Teresa Lourenço, became Master of the Order of Avis and eventually King John I, who married Philippa of Lancaster and founded the great Avis dynasty.

With Ferdinand the project of union with Castille reappeared. When Alfonso XI died in 1350, Peter the Cruel succeeded as legitimate heir to the throne of Castille, but the succession was disputed by Henry of Trastamara, his bastard brother, and a civil war followed. Peter was the better commander, but allowed himself to be surprised and captured at Montiel in 1369; he was stabbed in an undignified scuffle with his brother, aided at a critical moment by someone who was standing by. Ferdinand of Portugal entered into an alliance with the Kings of Aragon and Granada against the Trastamara, and invaded Galicia and Castille. Henry, however, counter-attacked vigorously, and Ferdinand had to sue for peace.

John of Gaunt was pretender to the throne of Castille, through his marriage to a daughter of Peter the Cruel, and Ferdinand now entered into a military alliance with him; but before any English troops could be sent, Henry invaded Portugal once more as far as Lisbon, and once more Ferdinand had to sue for peace. On the death of Henry of Trastamara, Ferdinand tried the English alliance again; but before English aid arrived, Ferdinand lost his fleet of galleys in an engagement with the galleys of Castille; and the 'picaresque English force', when at last it arrived, did more damage in Portugal than in Castille.

Troubles came to Ferdinand from his unwise and precipitate marriage to Leonor Teles. She was remotely of royal descent, ambitious and irresistible, with a fair share of human frailty; only Shakespeare, or Euripides, could have done her justice. She had originally been married to João Lourenço da Cunha; but when the King saw her in Lisbon, on a visit to her sister, he first made her his mistress, then had the marriage annulled and carried her off to a church near Oporto, where he married her himself. Their daughter, Beatriz, had been married to that 'melancholy and incompetent fanatic', Juan I of Castille, and now, on Ferdinand's death in 1381, Don Juan I of Castille became legitimate successor to the throne of Portugal.

4

Here the Portuguese people come upon the scene. They had protested against Ferdinand's marriage with Leonor Teles: a royal mistress was all very well, but it was not well for a King of Portugal to marry the wife of one of his vassals. A tailor who had protested too much had been hanged – through the Queen's influence, it was said; and now it was common knowledge that she had taken as her paramour – even before the King's death – Count Andeiro, a Galician, a Castilian subject and therefore a traitor. The Lisbon crowd was not far from rebellion, and leadership was provided by the *letrados* (lawyers and officials) and the commercial bourgeoisie.

The King of Castille wished to take possession of what was now his by right. Leonor, however, wished to continue as Queen regent, and in the autumn of 1381 appointed commanders to posts on the Spanish frontier, among them being the twenty-six-year-old Master of Avis. Most of the Portuguese nobility had opted for legality, i.e. the King of Castille; but the commercial interests demurred, and gave all their support to the forces of popular unrest. In Lisbon their chief was Alvaro Pais, who had been Chancellor under two reigns and was old and gouty, though still vigorous. He was the step-father of João das Regras, a clever lawyer trained in Roman Law at Bologna, who was to be the brain of the Revolution. Another acquisition of the revolutionary party was the young noble Nun' Alvares Pereira, whose family were all on the other side, but whose exalted faith and passion for Arthurian chivalry did not cloud his clear, tactical intelligence, and he provided the revolution with a brilliant commander in the field.

Alvaro Pais had decided that the Master must murder Count Andeiro, who, being a subject of Castille, was certainly disloyal to Portugal. The Master was on the point of leaving Portugal for good, and offering his services to Richard II of England. He had two ships waiting in the Tagus, loaded with all his movable property, and protested that he was not in the habit of murdering his enemies; but he was overruled by the irascible ex-chancellor and by a friar, João da Barroca, who had been hired by Alvaro Pais to announce to the Master (as if it had been a divine revelation) that it was his mission to save the country. He made some show of leaving for Alentejo, to take up the command to which the Queen had appointed him, but turned back suddenly and begged for a further audience. The Queen received him in some surprise seated on an *estrada* with her ladies, doing needlework and chatting with Count Andeiro. Why had the Master returned so unexpectedly? Why were he and his attendants armed, and 'not wearing gloves as the English do'? The Master was nonplussed, until one of his attendants explained that the English, being always in a state of war in their own country, delighted when abroad to appear in the habiliments of peace, while the Portuguese, being by nature men of peace, could afford to wear arms, especially when on the way to a post of danger. Count Andeiro unsuspiciously left the audience chamber with the Master, and was struck down in the corridor, the Master's half-hearted blow being followed by a more vigorous thrust from one of the attendants. The body was left lying in a corner, where it was presently found by the Queen; there was at that time such confusion in the palace that no one had thought of taking it away.

Meanwhile Alvaro Pais had sent a page through the streets crying, 'They're murdering the Master!' and himself followed the crowd on an old horse which he had not been able to mount for ten or twelve years. The Master was acclaimed at one of the palace windows: the 'quisling' bishop (another Castilian) was brutally thrown from the tower of the cathedral, and the Queen herself was lucky in being able to escape to Alenquer that night. The merciless Alvaro Pais, however, pursued her with the hypocritical proposal that she should marry the Master, for reasons of State, in spite of the fact that he had just murdered the man she loved, Andeiro. She was believed to be with child; and it would simplify matters if the child were born after she had married the Master. The populace, however, would not hear of the Master leaving Lisbon (for the Queen was still at Alenquer); and Alvaro Pais went himself, returning with a letter in which the Queen refused the proposed marriage, but promised the safety of the city of Lisbon – from the Castilians. The Master, warned by his Council, refused to read the Queen's reply, and publicly tore it up.

Within two months there were clearly two parties, and two policies: the Master of Avis and national independence, or the King of Castille and union with Spain. For the Master were the *letrados*, the noble Nun' Alvares Pereira, and the Archbishop of Braga; the rest – all those with money or influence – were for the King of Castille. D. Juan I crossed the Portuguese frontier in the beginning of January 1384; he was at Santarém by the 12th, and by May Lisbon was surrounded. Alvaro Pais, however, had not been idle. He sent a popular orator round the country, speaking for the Master's cause; we can read what he said at Montemôr-Novo (Alentejo) in Gama Barros.[12]

The maritime bourgeoisie, preparing the alliance with England, brought the Master strong financial and military support, pledging the merchandise which they had in English ports for the enlistment of English archers; while the *letrado* Lourenço Eanes Fogaça and the Master of Santiago went to London to negotiate the alliance.

Whenever Portugal has been subjected to invasion, it is not on the frontier or at the usual entrances that the enemy has been stopped. Henry of Trastamara in 1369 had met with no resistance until he reached Guimarães. In 1372–1373 the Castilians had approached Lisbon without difficulty, as they did now, in 1384. In 1385 there was no hindrance before Aljubarrota, and in 1810 Masséna was allowed to reach the lines of Torres Vedras. In 1384 there was one exception. At Los Atoleiros in Alentejo, on the 6 April 1384, the Constable Nun' Alvares tried out the new English tactics of dismounted men against heavy mounted men-at-arms. It was only a small engagement, but completely successful; the horses floundered among the hurdles and shallow entrenchments, and the raiding party lost many men and most of their mounts.

The King of Castille was already at Santarém, where he had forced Leonor to renounce the throne. He pushed on to Lisbon and surrounded the city, though his blockade was not quite complete, and a few food ships managed to get through. The siege went on through most of the summer; but in the Castilian camp plague broke out, and by September the Spaniards were forced to retreat to the frontier, having lost their stoutest men-at-arms and their most experienced commanders. Next year the invasion was repeated; but for one reason or another the main

drive for Lisbon was not begun until August, and by that time
the Constable had chosen an admirable defensive position on
the main road south, at Aljubarrota.

Professor Russell has given so admirable an account of the
day and the events which led up to it that it would be useless
and unnecessary to attempt another; for, unlike most accounts
of medieval warfare, it reads like a real battle. This is due to
familiarity with the ground as it was a few years ago, and to a
historical vision of what it must have been like in 1385, and
also to exact knowledge of where the various formations were
posted and how they moved. The Castilian commanders were
mainly new, untried and rash; but they had the support of a
strong contingent from France under its own experienced
leaders. They realised that the Constable's position was going
to be difficult to attack, but, though impossible from the front,
might be taken in the rear. While they were manœuvring,
however Nun' Alvares reversed his dispositions, and by six
o'clock in the evening it was clear – to the French commanders,
at any rate – that it would be folly to attack a prepared position
with troops exhausted with marching and countermarching at
the end of an August day. They succeeded in convincing the
King of Castille; but suddenly, without waiting for orders, some
of the junior Castilian commanders went into action. The result was what the Constable had foreseen: the superior Castilian
and French forces were crowded into a narrow space; their
horses were killed and their riders slaughtered. The French
losses were particularly heavy. The English archers – fewer
than is generally supposed, and not sent by John of Gaunt but
privately recruited in England by Portuguese merchants –
were in an exposed position on the Portuguese left; but they
were well supplied with ammunition; 'boxes of arrows' appear
on merchants' bills of lading.

The rout was complete. Aljubarrota is one of the decisive
battles of western Europe, and it owes nearly everything to the
tactical skill and personality of the Constable Nun' Alvares.
The chronicler gives a picture of him riding through the lines,
'The Constable of Portugal got on a horse . . . to see if each
man was correctly in that good and sagacious order in which
he had first posted them. He said that all should keep steady
when the Castilians moved; and in engaging the enemy they

should stand firm on their feet, holding their lances straight before them, supported under the arm and as far forward as they could.'

5

Fernão Lopes, in the *Crónica de D. Fernando*, gives the impression that after the wars of that monarch the world was very different from what it had been before, now that the easygoing years of his father's time were over.[13] In the chronicle of the next King, however, he takes the view that the new age really began in the time of the Master of Avis. What most impressed him in the first period was the economic and social crisis. He did not perceive its origins, only observing the last phase in its effects on the men at Court and in the coast towns. He was also aware that the new generation had risen to a higher cultural level.

The transformation observed by Fernão Lopes shows the aggravation, and finally the explosion, of a situation which had been developing since the middle of the century. It was hidden from the eyes of the well-to-do by the flourishing state of the exchequer, combined with the ostentation of the newly rich and the prosperity of the cosmopolitan maritime bourgeoisie engaged in overseas trade; but, examined more closely, the social situation is seen to be one of class warfare and economic disturbance, caused mainly by the Great Plague of 1348. The larger proportion of victims came from the poorer classes, and at least one-third of the population had died. This led to an acute shortage of labour and a steep rise in prices. There were not enough workers for the land, and the survivors naturally refused to work at the old wage-scales, although (as in England) the landowners claimed the right to force them to return to conditions as they were before the Black Death, and work for the same wage.

This head-on collision of interests and acute dissension between the different classes finally led to revolution. The rich were richer than before, through the accumulation of inheritances due to deaths from plague; but when the former landworkers tried to better themselves at the seaports, they found that they were being exploited by the *homens bons* (as they were called) of the councils, who were lined up with the nobles.

The revolution when it came was directed by the shipowners and merchants of Lisbon and Oporto; it was organised – for it was profitable to them politically – by the bourgeoisie of the seaports, under the shadow of the Master of Avis. The first outbreak was in Lisbon; but no sooner had Alvaro Pais called out the inhabitants than the provincial workers turned and showed the accumulated resentment of thirty years against their employers. Whenever they could, they avenged themselves with the utmost violence; in the country there was complete anarchy and in Lisbon much looting. In the villages the 'best and most honoured men' went in peril of their lives and were often robbed of all that they possessed. Some fled to those towns which, in the emergency, had declared for the King of Castille; others abandoned Portugal altogether, leaving their lands and goods to be taken over by the Master, who gave land to any who asked for it. There were also direct expropriations by the Master himself. Alvaro Pais had found the formula: 'Sir, listen to my advice, and it will help you. Give away what is not yours, and promise what you have not got; forgive him who has done you no injury.'

In Spain, Professor Russell observes, the forces of tradition won; but they were not destined to do so in Portugal. Just as, in Castille, fate had decreed that the aristocratic John of Gaunt should become titular head of a party hostile to the unlimited pretensions of the magnates, so, in Portugal, the government of Richard II and his friends espoused the cause of elective monarchy and aided the overthrow of a landed aristocracy in favour of a bourgeois state. He sees no reason to dispute the conclusion of António Sérgio that Portuguese nationalism in 1383–1384 was derived from the opposition of the mercantile bourgeois of the cities – notably Lisbon and Oporto – to the traditional power and influence of the officials of the small towns. The bourgeoisie was strongly nationalist, and behind it were the city mobs which knew nothing of feudal obligations. Behind them also were the surviving landowners who had suffered severely from the rulings of rural and urban officials responsible for fixing wages, the men who had had to implement the restrictive labour legislation introduced to deal with the scarcity of manpower brought about by the Black Death.

Oliveira Martins sums up the period by remarking that it

was John I's companions and his Queen, Philippa of Lancaster, who made him, in mature age, a wise king. After Aljubarrota the feeling for national independence became popular; for the revolution which had brought the Master to the throne coincided with the particular interest of the Portuguese people.

6

Aljubarrota consolidated the independence of Portugal. But neither this nor the fact that Portugal became more and more cosmopolitan in appearance and outlook could destroy certain basic conditions common to the whole Peninsula. We should not forget that, until the middle of the seventeenth century, Portuguese, Castilians and Catalans lived intellectually in much the same civilisation, though in Portugal and Catalonia the bourgeoisie were more prominent and had a more liberal and humanist outlook.

The Trastamaras' matrimonial schemes, as we saw, included Portugal, and they were not deflected from their main purpose by Aljubarrota or the change of dynasty. Thus Juan II of Castille married a Portuguese princess who became the mother of Isabel the Catholic, and Enrique IV married the sister of Afonso V (1455). These repeated marriages between near relations may have contributed to the rapid degeneration of the Trastamaras; but there was no sign of it in Isabel, who was to make Castille the leading kingdom in Spain and, indeed, in Europe. The death of the Prince of Viana, the suitor for Isabel preferred by Enrique IV, favoured her proposed marriage to Afonso V of Portugal. 'Only the projection of the facts of the present into the past, and the modern idea that Portugal is not Spain, can have led so many writers to consider that no other marriage of Isabel of Castille save that to Ferdinand of Aragon was "patriotic", in the sense of being favourable to Spain.' [14] They rejoice in the failure of Enrique IV's schemes and the obstinacy of Isabel in not accepting the Portuguese marriage. Regarded in the light of the unity of the Peninsula, the Portuguese marriage was the one that was most urgent, though it offered the greatest difficulties. It was necessary to take the chance of union with Portugal while it offered, and then accomplish the union of Castille and Aragon with the acquiescence of the Portuguese and the good will of their king. The opposition of Isabel and her supporters to the Portuguese marriage was considerable; and it led eventually to the union of Castille with the eastern provinces but not with the kingdom in the west. Enrique cannot be blamed for having opposed the Aragonese marriage in the name of union with Portugal; for if this had been achieved just then, under the Portuguese dynasty of Avis and with Portugal for the senior partner, it would have been more likely to last than under Philip II, III and IV. Later, when Ferdinand and Isabel wished once more to achieve this union through matrimonial alliances, fate intervened and the scheme came to nothing.

Portuguese historians, and Spanish historians as well, are apt to forget how slender the thread of Portuguese separatism was, even after Aljubarrota. It depended on the whim of a determined young woman of nineteen, brought up in Old Castille and speaking with what Toledo regarded as a provincial accent. The reasons were not only political; there were personal feelings as well. Of all the suitors, Ferdinand was the only one who was physically attractive; the King of Portugal was getting on in years and the Duc de Guyenne not quite right in the head. She chose a moment when the King of Castille was out of the way, in Andalucia; and Ferdinand had just sent her a collar of pearls and rubies worth 40,000 gold florins. He came to Castille disguised as a muleteer in the company of some Catalan merchants, reached Valladolid on 14 October 1469, and they were married on 19 October. There was no papal dispensation for the marriage; the bull was made out in the name of Afonso V of Portugal; but Isabel without hesitation had one forged in the name of Ferdinand. Both, of course, were excommunicated; in ecclesiastical law the union was 'incestuous concubinage'. They had very little money, and lived for some time as guests of the converted Jewish Admiral of Castille. The King meanwhile hastened to declare his putative daughter, Juana 'la Beltraneja', heir to the throne, and pushed on with his preparations for marrying her to the King of Portugal. When he died in 1474 – with all the symptoms of poisoning – Afonso V became the champion of Juana's cause and the Portuguese form of union between Portugal and Castille; but he was defeated at Toro in 1476, renounced his claims, and Juana la Beltraneja retired to a convent. Ferdinand and Isabel set about making

Castille the senior partner in union with a wasted Aragon and a Catalonia whose Mediterranean trade had been ruined. Their extraordinary luck is another story; but the independence of Portugal in the Peninsula was a very near thing.

Meanwhile the fortunate marriage of John I (the Master of Avis) with the daughter of John of Gaunt changed the customs of the Court and of the governing classes in Portugal. The King was not remarkable for intelligence, or for quickness of decisions taken in the field; but he had (Sérgio considers) a moderate dose of good sense not amounting to genius, and this enabled him to adapt himself to the ideas of those who assisted him. His children were naturally gifted, and received an excellent education in the surroundings created by Queen Philippa, who became, in fact, governess to the whole Court.

The Court eventually became an academy; the Infantes were not only cavaliers, but educated men: thinkers. D. Duarte, the eldest, was a man who paid great attention to detail and almost morbid in his scruples: he wrote 'The Loyal Counsellor' (*O Leal Conselheiro*), and also a book on the art of riding. The second, D. Pedro, was interested in sea voyages, studied the geographers and also the moralists and composed a moral treatise, *La Virtuosa Bemfeitoria*. The third, Henry 'the Navigator', was reserved, tenacious, hard; the moving spirit in promoting voyages of discovery. D. Fernando, the 'Constant Prince' of Calderón's play, met a martyr's death in Morocco, while D. João left on his contemporaries an impression of exceptional talent.

NOTES TO CHAPTER 7

[1] A. da Costa Lobo, t.c.
[2] Gama Barros, t.c., I, 483 ff.
[3] V. Rau, *Sesmarias medievais portuguesas* (1946), 66.
[4] Gomes Ramalho, t.c., I, 185.
[5] *English Social History* (1944), and Sir John Clapham, *A Concise Economic History of England* (Cambridge, 1949).
[6] Among the celebrations which took place to commemorate the thousandth anniversary of Guimarães was the unveiling of an obelisk to mark the signing of the first Anglo-Portuguese treaty of alliance. *The Times*, 14 July, 1953.
[7] *The English Intervention in Spain and Portugal in the time of Edward II and Richard II* (Oxford, 1955).
[8] Rymer, *Foedera*, III, 88; Gama Barros, IV, 423–424 (1st ed.); J. Cor-

tesão, t.c., 78; R. Jorge, 'Origems e desenvolvimento da populacão do Pôrto, in *Anuário de Câmara Municipal do Pôrto*, 1923, p. 39.

[9] C. R. Beazley, *Prince Henry the Navigator* (1895).

[10] Rodrigues Lapa, *Lições de Literatura Portuguesa: época medieval*, 4th ed. (Coimbra, 1954).

[11] A. Sérgio, *Historia de Portugal* (Madrid-Barcelona, 1927).

[12] Gama Barros, t.c.

[13] A. Sérgio, *Ensaios*, VI (1946) and prologue to *Chrónica de D. João I*.

[14] F. Soldevila, *Historia de España*, II, 334, 374 (Barcelona, 1952).

E

Chapter 8

Discovery and Pepper

I

THE EPOCH beginning with the House of Avis is characterised by expansion overseas and a new turn to the many questions involved in European trade with the East.

In spite of religious barriers, the trade of the tropical countries formed a whole; the great maritime states of the Mediterranean – Venice, Genoa, Catalonia – directed their energies to North Africa as well as to the Levant; the rich trade of Christendom had in view both the eastern Mediterranean ports and those of North Africa. From the time of the first Crusade, this trade had been quietly gaining in importance. As the well-to-do in European towns progressed, Christians began to demand the more refined products of the East, and the wives of crusaders were longing for the soft silk undergarments and other comforts made and marketed by the very men whom their husbands had gone out to kill. Many of their products had become indispensable to the basic industries and occupations of the time, others, like spices, were essential for cooking. Above all, there was pepper, important in a way that is difficult for us to imagine to-day. It was not only a condiment for meat (particularly when the meat was none too fresh), but was also used in wine and pastry. It became so widespread that it was accepted in payment of fines and taxes, freight charges and debts between one state and another.

In times of famine, Mediterranean countries had recourse to North Africa; and Christians were glad to trade with Moslems for another reason: the gold, in bars or nuggets, which the Moslems brought from the Sudan.[1] Moslem ships often came into Christian ports; and there is evidence that much of the gold coinage circulating in Portugal at the close of the Middle Ages came from Moslem states in North Africa. As early as Afonso IV (1325–1357) the Portuguese had sent an expedition to the Canary Isles; and in the same century they seem to have known Madeira and some of the Azores. In 1415, to free commercial navigation from the attentions of Barbary pirates and intercept caravans coming up from Morocco with gold and the cereals so necessary to feed Portugal, the bourgeois merchants of Lisbon and Oporto induced the King to take Ceuta.

Ceuta was the great commercial emporium for products of the East, while Lisbon already possessed a cosmopolitan middle class ready to push the nation on to audacious undertakings overseas. The reasons why the idea of the conquest of Ceuta appealed to the traders rather than the nobles, why the commercial middle classes were so anxious for the expedition, and the financial manipulations which the King employed to obtain the necessary funds [2] are clearly stated in the Chronicle of Azurara. But above all there was the need for the Portuguese to act quickly, on account of the enterprise of their Castilian neighbours, who seem to have got off the mark first. It is doubtful (though the claim has been made) whether a Castilian fleet attacked Tetuan and temporarily cleared the Straits of pirates; but from 1403 to 1406 the King of Castille, aided by Jean de Béthencourt and Gadifer de la Sale, achieved the conquest of the Canaries. He also sent embassies to the East, the last of which, under Ruy González de Clavijo, visited the Court of Timur Beg ('Tamburlaine') at Samarkand, the centre of Asiatic trade.

The death of Enrique III in 1406 and the troubles which ensued in Castille prevented this movement from being followed up; but information of what the Castilians were about fully explains Portuguese secrecy over the conquest of Ceuta, and disposes of the theory that the voyages were a psychological product of 'the Celtic character of the Portuguese adventurer and dreamer', in opposition to the 'Gothic' Castilian – a theory always condemned by António Sérgio.

For Jaime Cortesão, the main reason for the conquest of Ceuta was to avoid the 'commercial asphyxia' to which the Barbary pirates had reduced the trade in Oriental products; and secondly to prevent Castille from forestalling Portugal in discovering the way to India.

The first result of the occupation of Ceuta was that the Moorish tribes ceased to go that way, and took their saleable produce

elsewhere, where Christians had not yet penetrated. Professor
Ganshof, in *The European Heritage*,[3] explains how the supply of
currency in the fourteenth century had grown inadequate.
The main reason was the increasing scarcity of the Sudanese
gold, formerly acquired in North Africa by merchants from
Genoa, Venice, Catalonia and Provence. This had been used
chiefly to balance the perpetual deficit of Eastern trade. The
shortage was apparent about 1440, but fell after 1460; and it has
been conjectured that a considerable portion of this Sudanese
gold was appropriated by the Portuguese, as they ventured
southwards along the West African coast, and that they spent it
at Bruges and Antwerp. This shortage of Sudanese gold led to
the introduction of new silver currencies in Europe (e.g. the
Thaler) and the rise of great banking houses like the Fuggers of
Augsburg, who deposited large sums in Bruges and Antwerp,
to maintain contact with the new colonial trade now being
handled by the Portuguese through their geographical discoveries; and this can be partly explained by the increasing
difficulty of procuring Asiatic products, particularly silks and
spices.

In the second half of the fifteenth century the direct conti-
nental routes were closed by the Turkish wars in the East, the
fall of Byzantium (1453), Trebizond and the shores of the
Black Sea. Trade became increasingly difficult and uncertain,
not to say hazardous, while the old spice-route through Egypt
depended on the caprice of individual rulers. Gradually the
Arab merchants were replaced by the purely military Turks and
produced a commercial crisis. The traders, bankers and shippers tried to find another way round; began to think of Cadiz
and Lisbon as the successors of Genoa and Venice, and of Antwerp as the terminus of a sea-line of commerce.[4] The price of
those products which ultimately reached Europe was exorbitant.
Attempts were therefore made to restore direct contact with the
East, and this was accomplished by the Portuguese.

2

From now on we begin to see the efforts of Portugal to solve
the problems, not only of feeding itself but of dealing in its own
way with the commercial crisis of the whole of Europe. Prince
Henry 'the Navigator', backed by a cosmopolitan bourgeoisie,

collected round him at Sagres geographers, astronomers and traders; established an observation post on Cape St Vincent, and engaged the most famous cosmographer available, the Catalan Jewish Jafuda Cresques, from Majorca, known after his conversion as Jaume Ribes. The Infante's real objects were kept secret; but, according to Sérgio, from the beginning his idea was to reach the Far East and take possession of Eastern trade. The idea of conversion and the propagation of the Gospel was also mentioned – perhaps as a sop to the ecclesiastical authorities – and this afterwards became the official view; moreover the Infante counted on the help of 'Prester John', a Christian monarch said to rule somewhere in those parts and perhaps to be identified with the Emperor of Ethiopia.

The Portuguese discoveries of the fifteenth century were undertaken by methodical men, gifted with a cool, political intelligence and a lucid vision; precise in their view of the practical objectives, of which they had made an exact and detailed study. They had a far-reaching plan, prepared by men with an exceptional capacity for organisation, and with nothing of the unconscious adventurousness attributed to them later. Every year ships went to Africa with orders to go as far south as they could without losing sight of the coast. The greatest obstacle was Cape Bojador, (in what is now the Spanish possession of Rio de Oro,) some way north of the Tropic of Cancer, and the subject of terrifying legends. There the land seemed to fall away in an immense curve, and there was a wide stretch of white spray, giving the idea that the ocean from there onwards was always on the boil from the torrid heat of the sun. This cape was passed in 1434, and the commercial exploration of the West African coast led to the colonisation of the Atlantic islands: Madeira (1420), the Azores (1437) and Cape Verde Islands (1456). Plans for the first expeditions were prepared by the group of pilots, mathematicians and cartographers whom 'the Navigator' gathered round him; under John II, the later voyages were worked out by other expert groups, including the cosmographer Martin Behaim of Nuremberg. The second half of the fifteenth century brought fresh discoveries, including the mouth of the Congo (1485). Bartolomeu Dias rounded the Cape of Good Hope (1487) and Vasco da Gama finally reached the west coast of India in 1498.

The Portuguese success in these maritime undertakings and
adventures in navigation was due to science; and the science of
the day, however rudimentary, had led to a series of technical
improvements in ships and how to sail them. Most important
were the axled, hinged rudder, and the mariner's compass.[5]
The former had been in use in the North Sea and Baltic as
early as the thirteenth century, but it only came into general use
in the fourteenth. It was this rudder that enabled comparatively large ships, like three-masted caravels, to be sailed out
into the ocean. The mariner's compass implies not only the
magnetic needle (which had been already known to the
Vikings), but one fixed on a pivot, independent of the ship's
movements and used in conjunction with a compass-card. It had
been invented in the fourteenth century, but was not widely
used until the fifteenth. Without it, it is safe to say that the Portuguese discoveries would have been impossible; but their
nautical science was up-to-date because they were aware of
what was being done in other countries and willing to invite
foreign specialists to come and help them.

From the beginning the discoveries produced important
economic results. Colonial products such as sugar were eagerly
taken by North-West Europe: a little later came the first gold-
dust. The first convoy of black slaves reached Portugal in 1441.[6]
Three years later, at Lagos (Portugal), there was a company
of slavers. In the matter of slavery, Portugal is like the woman
taken in adultery: unquestionably guilty; but can any other
people in Europe – or for that matter in Africa, India or
America – throw the first stone at her? It would be something
if it could be proved that the Portuguese treated their slaves
better – or worse – than any other people; but proof is impossible. All great civilisations, not excluding Greece, Rome and
China, have at one time been based on slavery; it was only the
idealism of the eighteenth century and the practical humani-
tarianism of the nineteenth which eventually put a stop to it.
Yet we have seen, in the last twenty years, a recrudescence of it
in war-time Europe, while in Arabia (in 1955) there were still
said to be from 750,000 to 1,000,000 persons who had been
deliberately sold into slavery. The Portuguese were only following the custom of the time and the country, while the
Church seems to have been unable to do anything to stop it.

To the port of Lagos came a fleet of caravels: ships of all nations, but principally from Venice. One-fifth of the captives
went to the Infante and were sold on his account; the rest of
the wretched *moiros* were divided up on the beach: husbands
and wives and children torn apart and separated, in much the
same way that the Nazis, 500 years later, were to treat the Jews.
The slave-trade became a most profitable business. Every year
some 700 or 800 were imported from Guinea; but there were also
musk, *malagueta* (an 'Ersatz' pepper sold in Lisbon about 1460 and
soon after in Antwerp), *unicornio*, spices, precious stones, ivory; but
all these things had to be sold to the King. The business was at
first efficiently managed and immensely profitable to the Crown.

On the second expedition to Morocco (1441), the Portuguese
were surrounded by an army of Moorish tribesmen who cut
their communications with the sea. They could only re-embark
on the promise of surrendering Ceuta, and left as a hostage the
Infante D. Fernando. Ceuta was not surrendered, and D. Fernando, the 'Constant Prince' of Calderon's play, died, or was
made a martyr, in 1443. The definite impulse to open the way
to India came in 1487 with the voyage of Bartolomeu Dias.
After the Cape of Good Hope had been passed, the chief
nautical and geographical problems of the way to India were
solved. Bartolomeu Dias was the last of the type of discoverer
created by Henry 'the Navigator': men of modest condition,
who were sailors first and last. In future the problem was not
to discover, but to organise: to see to the purchase and transport of merchandise and negotiate by diplomatic means with
oriental potentates. For this reason, the King chose as leader of
the expedition to India not a seaman but a noble capable of
acting as his ambassador: Vasco da Gama.

Gama's mission was completed by Pedro Alvares Cabral and
João da Nova. It was necessary to establish trading-posts; and
Cabral's expedition (1500) was the largest which had ever set
out. He sailed in a south-westerly direction to profit by the
trade-winds, and accidentally (so it is usually thought) struck
the coast of Brazil. That fact, however, was hushed up, for what
would now be called 'security reasons'. In neither of the accounts of the voyage is there any particular excitement at
touching Brazil; it does not seem to have been anything out of
the way, indeed it is possible that the coast of the American

continent was already known to the Portuguese, not only before
Cabral but also before Columbus. It was probably due to fear
of foreign competition that they concealed a great part of what
they were doing.[7] There is no better proof (Cortesão observes)
of the methodical secrecy with which Portugal surrounded her
nautical knowledge, in the last quarter of the fifteenth century,
than the ignorance of Columbus of the new methods of navigation. Gifted with a great curiosity for scientific facts and considerable qualities as an observer, Columbus, though he had
sailed with Portuguese pilots during the reign of John II, re-
veals in his marginal notes how far behind the times he was in
navigation and cosmography. His errors in latitude are frequent and startling; and among the 250 notes referring to
astronomical studies in the margins of his books, there is nothing to show any knowledge of the calculation of latitude from
the altitude of the sun, though it was in this that the Portuguese
first began to show their superiority.

3

Portugal overseas is not the subject of this book. That has been
admirably treated by many writers, and notably by Professor
C. R. Boxer, who, through his knowledge of various oriental
languages as well as Portuguese, has been able to penetrate into
the documentary evidence more deeply than any previous
historian. Here only the first steps will be indicated and, later,
their effect on life in Lisbon and in Portugal itself.[8]

The fundamental fact is that the Portuguese first went to the
East as traders. They were not aiming at conquest or colonisation, or, primarily, at the propagation of the Gospel. But it was
necessary, in an Eastern country, to acquire prestige, and the
only form of prestige which counted was military. The first
great soldier who upheld it was Duarte Pacheco Pereira. Left
alone to protect the fortified Portuguese 'factory' at Cochin, he
was attacked by an Indian ruler, the Samorim of Calicut. Short
of men and supplies, and with no superiority in weapons or
armament, he yet defeated the Samorim in person, to the
amazement of all the inhabitants. He was a gifted tactician;
but he was also possessed of an indomitable, Spartan courage.
The Government in Lisbon saw that larger forces were necessary, and sent out (1505) Francisco de Almeida as first Viceroy.

He was appointed for three years, and took with him 500 men, mainly young gentlemen and courtiers who had entered into a three-years' engagement. In East Africa, Quiloa proved hostile; it was taken and confided to a friendly African chief. Mombasa also had to be taken; but the King of Melinde remained faithful, and in his great poem Camoens makes Gama tell him the whole history of Portugal.

Almeida's object was not conquest, but the freedom of the seas, with points of support on the mainland at which pepper might be loaded and ships repaired. The Arab merchants were now prevented from leaving the Red Sea and supplying the markets of Egypt, and they complained to the Sultan, whose forces, at that time a menace to Europe, were finding themselves attacked in the rear. It was they, and not the people of India, who were the enemy, and they were joined by the Venetians who had formerly picked up pepper in Cairo and Alexandria but were now being deprived of that profitable trade. Powerful Moslem squadrons were sent to India to expel the Portuguese traders; Almeida's son was surprised and killed. His father rapidly collected ships and men, sought out and engaged the 'Moros' at Diu, and destroyed the combined fleets of the Sultan, Diu and Calicut (1509), in spite of their artillery and Venetian gunners. This victory, more than any other, gave the Portuguese the prestige of invincibility.

Albuquerque, Almeida's successor, brought a new plan to meet the difficulties of administration. He had the qualities of a statesman as well as of a soldier; but his instructions were to make the overseas possessions pay, and he had therefore to create fresh sources of income. This, he found, could only be done by the conquest of new territories and the imposition of tribute upon their rulers. It was a departure from the simple trading posts of the past; but the plan might have succeeded if the Crown had given it more support from home; or if there had been any real stability in the economic life of Portugal itself. As things were, not even the profits from pepper could cover the expenses and losses inevitable with the methods employed. Albuquerque created an empire, and when he died in 1515 the plan was beginning to succeed. His capture of Ormuz in 1507, with the destruction of the Moslem fleet, and his appointment in 1508 as Governor of India, at last enabled him to realise some of his projects. He chose Goa as his capital, half way down the west coast, and took it by surprise in 1510. He began forthwith to make it a Portuguese city, but (unlike the British) encouraged marriage between his Portuguese troops and Indian women, so that the population, from that day to this, has not been Indian, but Eurasian. He would not allow the Portuguese to go into business; and this ban, whether wise or not – for it encouraged idleness, robbery and looting, inevitable among troops at that time, even in their own country – yet had the effect that they were regarded by the inhabitants as *cavaleiros* and not tradesmen, and worthy of the highest respect. The original inhabitants, meanwhile, lived on in freedom, in the practice of their own religion (the Inquisition only came later), and with their property guaranteed to them as subjects of the King of Portugal. Albuquerque died on the voyage back from a successful attack on Aden, 'out of favour with the King for his love of men, and out of favour with men for his love of the King'. His memory became a legend in Goa, and the inhabitants went to his tomb to pray; for they believed that the 'sea-lion' was still alive, though changed into a great fish which swam up and down the Indian Ocean. He only ceased to work miracles when Goa came to have a genuine holy man, St Francis Xavier, whose incorruptible remains, duly honoured in procession, have twice saved the city from capture: once, in the eighteenth century, from an army of Marathas, and again, in 1954, from the peaceful aggression of unemployed Indian '*satyagrahis*' acting for the Indian Union.

In the last days of Albuquerque the Portuguese Empire knew hours of triumph. From all sides there were applications for maritime safe-conducts – Portuguese 'navicerts' – for ships trading anywhere between Ormuz and Malacca. Oriental potentates paid tribute and sent ambassadors, the Shah of Persia came to Goa, the ruler of Calicut and the Queen of Ethiopia to Lisbon, the King of Siam to Malacca. 'The Portuguese', it has been said, 'spread over the East; sailing, trading and fighting; a life of reckless adventure, full of fantastic stories and unforeseen events in endless variety; full of picturesque and heroic energy.' The memorial of this is Mendez Pinto's *Pilgrimage*; but the long sea-voyages, with their 'ardours and endurances' – and horrors – provided another of the masterpieces of Portuguese literature; the circumstantial, eye-witness accounts of shipwrecks, afterwards collected in the *História Trágico-Marítima*.

Thomas Stevens, a Jesuit missionary and the first Englishman, apparently, to set foot in India, wrote from Goa of the gravity and pomp with which the fleets of Portugal went out. 'The setting forth from the port, I need not tell you how solemn it is, with trumpets and shooting of ordnance.' His own voyage in a Portuguese ship, he thought very good.[9] Even when the Empire was slipping away, after the disastrous Spanish occupation of Portugal (1580–1640), the Portuguese in India excited the admiration of their enemies. 'I never see men fight with greater resolution than the Portugals; therefore not to be taxed with cowardice as some have done.'[10]

Four hundred and fifty years afterwards, the Portuguese enclaves in India still have a Portuguese look and a Portuguese mentality: the Eurasian inhabitants genuinely feel themselves to be Portuguese. They have had, for some centuries of their history, a type of rule and culture which has given them an affection for the European side of their ancestry; they think like Portuguese, though they speak to one another in an Indo-European language of their own: Konkani. The Goanese are not a creation of the new Indian Union; they are the creation of Albuquerque; indeed the difference in mentality from any of the inhabitants of the India of Dr Nehru is always becoming greater, for the national characteristics of the Goanese – whether they live in Goa or Bombay – are very different from those of the Union. They have no caste-system, and their religion (which is mainly Roman Catholic, though some are Hindoos or Moslems) renders them incapable of understanding a new religiosity of peace and non-violence which yet can be used as a means of aggressive imperialism. A parallel with what was once British India should not be drawn; the Hindoos never considered themselves to be British. The Goanese on the contrary wish to be, and in any justice should be, Portuguese. Albuquerque is the peer of the great British Viceroys; but the system by which the British ruled, and the India they served, were different, and Albuquerque's has lasted longer. Professor Boxer once remarked that the Portuguese, who were the first Europeans in Asia, were likely also to be the last.

4

Much has been written on Portugal's 'destiny' or 'divine
mission to discovery'. Some would even trace it back to the days
of D. Denis. Yet it cannot be deduced from Portuguese psychology. It is in folklore and folk-memory that we might expect
to find Portuguese psychology in its most spontaneous and un-
guarded manifestations; yet this voice – 'the voice that is now
silent' [11] – seems to have been opposed to all official views of
discoveries and even to the mere adventures of the voyages.

There is, of course, a patriotic literature, exalting besides the
discoveries the propagation of the Faith and the foundation of
the Empire; and we know that from such ideas and such literature an epic was really born. The *Lusíadas* is a work full of refined University learning; it condenses, in a classical form, the
national legendary values which do not – on this occasion –
come up from the anonymity of the people like ingenuous pieces
of folklore, but are generated in a spiritual zone which is higher
in the intellectual scale. And this is curious, because the *Lusíadas*,
unlike the *Æneid*, is not the tale of one man, but of all the men
of Lusitania who took part in the epic of India.

Now the process of making a myth for an epic of voyages and
discoveries comes up against a serious obstacle. The thing that
is most alive in it, and most likely to remain in the memory, is
the bitter prose of the reverse of the medal: not Mendez Pinto
but the *História Trágico-Marítima*. The first collector of Portuguese ballads, Almeida Garrett, was surprised to find so few
on the presumably epic subject of voyages and discoveries. The
reason may be that all Portuguese are content to accept the
prodigious achievement of the discoveries as the work of the
chosen few, knowing (or hoping) that if they had been there
they would have done the same; and so it was really the work of
the whole Portuguese people. Carolina Michaelis de Vasconcellos, another great authority on Portuguese ballads, was
equally surprised when she inquired why the discovery and conquest of 'strange stands' outside Europe did not inspire, among
the people of Portugal, sentiments like those produced by the
Reconquista in Spain. There was a Portuguese ballad, once common on the coasts, but now heard no more, *O Capitão de Armada*;
but that apparently referred to the Battle of Lepanto (1571)

against the Turks, and had nothing to do with the history of
Portugal. The famous *Nau Catrineta* – the 'Ancient Mariner' of
Portuguese literature – has no definite relation to the dis-
coveries, and seems to be connected with a stormy voyage from
Brazil to Lisbon in 1565, related in the *História Trágico-
Marítima*.[12]

Perhaps the need for expansion was already there as soon as
people were wishing for more money to spend, and more things
to buy – or sell. But the development of towns and seaports was
not enough to accomplish anything, as things were. The idea
of tropics and discoveries had to be raised from a material
necessity to something higher, and the Church could do nothing
to help, except perhaps in the pilgrimage to St James of Compostela in Galicia, which was never so much of a voyage or so
popular with the Spanish or Portuguese as it was, for instance,
with pilgrims from Canterbury.

There was certainly a religious side to the discoveries; but
it was not the awe-inspiring legends of the *Mar Tenebroso*, the
sea where all was dark; the fabulous monsters, the fogs which
never lifted, the seas sown with sunken rocks, or the whirlpools
which swallowed up sailors 'quick into the pit'. Nor was it the
Catholic idea that this earth is transitory, a place of expiation
to make its inhabitants worthy of the glories beyond the grave.
The religious side came from St Francis of Assisi.[13] Before the
time of St Francis, Christians hardly knew the feeling for nature,
or the love of it; they had never looked at it with the loving eye
of a 'primitive' painter, for instance. Nature was something in
which the serpent had snatched the forbidden fruit and deprived
man of his pristine innocence. It was St Francis and his companions and followers who changed all that, St Francis who may
claim a degree of saintliness equal to that of any of the holy
men of India – the only country, we are frequently told, where
the religious sense is really at home.

Few, except Renan, Thode and Emile Mâle, have so far considered the new sensibility which Franciscan ideas brought to
the medieval spirit. The religious significance of man and
nature, the approximation between one and the other, the
ardent proselytism, avidly extended to all religions and peoples,
the passion for voyages – all these are essential spiritual factors
in the expression of medieval life. I myself once tried to trace it

in the medieval Spanish poet Gonzalo de Berceo. It is enough, here, to recall (with Dr Cortesão) that the advent of Franciscanism marks the beginning of a whole literature of geographical discovery, of an optimistic and attractive character, in which observation of nature is mixed with enthusiastic exaggerations of reality and great plans for the expansion of Christendom. It is not only that the first of these, already mentioned for its startlingly new tendencies, belongs to a Franciscan; but also that, apart from the altogether exceptional travellers (like Marco Polo), many of the great works of geographical literature and the expansion of Christendom during the last three centuries of the Middle Ages were also the work of Franciscans, however far these fellow-travellers of the Man of Assisi may have fallen behind their founder to other ways.

There was a new sensibility, an awakening of the feeling for nature which led, among other things, to a rebirth of the arts in Italy. Cortesão believes that this spiritual renovation extended to the whole of Europe, and more particularly to countries like Portugal where there was much Franciscan influence; and that this in its turn powerfully affected the genesis of the discoveries. This, at any rate, is where the religious significance of the discoveries really lies.

NOTES TO CHAPTER 8

[1] J. Cortesão, *Hist. de América*: *III*, 'Los Portugueses' (Barcelona, 1947) 504–506.

[2] A. Sérgio, *Ensaios*, IV, 233.

[3] François-L. Ganshof, in *The European Inheritance* (Oxford, 1954), III, xvi, 480.

[4] A. Sérgio, *Considerações Histórico-pedagógicas* (1915).

[5] François-L. Ganshof, t.c.

[6] A. Sérgio, *Hist. de Portugal* (Madrid-Barcelona, 1927), 83.

[7] J. Cortesão, t.c., 548.

[8] See his admirable chapter in *Portugal and Brazil* (Oxford, 1953).

[9] Edward Thompson and G. T. Garratt, *The Rise and Fulfilment of British Rule in India* (1934), 4.

[10] Sir William Foster, *Letters received by the East India Company*, 186–187; ibid.

[11] Amorim de Carvalho, *O Ethos nacional e a épica dos descubrimentos* (Diario de Lisboa, 9 August 1955).

[12] The dialogue with the old sailor recalls the Spanish ballad of *Valdovinos* and versions of the *Bela Infanta*; the celestial intervention is not unlike that in *O Mouro* and the ballads of *Santa Catarina*. There has evidently been a certain amount of contamination.

[13] J. Cortesão, t.c., 510.

Chapter 9

The Age of Camoens

I

S PICES HAD been sought from the earliest times. Even in the Dark Ages they had reached London. In the ninth century, 'men of the Emperor' from inner Germany had brought pepper which must have come through Venice and the East and across the Alps. Later there was a London guild of 'Pepperers'.[1] The pepper came by various routes, but latterly by long sea voyages in Genoese *carracks*, in Catalan vessels, or, from 1317, in ships from Venice. But the Portuguese diverted most of the traffic, and in 1503 the first cargo of spices sailed up the Thames direct from Portugal.

As we have seen already, the appearance of the Turks slowed down the oriental trade of the Venetians. Pepper, which had come from Suez in 'the ships of Mecca', was subject to heavy duty and transport charges in Arabia and Egypt, and was sold in Cairo and Alexandria at very high prices. When the cost in India was equivalent to 2 or 3 *cruzados* a bale, there were occasions when the price in Egypt went up to 80 *cruzados*. To this it was necessary to add, for the purchaser in Europe, the cost of transport to Italy, customs duty in Venice and the profits of the importer. After the voyage of Vasco da Gama pepper was offered in Lisbon for 30 *cruzados*, or less; and the prices of cinnamon and ginger went down in the same proportion.

Gama's voyage made Portugal the great intermediary between East and West, and Lisbon the entrepôt for an immense trade, which brought swarms of ships and traders from all over Europe. It became an important financial centre; in 1504 the great mercantile and banking houses of Germany obtained permission to establish branches in Lisbon: Welsers, Höchstetters, Imhofs and Fuggers, the bankers of Pope Leo X and the Emperor Charles V.[2] The Welsers were already established at Antwerp, where, since the fifteenth century, the Höchstetters had directed commercial relations with Lisbon. The great business houses of Italy were also there, and the Portuguese 'factory' was busy in Bruges.[3] For over 200 years Portuguese interests in Flanders had been important. In 1293, merchants of Lisbon resolved to found a *bolsa de comercio* to provide a financial backing for their northern trade, and there was a branch of it in Flanders. The first Portuguese 'factor' was sent by John I 100 years later; and in little over a year, fourteen Portuguese merchant ships appeared in the port of Bruges.[4] A large part of the goods in transit belonged to Portuguese gentlemen and courtiers, so that Oliveira Martins could remark that it would have been better and more decorous if they had gone on in the same way, as merchants, instead of being let loose in India to rob, as officers and gentlemen.

Discoveries on the coast of Africa enabled them to extend this Flanders–Lisbon line, and include products from overseas: malagueta-pepper from Guinea, sugar from Madeira. On a small scale, also, the Portuguese traded in the Mediterranean; the 'Nazareth', for instance, in 1445 had made four voyages to the Levant besides four to Flanders. When Vasco da Gama's ships returned to Lisbon in 1498, something like panic shook the Italian trading cities. Braudel,[5] however, considers that the voyages to India did not immediately put an end to the Mediterranean trade in pepper, though this has often been claimed. Germany did not stop receiving spices from Venice; in fact the Portuguese did not gain possession of all the streams of this precious traffic. Portuguese success certainly produced an acute crisis in Venice: falls in price and bankruptices, above all in 1504, when the King of Portugal fixed the price of pepper, and then converted the spice-trade into a royal monopoly. In 1504 the Venetian galleys on the usual runs to Alexandria and Beyrouth found no spices left. The Portuguese certainly gained possession of a considerable part of the European market; and in 1515 Venice itself imported the balance of its needs from Lisbon. Twelve years later the Venetian Senate proposed to John III that they should buy up at a fixed price all the pepper reaching Lisbon, separating first the part needed for consumption in Portugal; the proposal was not accepted. Eventually there was a return to higher prices (1530), and this began to damage Lisbon's prosperous trade. Rumours were put about that Portuguese pepper was of an inferior quality, or, because of the long sea-voyage, had lost some of its flavour; and the Arab intermediaries of the Venetians were able to recover some of the trade by paying more at the ports of embarkation – Goa, Cochin and elsewhere – for products of a better quality. Perhaps Portugal had gone too far in trying to keep the purchase price low; at any rate, the old spice-route recovered to a large extent, and from the mid-century the Mediterranean regained a good share in the traffic.

Spices and pepper had to be paid for in precious metals. The Portuguese had gold from Guinea; but the East preferred silver, and it was in that metal that the West made its purchases. Guinea gold was a means of exchange to obtain silver, provided particularly by Antwerp from the mines of Germany. Trade in the Indian Ocean, Braudel points out, was for the Portuguese only a new way of investing capital, which consisted of that African gold which they had been acquiring for the last half-century. As soon as the first Portuguese spice-ships reached Antwerp, the *Casa da Guinea* there was transferred to Lisbon and became the *Casa da India*: the India House.

2

It is impossible to estimate the vast sums of money which poured into Lisbon between 1497 and 1521. Spices alone produced a fabulous sum. Damião de Goes says that he often saw, at the India House, merchants coming with sacks full of gold and silver to pay what they owed, 'and this money the officials told them, they should bring back another day, because there was no time to count it'.[6] But were the Portuguese well-off with so much money? They were miserable. On the Antwerp market a thing more important than pepper was English cloth; and this shows the Achilles heel of Portuguese prosperity. They did not produce anything at home, in agriculture or manufacture; and in the midst of what seemed a perpetual carnival the nation was begging its bread. The King sent to Flanders for ships of corn. After the famine of 1503–1504 came the plague of 1505. The immense wealth of Lisbon was useless. In 1521 the pressure of hunger was so great that poor people, wandering in bands through Lisbon, fell dead and remained unburied. Corn continued to be bought abroad: Portugal began importing wheat and barley from France and North Africa as well as from

Flanders. By 1543 so much was owing in the latter country that the rate of interest went up to 50 per cent. Portugal had had a rake's progress, and was now in the clutch of the money-lenders.

Such a state of affairs was disguised by a permanent masquerade. By day there were triumphal processions, with musicians and singers from all parts of the globe; processions in which shone the rubies of Pegú, the diamonds of Naringa, the sapphires of Ceylon and the emeralds of Babylonia; rich stuffs from Bengal, velvets, lace and rings. By night there were diversions on the Tagus, parties at the Palace, masques and mimes which were the wonder of the world. In 1608 an observer wrote:[7] 'The price of the brilliant discoveries, the bravery and endurance, was that as we went forward in the discovery of the world, the cultivation of Portugal grew worse and the rural population diminished. India was a dazzling hallucination. 'If we consider what is to be seen in this city (of Lisbon) from the East Indies: spices, amber, pearls, precious stones and other things of great esteem, and gold from the mines [the Brazil gold-fields had not yet been discovered] it will be seen to exceed greatly what could have been imported by the fleet of Solomon. Yet all this wealth from the conquests in India, which brought to Lisbon parrots in golden cages, gave us no fields in which to sow or to pasture cattle, or labourers to cultivate fields. On the contrary it took away those who might have served us in this.'

There were many wild tracts of land which once were cultivated; but now they had reverted to copse. 'I do not put much faith in Indian things. Let men occupy themselves with the things that they have at home. . . . For a state cannot be great and prosperous without an abundance in itself, and all the things that are necessary.' The writer was not preaching without book. The discoveries brought ever-fresh discoveries, which dispensed the people from having to cultivate the soil or work at trades or skilled employment.

One hundred and seventy years later, another writer came to the same conclusion. He was examining 'the true reasons why luxury has been harmful to the Portuguese':

'The era of luxury among us should be put in the reign of D. Sebastian. Preachers, even, pointed it out to him. But the love

of leisure had come to many from the remote past, and therefore the remedy was the more difficult.'[8]

Under the Spanish government (1580–1640) the old orders
to till abandoned properties remained ineffective, and the disorder continued long after the Spaniards had gone. Meanwhile,
in Lisbon, people died of starvation in the porches; barbers,
shoe-makers, skilled workmen of all kinds came from abroad.
Thousands of orphans and widows perished in idleness; and
the parvenu who went out on a mule with gold harness and
liveried servants went home to fast, instead of to dine. The
Flemish humanist, Cleynarts,[9] tells of the disorder of domestic
life, and being from the Low Countries, he particularly noticed
it; the carelessness and neglect of the ladies of the house; the
penury, discomfort and dirt of the rooms; the unbridled pros-
titution.

The situation was aggravated by persecution of the Jews. To
live exclusively on overseas trade (which might have been
possible) would have meant the encouragement of the only part
of the population which had any real aptitude for commerce.
A Spanish writer [10] saw this clearly in 1622; but Jews were always despised by the Portuguese no less than by the Spanish,
and treated as if they existed only to be assaulted and robbed.
There were pogroms in Portugal in 1449 and 1506; the uncon-
verted were expelled in 1496; and when, after a long struggle
with Rome, the Portuguese kings at last received permission to
have an Inquisition of their own, it only legalised the anarchy
and robbery of popular anti-semitic outbreaks. John III was a
faithful interpreter of the baser passions of his people, for they
hated the Jews with all their hearts and lost no opportunity of
looting their possessions. The King fought with Rome for
twenty years to extract its consent to the extension of the Inquisition to Portugal, with an insistence which the Pope himself described as satanic. He began with an attack on Damião
de Goes: the charge being his acquaintance with foreign
humanists: 'un-Portuguese activities'. Two hundred years later
the same was said of the reforms in education introduced by
Pombal, who had become *estrangeirado* (made to think like a
foreigner) by his missions to foreign courts.

Portugal's population at the end of the sixteenth century was
about a million, compared with Spain's 8 million, Italy's 12

or 13 millions, and France's 16 millions; and the scanty population grew even less in the south: Algarve, Alentejo and also in Beira. The cause was not as in the Mediterranean countries, over-populated for their resources; Braudel inclines to the belief that, in the expulsion of the Jews, religion was a pretext for forced emigration no less than a cause of persecution. So it was that the law of numbers came into play against the Moriscos in the Spain of Philip III, and the Huguenots in the France of Louis XIV.[11]

3

The master-works of Portuguese Renaissance literature came from the voyages. We have already mentioned the eye-witness accounts of shipwreck, brought together as *História Trágico-Marítima*. The soul of the nation, it has been said, was shipwrecked too, and henceforth was separated from its natural surroundings which had originally been humanist: a spirit of free inquiry and free criticism to which navigation and sea-faring had led it.[12] The sense of cohesion, gained in the struggles and campaigns of the first line of kings, was lost in the sixteenth century through imperialism and Jesuit education. Portugal was coming to an end; the *Lusíadas* was its epitaph.[13] If it had not been for the Counter-Reformation, if the seed of humanism had been allowed to germinate without the crushing weight of theocracy, the natural direction of Portuguese thought would have been towards that experimentalism which, so far as method goes, has characterised the British. In philosophy it might have led to a school of Spinoza, who came of a family of exiled Portuguese Jews but was excluded for 'modernism' even from his own community in Amsterdam.

Portuguese humanism culminates in the speech of the 'Old Man of Restelo' in the *Lusíadas*. Camoens, describing the departure of Vasco da Gama, unexpectedly and dramatically condemns the whole idea of exploration, out of the mouth of a man of age and experience who has come to see them off – condemns the very achievement which he is about to celebrate. It is certainly an interesting problem, and several solutions have been attempted. Camoens had proposed in his epic to extol the valour of his countrymen in the great enterprise of discovery and conquest, the main theme of the poem; but he wished also

to provide a model of magnanimous wisdom, great experience
and a lofty sense of honour; and he has done this in the vener-
able figure of the Man of Restelo.

What does Camoens really think? Does he praise the great
adventure or condemn it? At a first hearing he seems to be doing both at the same time; for the two aspects of his thought do
not coincide. One must distinguish (he seems to say) between
the endowments which we reveal through our actions, and the
end at which we are aiming. Energy, courage and exact knowledge; audacity in conception and firmness in execution – these
were some of the virtues which the Portuguese showed themselves to possess, virtues worthy of an epic poem. But there exist
other aims which are higher; and these epic virtues are precious,
because they may be applied to ends of a great human value.
Above the aim of material success – seamanship, trade and
victory – there are also the aims of fraternity and goodness,
equality and friendship; of the tenacious daily effort to make
our society better, and more just.

These are some of the things of which the Man of Restelo
seems to remind the poet; and it is part of the greatness of
Camoens that he does not taken them on trust, dogmatically,
but is thinking them out for himself, which, however, makes
them more difficult to follow. The mental endowments from
which come technical and scientific superiority – in navigation,
trade, diplomacy or war – are not such as to confer on our
actions a superiority that is human and absolute. We observe
further that what is expressed in the old man's words is not fear
that the enterprise will not succeed, but moral condemnation,
not only of that particular undertaking, but of the whole
cobiço de mandar – 'the passion for ordering people about', to use
words less dignified than those of the poet – and that this is
coming from a man of the greatest moral authority.[14]

One of the things most characteristic of the intellectual revolution brought by the Portuguese voyages is the feeling that
nature has a divine power in it, a 'majesty'. Such an idea may
have been vaguely felt by the men who made the voyages;
but the way in which it is expressed by Camoens shows a tendency to see in nature a 'majesty' which is immanent and
autonomous, and perhaps playing the part of providence in
the function of creation. This conception is in harmony with

theological doctrine and is strengthened by it, not destroyed; and this juxtaposition of both ideas is characteristic of the age.

It is in the light of these considerations that we should regard a problem much debated by literary critics: the existence in the *Lusíadas* of pagan mythology side by side with the mythology of Christianity. The question goes deeper than a mere problem of literary theory. The feeling for 'the majesty of mighty nature' and its autonomous powers obliges the poet to treat nature as an independent kingdom – a circumstance which he reproduces artistically in the adoption of the Greco-Roman gods who come, in the end, to be forces of nature personified, like Venus in Lucretius. Pure nature-worship and pure Christianity, considered separately, give a false picture of the mental state produced in the Portuguese by the long voyages, which Camoens, too, had made. The Portuguese, without ceasing to accept 'the wise men of Scripture', face them with new problems derived from 'the secret power of natural forces':

> Digam agora os sabios da Escritura
> Que segrêdos são êstes da natura.

The voyages, in fact, conferred on Portuguese literature the qualities in it which are most characteristic.

Meanwhile the social effects of the discoveries inspired much of the Erasmian wit of Gil Vicente and the more laboured compositions of Sá de Miranda, who introduced into the country the classical and Renaissance manner and gave expression to a view of life which, after all, has much in common with the basic ideals of Camoens and of João de Barros, the main historian of the discoveries. Renaissance Europe had gone to school with the Italians when mysticism gave place to the observation of nature and the study of man. But Portugal soon ceased to collaborate with the rest of Europe. At first, Italians were duly invited to Portugal, and Portuguese studied in Italy. In the collegiate schools of Coimbra (where Camoens once had been a student) they spoke Latin and commented on the Greek text of Homer. In 1489 the sons of the Chancellor, João Teixeira, had for their preceptor in Italy none other than Politian;[15] there is a letter from John II of 23 October 1491 telling him about the boys. His Queen encouraged the printing press and Gil Vicente's

plays and insisted that her ladies-in-waiting should come to
see them. There were learned ladies also about the Court.
While Portugal was discovering new worlds, Portuguese stu-
dents were sent by John III, at his own expense, to Paris; Sá de
Miranda went to Italy and learnt to read Homer in the original
Greek, and some Portuguese taught in foreign universities.
Andrea de Resende and Damião de Goes were followers of
Erasmus. Francisco de Holanda (whose book on painting was
translated by Aubrey Bell) had met Michael Angelo. Pedro
Nunes (Nonnius) was professor at Salamanca.

This fine dawn was brought to nothing by the Inquisition
and the Jesuits. The University was transferred once more to
Coimbra in 1547; but as soon as the great rector, Andre de
Gouveia, died, persecution began. Diogo de Teive, João da
Costa and the Scotsman George Buchanan were arrested on
the trumpery charge of eating meat on meatless days, and
imprisoned by the Inquisition. Diogo de Teive was ordered by
the King to hand over 'the college of arts and the government
thereof in its entirety' to the Provincial of the Company of
Jesus (1555). Cut off from Europe, Portugal (it was bitterly
remarked) had nothing to lighten its intellectual darkness but
the homicidal fires of the Inquisition. Camoens died in poverty
and neglect.

4

The maritime discoveries, firmly founded on nautical and
geographical science and full of economic and civilising possibilities, are an event of capital importance in the history of
Renaissance Europe; but the architecture of the discoveries is
the opposite, both in spirit and inspiration, to that of the Renaissance in Italy. There, art was born again, largely through
the rediscovery of the ancient world; in Portugal, the Manueline Renaissance arose from the discovery of worlds which were
new. It is an art which is not Mediterranean, but Atlantic.
The style is neither Gothic nor Baroque, but rather 'the majestic
simplicity of Romanesque . . . overlaid by great exuberance of
decoration': with types of ornament mainly based on motives
which are nautical.

The essential buildings in the Manueline style are the
Jerónimos (the Hieronymite monastery) at Belém, Batalha

(the 'Battle-Abbey' built near the field of Aljubarrota), the former Templars' church at Tomar, and the Tower of Belém at the entrance to Lisbon river. The architects were Diogo Boitaca, Mateus Fernandes, and the two Arrudas, Diogo and Francisco. The most notable things in the style are the pillars, vaulted roofs and portals. The pillars are stout and rolled spirally, covered with strings of pearls, laurel leaves or over-lapping scales; or they are twisted like a ship's cable, worked over and almost 'corroded with ornament', interrupted at every moment by rings which cut them into broad bands. The windows, arches and ribs of the vaulting often have a design of plaited cord.

Boitaca's favourite decoration was the armillary sphere, sym-bolising navigation, with artichokes, maize-cobs, poppy-heads and the initials of King Manuel, entwined with roses, fleurons and foliage. The friezes of artichokes and maize-cobs at Belém are by him, and so is the whole church at Setúbal and the unforgettable 'Unperfected' Chapels, *Capelas Imperfeitas*, at Batalha.

Mateus Fernandes was clerk of works at Batalha from 1490 to 1515. He was brought up on Gothic work in the monas-tery in the traditional pointed style, and he developed a moder-ate naturalism with geometric leaf-patterns or motives from calligraphy. Each archivolt with its supports seem to develop a pattern of its own without interruptions or sudden breaks, treated with the continuity of the composer of a classical sym-phony. In this he is distinguished from the Arrudas, whose restlessness shows at every moment in the broken rhythm of their forms.

The architecture of Tomar is a reflexion of the history of the two military orders: the Order of the Templars and the Order of Christ: two chapters in the history of Portugal at two decisive moments. The Reconquest is reflected in the austere sanctuary of the twelfth century, with its solid battlements and buttresses. But the Manueline building grafted on to the ambulatory is like the Order of Christ grafted on to the Templars; it repre-sents the zenith of Portuguese expansion, and the obsession – which was to prove so fertile – with things of the sea. The Por-tuguese in the time of D. Manuel, Dr Reynaldo dos Santos says, 'feeling the stiff breeze of a new ambition and a new art, broke out of the ambulatory and expanded into the nave, as the boundaries of the nation expanded overseas'. The Round Church at Cambridge is like a miniature on something like the same plan.

The chief monument of Francisco de Arruda was the Tower of Belém. Cork-trees and their roots, collars hung with jingles, branches of coral – all these appear together on the window-frames of the principal storey. Tongues of fire, luscious sea-weeds from the water below, wave-borne fish on stylised breakers, cables and hawsers engirdling the ship and made fast in gigantic knots. 'A surrealist's nightmare, one would say, as if the nave of Tomar were not only the symbolic ship of St Peter, but had become another ship as well, sunk to the bottom of the sea, with the great crosses of the Order of Christ like banners on the walls for the spiritual defence of the harbour.' The orientalism of the Tower of Belém did not come from India but from Morocco. The architect had just come back from Safi and Azamor on the Atlantic coast; and the balconies, verandahs and little towers seem to exhale a faint, tradition of sandal-wood, like the Gothic of Venice.

The *Capelas Imperfeitas* at Batalha – 'unperfected' rather than 'unfinished' – are a symbol of the Portugal of the House of Avis, the Pantheon of the discoverers. The Tower of Belém is Portugal in the Algarve and in Morocco, 'on this side of the sea and that'; but the Jerónimos is a King's College Chapel which has been sunk to the bottom of the Indian Ocean and come back as something rich and strange, encrusted with sea-beasts and nautical gear and all the paraphernalia of a voyage of discovery – like the Virgilian epic which has so strangely become the *Lusíadas*.

5

It was not the Unperfected Chapels that were to blame, but the Tower of Belém, which failed to protect Lisbon from Morocco. In 1579 the Portuguese suffered a shattering defeat under the maniac, pathological leadership of D. Sebastian, near the walled town of Alcázar Quibir.[17]

Yet it was not done without preparation: there was the engagement of mercenaries, Castilian, German and Italian, the purchase on a large scale of arms and munitions, the moral and

material support of Gregory XIII and Philip II – and all of
these caused preoccupation and distrust in England, where
Elizabeth feared a Catholic invasion. D. Sebastian was so
chivalrous that he could easily have thrown over the English
alliance for the sake of the Church; the expedition had the
papal benediction, the bull of excommunication against Elizabeth was renewed, and command of the papal contingent was
given to the fantastic English papist, Sir Thomas Stukeley.
Secret Service reports stated that the concentration of Catholic
forces in the Tagus was intended for an invasion to save England from heresy; Africa was camouflage, for the real place
where the blow was to be delivered was the West of England.
Yet for once the Secret Service was wrong; the real objective
was Larache, west of Tangier. In view of the formidable preparations reported from Lisbon, the enlightened Moorish
governor thought an unjust peace preferable to a just war, and
proposed to cede to the Portuguese any town on the coast that
they wished, with 10 miles round for cultivation. But this advantageous offer was frivolously rejected. The main Portuguese
object was religious; what D. Sebastian wanted was to fight
infidels and kill Moors.

We need not follow the fate of the expedition any further:
the incredibly, and ridiculously, sumptuous force of 30,000 men
(only about half of whom were combatant troops), was over-
whelmed in the heat of a Moroccan August by a Moslem force
of some 60,000, of whom 25,000 were mounted. The whole
expedition was routed, captured or annihilated, with all its
arms, baggage and camp-followers. D. Sebastian was lost and
never seen again. The details of the disaster were, as far as
possible, hushed up. The tragic and unnecessary adventure
brought Portugal the crisis of its history; and two years afterwards, Philip II put an end to its independence.

Portugal was not equal to the test of Alcázar Quibir. The
empire was mainly supported by exchange of goods, the most
important being the sending out of gold and silver from the
Atlantic, which returned in the form of spices and pepper. But
the African trade had also played a considerable part, and now
the economic machinery was broken. Besides, a large part of
the nobility remained in Moorish hands. To pay their ransoms,
so enormous that they could not be paid in cash, the country

was deprived of all its ready money and had to send jewels and precious stones to Morocco and Algeria. The distress of the little kingdom can hardly be measured.[18]

It is inaccurate to speak of the 'conquest' of Portugal by Spain. It was not incorporated with the Crown of Castille, but preserved its administration, councils and justice, like Aragon, and remained itself, in spite of personal union under Philip II. India accepted him and gave him the second of the great empires of the century, both based on the sea: the 'universal monarchy' with its centre at Lisbon, where he spent the years 1580–83. It was an admirable point from which to govern the Hispanic world. From his palace windows he could see the incessant coming and going of ships which he describes in his charming letters to his daughters, 'a daily lesson on the economic realities which supported his empire'. It was a far better observation-post than the Escurial.

In Portugal itself, the defeat and death of D. Sebastian gave rise to a very curious and interesting phenomenon which has not had enough justice done to it by foreign historians. This was *Sebastianismo*: the belief that D. Sebastian was not dead but would come again, like Jesus Christ or King Arthur. Oliveira Martins considered it 'a characteristic and natural product of the Celtic race'. But Sérgio,[19] long before the Nazis, rightly insisted that we must avoid all dealings with 'the dishonest mystique of races', a study which, we see now, will only make sense if checked with the biological and genetic evidence of blood-groups. *Sebastianismo*, far from being the effect of a racial Portuguese spirit, was merely an idea which came with the economic decadence. In part, it was Hebrew messianism, preached in the doggerel verses of Bandarra, a mad cobbler and fraudulent prophet full of Old Testament sayings. Those chiefly responsible for spreading it were 'New Christians' (converted Jews); but it had begun long before D. Sebastian, and only received popular support when the disappearance of the King and loss of independence made it seem to have some truth. To the Biblical prophecies were added the Spanish idea – imported from Castille about 1520 – of the *Encoberto*, the hidden or secret one who would one day be revealed. It was a Spanish Jew who, filled with the illusion of his mission, led the rebels for two years at Valencia in 1532; and Isaac Abrabanel (the father of León

Hebreo) had prophesied the coming of the Messiah in 1503 (one actually appeared in 1502 in Istria), and David Rubeni was 'revealed' in Portugal in 1526.

After Alcázar Quibir, the idea was applied to D. Sebastian. Was he alive? Why not? Thus the messianic doctrine of the *Encoberto* acquired a still greater capacity of absorption. The throne without an heir; the stranger at the gate; a king who had disappeared but might come again at any moment. The moral climate of Portugal became identical with that of the Jews; and the popular Biblical *bandarrista* messianism contributed greatly to the credit of *Sebastianismo* – so long, that is, as its hopes held an element of possibility. After these faded – for D. Sebastian would now be too old, or dead – *bandarrismo* was deliberately cultivated with a political intention, and it was used in this way by the monks in the campaign to restore the monarchy in the person of the unwilling Braganza. Even the Jesuits instructed people in the cobbler's prophecies, and showed them that they predicted the Restoration.

In general it may be said that Portuguese messianism (of which *Sebastianismo* was only one phase) originated not from the psychology of the 'race', but from social conditions like those of the Jews. Belief in a Messiah, a long-desired Redeemer, is common to many peoples; but the national situation of the Jews and of the Portuguese intensified a common state of mind which did not satisfy patriotic feelings. The ancient dream lived on and imposed itself on the imagination, in a comparison of the ephemeral greatness of the past with the lugubrious decadence of their own time. Indeed, it is only for the last thirty years or so, in a healthy economic and scientific reaction against the 'fumes of romanticism' that Portuguese people are no longer *Sebastianistas*.

The economic historian Lúcio de Azevedo made the point that it all began before D. Sebastian, and recalled the legends of King Arthur, which (curiously) seem to come up in Britain about every 200 years. In Portugal it is clear that messianism spread, by contagion, from the New Christians; while the Jesuits encouraged it for political purposes and even Pombal admitted that the Restoration was largely their work. Soon afterwards, the daughter of a guitar-player, living in the Chiado, declared that she had actually been to the *Ilha Enco-*

berta, the Hidden Isle; had spoken to D. Sebastian and seen King Arthur. Unfortunately, she added Enoch, Elijah and St John the Divine; and her reference to persons from the Old and New Testaments, still living on a misty island in the Atlantic in 1666, brought in the Inquisition which had her scourged at an *auto da fé*. Even after 1808 and the Napoleonic War there were messianic hopes which soon fell into ridicule. In 1813 a madman dressed as a Moor appeared in the streets of Lisbon, saying that he was the envoy of D. Sebastian. He was not scourged; but prints were made of him, and statuettes. He was the last *Sebastianista*.

NOTES TO CHAPTER 9

[1] Sir John Clapham, *A Concise Economic History of Britain* (Cambridge, 1949); 60, 170.

[2] R. Carande, *Carlos V y sus banqueros* (Madrid, 1943).

[3] The Portuguese factory in Bruges was at first in the Rue Kipdorp, in a house belonging to Gil de Schermere. A Braamcamp Freire, *Arq. Hist. Port.* (1908), VI.

[4] By 1387 the Portuguese merchants had their house in Bruges, first in the Rue de Saint-Jean at the corner of the Rue des Anglais down to 1445, when they built their own factory behind the Grande Place. The first Portuguese factor in Flanders was Pedro Eanes, a dependent of John I. A. Sérgio, *Considerações Histórico-pedagógicas* (1915). J. da Silva Figueiredo, *Os Peninsulares nas 'Guildas' de Flandres*: Bruges e Antuérpia (1941).

[5] F. Braudel, *La Méditerranée . . .* (1949), I, iii, i; pp. 421 ff.

[6] A. Sérgio, t.c.

[7] Luis Mendez de Vasconcellos, *Diálogos do sitio de Lisboa* (1608), ap. A. Sérgio, *Antologia de Economistas portugueses* (1924).

[8] *Memorias Económicas da Acad. Real das Ciencias de Lisboa* (1779).

[9] M. Gonçalves Cerejeira, *Clenardo e a Sociedade Portuguesa do seu tempo* 3rd ed. (Coimbra, 1949).

[10] Gomez Solis, *Discurso sobre los Comercios de las Indias* (1622).

[11] F. Braudel, t.c., 348, 351, 358.

[12] A. Sérgio, *Hist. de Portugal* (Madrid–Barcelona, 1927), 112.

[13] Oliveira Martins, *Hist. de Portugal*.

[14] *Os Lusíadas*: os seus mais belos trechos, ed. A. Sérgio (Lisbon, 1940), 65–66.

[15] A. Sérgio, *O Problema da Cultura* (1914).

[16] Reynaldo dos Santos, *O Estilo manuelino* (Lisbon, 1952). The style cannot be appreciated even on the spot, without a careful study of the exquisite photographs in this book.

[17] E. W. Bovill, *The battle of Alcazar: an account of the defeat of D. Sebastian of Portugal* (1952). See also the review in the short-lived periodical *Ler* (Lisbon, August, 1953). The author has made use of new or little-known sources, English and Arabic; the Calendar of State Papers, and Castries' *Sources inédites de l'histoire de Maroc*.

[18] F. Braudel, t.c., 1023–1024.

[19] A. Sérgio, 'Interpretação do Sebastianismo': *Ensaios, I* (1917), a review of L. de Azevedo, *Evolução do Sebastianismo* (1917; 2nd ed. 1947).

Chapter 10

The Restoration, Methuen, Pombal

I

THE RESTORATION is a grim period in Portuguese history. It was a Restoration with no 'Merry Monarch'; yet even Charles II in England had a seriousness and a sense of duty which seem to have been entirely lacking in the first Braganzas. John IV (1640–1656) was mainly interested in big business; though he also formed one of the largest music libraries of his time, and we can see from the catalogue (printed in 1649) how great was the loss when it was destroyed in the Lisbon earthquake. John V (1706–1760), the brightest – or least ponderous – of his line, could prompt Voltaire to the quip that his gaieties were religious processions; when he took to building he built monasteries, and when he wanted a mistress he chose a nun. His life was 'a tedious mixture of devotion and sensuality'. By the time of José I, however, (1750–1777) and Maria I (who ceased to reign in 1792) Portugal – we see it in the time of Beckford – was endowed with 'a peculiar quality of crazy beauty'.[1] Its gardens are still a joy.

With Alcázar-Quibir (1578) and the Spanish occupation (1580–1640) something had gone. It was not so much under Philip II as under his successors, Philip III and Philip IV, and their great minister Olivares, that Portugal was exploited for a bankrupt Spain. The Empire, now that it was under the Spanish Crown, had become the legitimate prey of the English and Dutch whenever they were at war with Spain; and what the English and Dutch did not destroy was ruined by the Inquisition. In 1640, when revolts against Spain broke out simultaneously – the simultaneity was not well synchronised – in Catalonia on the east and Portugal on the west, the Catalans felt the full force of the repression, owing to their nearness to France and the fear of French intervention. The independence of Portugal was only assured after years of desultory warfare in which neither side showed any great enthusiasm, and the sufferers, as usual, were the people in the country. The Braganza king did not show much enthusiasm, either. He was the richest man in Portugal, in any case; and the duties of kingship seemed merely a burden. His subjects were 'without hope, without help, without thanks':

> Every night and every morn
> Some to misery are born.

What taxes there were, and who collected them, what justice there was, and who did it, – these are difficult to determine and are usually passed over in silence. Most officials were infected by the disease which is paralysing modern England to-day: 'I couldn't care less'; while most traders had that other modern English disease: 'You can take it or leave it'. If the English diplomats and merchants succeeded in the seventeenth century, it was not so much because they treated Portugal like an English dependency, but because they did indeed care, and saw that English goods were taken and not left.

There was also something of 'the tarnish of achievement' in the 200 years of Portuguese history between the competent Master of Avis, who personified popular aspiration, and the pathetic or pathological lunacy of D. Sebastian, who was an absolute monarch. The achievement had been dazzling, and was due to the extraordinary energy of a nation of barely a million inhabitants and their leaders, resolved to do something and to be something, in spite of all historical probability and outward circumstances. In their greatest enterprises and incredible undertakings we find the fundamental conditions of the Peninsular family in its three distinct branches, Portuguese, Castilian and Catalan; for the Portuguese were hemmed in between the Old World and the Atlantic, and involved in the struggles of various medieval kingdoms and the disadvantages of the narrowest territory and the smallest population, always threatened in their right to their own independent existence. This gave a tone and quality to all their actions. From the very obstacles they seemed to derive a motive for making gigantic efforts, and their history deserves the admiration of all nations, especially those with whom it passes for a mere romantic legend. Like the Castilians and the Catalans, both of whom in a characteristic Peninsular manner had gone overseas, the one to

America and the other to the far end of the Mediterranean, the Portuguese were not mere adventurers. They were resolute men, conscious that destiny held something in store for them, and they thought out the problems of expansion before they attacked them.

But the Portuguese had shown their Peninsular parentage in another way: by the prominence of theocratic ideas. Catholic intransigence achieved the expulsion of the Jews and a total imperviousness to the criticism of the Reformation. Even in Spain things did not go so far as in Portugal, where popes dismissed kings and a cardinal occupied the throne; where clerics were the agents of princes, and Jesuits, without dissimulation or disguise, held the reins of government. Portugal seems exaggerated, compared with Castille; exaggerated in the violence which, in defiance of all sense and reason (at Alcázar), was put into a heroic effort; by their being cut off from the rest of civilised Europe, and from their having had to do without certain compensations which, in the history of Castille, have come from Catalan industry.

In the end, the Church had come to dominate every walk of life, annihilating all tendencies to original thinking. It insisted on political rights; and this theocratic absorption eventually included the absolute monarchy which had once upheld the common-law and resisted papal pretensions and clerical privilege.

The Restoration of 1640 brought the Braganzas to the throne and eventually led to the independence of Portugal; it seemed at first that the nobility had risen to the occasion and that the Côrtes had recovered its past importance. But the movement was only secondary to the new dynasty. The Duke of Braganza, made king by the nobles as John IV, was rich and pretentious but unworthy of the honour. Before accepting the crown he hesitated, if for no other reason than that his life might be endangered by the adventure. Then there was the fear of losing his immense wealth, accumulated over three centuries by capitalising the rents of the vast inheritance of the Constable Nun' Alvares. From the time of D. Sebastian the family had had the right to import 300 bales of pepper duty free,[2] which in itself was a small fortune, and this had been continued by Philip II and renewed from year to year right down to the Restoration. Once on the throne, no sacrifice – on the part of others – seemed too great to keep him there. He was not ashamed to enter into agreements to forgo part of the un-expected windfall, so as to enjoy the rest in peace and personal security, which he valued above everything. Twice he proposed to do a business deal with the throne itself, though stipulating that he should keep the title of king and, no doubt, some of the economic advantages of the 'royal fifth'. The first offer was to France: he was to be given an Orléans princess for his son, and a French prince to govern during his lifetime, the power re-verting on his death to the legitimate heir. The Braganza would retire to the Azores, which belonged to him, and would keep the vast domains of Maranhão and Grão Para in Brazil, which were his property and in which he shrewdly suspected there might be mineral wealth. When this came to nothing, he offered to sell the crown of Portugal back to Spain, marrying his son to the daughter of Philip IV, of whom no male heir was ex-pected; in this way the two crowns would be united once more. According to the diplomatic instructions issued to Padre Vieira, the great preacher and prose-writer who was negotiating the matter in Rome: 'The re-union of Portugal and Castille . . . would be achieved in this way, not only gently but with the greatest satisfaction to all, the war ending and all the conse-quences which it brought.' This cynical offer was refused, and so was the offer to France by the Prior of Crato, that he should cede Brazil if he might keep Portugal.[3] John IV had to continue on the throne and the Côrtes were dissolved in 1674, merely on claiming the right to inspect the public finances. The nobility, sure now of the royal protection, were satisfied to be left in the enjoyment of their properties; they built charming houses and planted wonderful gardens where immense pictures in blue and white *azulejos* shine out in a riot of flowers with a deep green foundation of foliage.

The expeditions overseas had contributed greatly to the depopulation and neglect of the countryside. Then, with the loss of empire and of independence, there came a general slackening of moral fibre, increased by the tyranny with which Spain had ruled the Lusitanian kingdom under Olivares. The whole economy of the colonial regime had, by this time, come to be inspired by a spirit of exploitation; and this not only put

F

an end to such agriculture as there was, but brought to the southern provinces the virus of African slavery with all its corrupting influences. The cumulative effects were disastrous, and by the middle of the eighteenth century it seemed – quite wrongly, as it turned out – that it would be impossible ever to rise again. The chief influences acting against these tendencies were both foreign, and each the extreme opposite of the other: the outward decency of English commercial life, and the inward cocksureness of Roman Catholic morals. In the Portuguese calendar more than a third of the year was taken up with festivals of the Church, which were like general strikes. Instead of bread and circuses there were free soup and convents. The Inquisition kept the fires burning, and prevented or frightened away anything like original thought; while the confiscated possessions of condemned heretics went to increase untaxed property and uncultivated land. Clerical celibacy, in a land where most of the young men were absent or idling on military service, led to no decline in the population but to a debasement of its quality; and the grossest sensual pleasures seemed to be imposed on Portuguese life as the chief aim of existence.

Moriscos and Jews, who had once maintained the high level of Peninsular craftsmanship and industry and had sought asylum in Portugal after their expulsion from Spain, were, through short-sighted clerical policy, persecuted and deported to Brazil or tortured in Lisbon. The infliction or spectacle of torture is, we know now, a form of sexual depravity, and it was one in which churchmen seem to have taken a special delight. Things are very different now: the present Cardinal-Patriarch, in his scholarly studies in Portuguese humanism, has ventured to question the value of the Inquisition itself. He maintains that, since the Jews were also Portuguese and resident in Portugal, their incomes and a great deal of their capital were in Portugal too; but after their expulsion, the profits from their trade and commercial activities largely went abroad, particularly to England. 'The Jews were, after all, Portuguese, while the English were not.'[4]

2

Soon after the Portuguese Restoration two commercial treaties were signed with England: 1642 and 1654. The treaty of 1654 was the more important, and it was to this that English merchants always appealed later in their controversies with Pombal.[5] Protestant worship was to be permitted in private houses in Lisbon and on board English ships in the Tagus. Sailors who deserted, and became Catholic to avoid the consequences, were to be handed over. English residents were to be allowed their own burial-ground. They and their servants could carry arms (unless their servants were Spanish) 'before as well as after the evening bell'. The English were given extraordinary legal privileges. Their interests were safeguarded by a special judge, the Conservador, to deal with all cases in which English nationals were involved. They were admitted to trade with Brazil; and by a secret clause, customs duties on English goods were never to exceed 23 per cent. The English community had a 'Factory' (chamber of commerce) with its own bye-laws, burial-ground, hospital and chapel; the Factory levied a small duty on all cargoes imported from England, which went to a fund for distressed seamen.

The treaty of 1654 was to some extent a reprisal. John IV had tolerated and encouraged the piratical career of Prince Rupert at Lisbon, where he seized Commonwealth shipping; his conduct even led Cromwell to a declaration of war. John hesitated for two years over the religious clauses, particularly the freedom of domestic worship. He wished to refer the matter to the Pope; but he had little understanding of the Puritan mentality or the personality of Cromwell, if he imagined that, in any circumstances whatever, they would allow the Pope to be brought into it. Mr Maynard, the Consul, was instructed to sign for England; but, as the delay continued, the Under-Secretary of State was sent out to support him. Portuguese authorities consider that Maynard, a rigid Puritan, drove a hard bargain. In fact, he was the more skilful negotiator. We should remember that, to an extreme Catholic country (like Portugal in the seventeenth century), the Cromwellians seemed as dubious as Communists to many people to-day; diplomatic relations were stiff and formal, and negotiations for a treaty only tolerated in matters of extreme urgency. Mr Maynard, in his black clothes, Puritan collar and steeple hat, must have seemed the representative of Anti-christ himself. His chief opponent was a Jesuit, arrayed no doubt in the sumptuous habiliments of a dignitary of the Church. Mr Maynard won.

In 1661, for the marriage of John IV's daughter Catharine of Braganza to Charles II, all that had been exacted by the hard bargaining of the Puritans was confirmed in a new treaty. The dowry included Tangier (which eventually had to be evacuated, under the supervision of Mr Pepys), and Bombay, 'to defend it against the Dutch'. The Portuguese Viceroy refused to believe that the city had been bargained away, and remained at his post for four years longer; but the concessions were partly in return for the renewed English promise to defend Portugal with all forces, on sea or land.

The first Methuen came to Portugal in 1691 as Minister, and was succeeded in 1697 by his son. He had tact and charm, and was known to the Portuguese – and even referred to in official documents – as 'Dom João Methuen'. He was sent out again in 1702, as envoy extraordinary, to persuade the Portuguese Government to break with Louis XIV in the war of the Spanish Succession, and join the other side, where, owing to the ancient treaty of alliance with England, it naturally should have been.

The famous Methuen treaty (1703), in its commercial section, consisted of three articles only, a model of precise draftsmanship. Portugal undertook to admit cloth and other English woollen goods, the import of which into Portugal had for many years been prohibited; England undertook to admit Portuguese wines paying only two-thirds of the duty payable on wines from France. If at any time the difference in duties was not maintained, it was for the King of Portugal to prohibit the entry of English woollens. The chief Portuguese fear was that, by encouraging the entry of English manufactures, they would ruin those just beginning in Portugal. But since the import of Portuguese wine into England at the lower duty immediately increased, owing to the war, the treaty at first gave satisfaction in Portugal: if the wine went out, why should not the wool come in? It seemed natural that 'Dom João Methuen' should be interested in wool, for he had a brother in the wool trade, his cleverness was that he had included wool and wine in the same treaty. The average merchant considered that England was taking what Portugal produced, and giving her what she needed.

Opinion in Portugal and other countries hardened, however, when the effects of the treaty were more fully understood. The Portuguese negotiators, they thought, must have been bribed, to admit English wool. There was the Jesuit, Sebastian de Magalhães, the King's Confessor, who was now able to provide magnificent dowries for his two 'nieces'. The Marquês de Alegrete, Foreign Minister, who had been accounted a comparatively poor man, now bought himself a fine house, while his daughter had certainly received handsome presents of jewellery from Methuen. This may, of course, have been idle gossip; but Methuen was generous enough to set tongues wagging, and he had a large allowance for expenses, both in gold and jewels.[6] The Portuguese objections have been well summarised by Sir Marcus Cheke. The commerce of both countries benefited. But since exports from Portugal did not suffice to pay for English imports, the balance had to be settled in gold. This fact continued to alarm Portuguese statesmen, whose ideas were still based on the mercantile theory: that a country was rich in proportion to the amount of gold and silver which it possessed. Again the stimulus which the treaty gave to the wine-trade in Portugal caused the conversion of cornlands into vineyards and further diminished the home supply of corn, already damaged by the effects of colonial expansion, by wealth in gold and silver. The Spanish writer, Rafael Labra, in an excellent though forgotten study of Pombal,[7] took the view, held by many others, that the Methuen Treaty contributed to the decline of Portugal. By concessions and preferences the London houses became the real directors of Portuguese commerce. The centre of European navigation passed from the Tagus to the Thames, and England became Portugal's banker. Money borrowed in London at 3 to 3½ per cent yielded 10 per cent in Lisbon. The annual imports from England into Portugal exceeded the exports of Portugal by something like an average of a million sterling. The difference had to be paid for in gold from Brazil (the mines were discovered in 1694); for England did not take either sugar or tobacco – articles in which preference was given to British Colonies. This lack of equilibrium sustained the high rate of exchange at Lisbon, and favoured the consumption of port wine in England.

The famous treaty has been variously judged. Some thought

it unfavourable to England; others harmful in the extreme to
Portugal, whose nascent industries it had destroyed. 'Mer-
cator's *Letters on Portugal and its Commerce* regarded it as an act
of treason to England carried through without a vote in Parliament'; [8] the negotiator (then dead) should have been beheaded.
Tories thought it favourable, defending the Royal prerogative
and therefore the legitimacy of the treaty; Whigs disapproved,
fighting for the rights of Parliament. Later, patriots and enemies
of France, supporters of the mercantilist system, extolled
Methuen because he had placed French wines in a position of
permanent inferiority. The coffee-house view was: 'Let the
Portuguese dress in English wool while the English drink port.'
The sunny Portuguese climate was admirable for viticulture and
voyages; the cold and damp of England was more suited to
indoor manufactures. Seventy years afterwards, however, Adam
Smith expressed his disapproval. Seen in the light of facts and
rationally considered, the Methuen treaty was certainly a mis-
take. 'This treaty', he wrote, 'is undoubtedly advantageous to
Portugal and disadvantageous to Great Britain. It has been
celebrated, however, as a masterpiece of the commercial policy
of England.' [9] The Edinburgh Scots clearly preferred claret.

Later on all the blame was thrown on the English. The
official prospectus, for instance, in which Fr. João de Mansilha
presented Pombal with the project of the Portuguese Upper
Douro Vineyards Company – even company promoters in
eighteenth century Portugal were friars – describes the ruinous
state of Portuguese agriculture, the general misery and the
abandonment of good agricultural land, all due to the usury and
oppression of the English. The peasants were even compelled
to sacrifice the honour of their daughters, if they wanted to sell
their wine: 'they [the English] only bought from growers who
allowed their daughters to dance with them'.[10] This looks like
making political capital out of old-time vintage customs. By
1803, after 100 years of the treaty, the example of the Upper
Douro had led to the growing of much excellent wine in the
Dão and other districts; while Portugal exported to its colonies
and islands almost as much wool of its own as that which came
from England and a quantity of its own manufactured goods as
well. Yet industry in Portugal never really flourished, though
there was certainly more in 1803 than there had been in 1703;

and the treaty can hardly be said to have ruined industries which did not exist. The economic problem of Portugal, Azevedo considers, was not that of industries but of something more complex and deeply-rooted: inefficient administration, a colonial empire disproportionate in size to the means of populating it or defending it; and the condition of the people themselves, more inclined – in those days – to a life of adventure and money made easily than to the slow, monotonous regularity and application which industry demands.

In 1842 Palmerston and Palmela signed an agreement revoking the Methuen treaty. It had not been entirely useless to Portugal, or a dubious achievement of absolutism. It was certainly responsible for great developments in the terraced vineyards of the Upper Douro, and in its time Portuguese industries had had a period of fugitive prosperity. It cannot be held that the treaty brought them to decline.[11] In exchange for a positive advantage to Portugal – preference for Portuguese wines – the treaty restored to England the Portuguese market for cloth. The economic and political predominance of England in Portugal was not established by the Methuen treaty; it was in the earlier treaty of 1654 that the obligations were imposed and the exceptional privileges created, through the hard bargaining of Maynard and in response to the unfriendly acts of a shifty king.

3

Pombal appeared at a moment when, to some writers on Portuguese history, things appear at their worst, both in the economic sphere and in the social. Whether they were really so may be doubted, or whether they seemed so to people living at the time. Yet Pombal laid hands on every branch of Portuguese life; and if the clock was put back as soon as he fell, that was due not to mistakes or poverty of ideas, but to the general weakness of Portuguese political institutions at the time. He still excites the passions of biographers. 'Everything that Pombal did', one writer has declared, 'was due to his dislike of the Jesuits.' His economic policy and his promotion of companies shows that he was 'bewitched by capitalism'. His attack on the nobility was due to 'personal spite'. Such personal – or 'personalist' – views give the impression that the usual historical processes and the development of society were set aside by an eminently 'personalist' power, and by the reforms which his experience abroad – particularly in London and Vienna – showed to be necessary in Portugal, in order to bring the country back into Europe.

There are many studies of Pombal the man, but few of the economic, social and administrative aspects of eighteenth-century Portugal. That gives some justification to those who write from the 'personalist' point of view: while one admirer, the economic historian J. Lúcio de Azevedo, had to admit that the economic action of Pombal was almost always unhappy; the measures on which he founded such high hopes gave in the end only precarious results, and, after having introduced grave disturbances into economic life, only brought general discontent. An exception is the recent study by Jorge de Macedo [12] to which reference is made later.

The first to feel that Pombal was a force to be reckoned with were the clergy and the nobility. That, we have just observed, was not due to personal spite but to the condition into which things in Portugal had been allowed to drift. His attack showed considerable courage. The Inquisition, besides its secret police who were active in the pursuit of heresy and modern ideas, exercised a blind censorship over literature, and a single sentence of which the 'familiars' disapproved – even if they could not translate it – sufficed to ban a book imported from abroad; while the few original Portuguese thinkers of the time – Verney, Sanches Ribeiro, the Cavaleiro de Oliveira and others – found it convenient to live abroad permanently. [13]

Pombal suppressed the *autos da fe*, and required all sentences of the tribunal of the Inquisition to receive the Royal assent before they could be carried out. He deprived the inquisitors of the right to confiscate the property of accused persons; but instead of abolishing the Holy Office, he converted it into a weapon for use against those whose ideas were disagreeable to the Government, as in the case of the aged and infirm Padre Malagrida, whose condemnation Voltaire considered to be an excess of horror joined to an excess of ridicule and absurdity. He had just expelled the Jesuits: it had been done in France and even in Spain; but that was only part of his policy, and not the main object of his career, as some writers would have us believe. He also dismissed the Papal Nuncio: withdrew the *exequatur* as if he were a mere consul and declared him to be *persona non grata*. He limited religious bequests, attempted to secularise education, and placed the jurisdiction of the bishops, in all save spiritual matters, under the Crown. He also issued new, lay statutes for the University of Coimbra, and created numerous teaching posts in educational institutions at other places.

The effect of these anti-clerical measures has been over-emphasised. They were incidental to Pombal's main policy, and not an end in themselves. He was far more interested in raising the standard of the middle class (not yet numerous or important), and he gave a helping hand to artisans and agricultural labourers. Personal merit was what counted with him, not hereditary honour. He humbled the older nobility by the trial and sentences (1758) which brought to the scaffold the Duke of Aveiro, the Marquis and Marchioness of Távora, the Count of Atouguia and others. The charge, it should be remembered, was one of attempted regicide, and the evidence, from intercepted letters on the way to Brazil, clear and conclusive; but the sentences were carried out with revolting barbarity. Pombal was not against the nobility, but wished to reform it. He created a special college for the sons of noble houses, to educate them solidly and fittingly to occupy important positions. There was no administrative or civil service tradition in Portugal; the Braganzas had been quite unable to create one, and the long and important reign of John V, with gold and diamonds rolling in from Brazil and the 'royal fifth' reserved for the king, became little more than an *opereta beata*: a pious parody of Gilbert and Sullivan.

Pombal, however, achieved something almost incredible in the Portuguese society of his day. Persecution of the Jews had been second only to what had been permitted in Spain, and descendants of 'new Christians' were living unobtrusively in Beira Baixa, often occupied in the manufacture of Portuguese cloth; there were African slaves, still, in the Algarve and Alentejo. He proclaimed the freedom of all men born or resident in Portugal, whatever their race or origin, and abolished the legal and social differences which had existed between 'new' Christians and 'old.'

After Pombal fell the Inquisition renewed its former activities. Anastasio da Cunha, an artillery officer and mathematician, was condemned for reading foreign books and associating with foreigners. The great botanist Brotero, and the Arcadian poet Filinho Elisio, had to fly to France (1778) to escape from this Portuguese form of McCarthyism. In the charge against the latter, one witness declared that he read French, Italian and English: three obvious sources of subversive foreign notions. It should be added that this new idea – or return to the old idea – of 'purity' was ridiculed in the University of Coimbra. The students performed a burlesque, *O Reino da Estupidez* (The Realm of Stupidity), which showed how that personage, banished from England, France and Germany, decided to seek her fortune in 'the Spains', accompanied by Fanaticism, Superstition and Hypocrisy who danced attendance on her. Although Lisbon was not the same as it had been ten years before – the almost European Lisbon, being rebuilt by Pombal after the earthquake – Fanaticism preferred Coimbra, where the Rector called a College Meeting to decide what ought to be done about the new arrivals. The Professor of Divinity opined that 'these modern studies', so much cultivated at the time, served no good purpose. Natural History, Anatomy, Chemistry, *Foronimia* (sic), with names difficult to pronounce and more difficult to remember, were good for nothing at all. Those were the sciences which foreigners were bringing in; and men who pursued them were obvious 'security risks'. It must have been a spirited performance, and – for the time – courageous.[14]

Pombal's greatest moment was the Lisbon earthquake of 1755.[15] He was one of the few who did not lose his head. The King moved out to Belém – unlike a later king of Italy, who went at once to Messina and telegraphed for 'shiploads and shiploads of quicklime'. Among the raging fires of Lisbon, the gangs of looters and the numerous clerics as well as laymen who courageously did all they could to help, it was left to the Marquis of Alorna to give the word – sometimes attributed to Pombal, and it shows Pombal's influence: 'Bury the dead, look after the living and shut the doors!' Pombal's plan for rebuilding the city, with straight north–south streets cut through the airless medieval labyrinth, was masterly; the so-called 'Pombaline style' of architecture is charming. The houses which remain – undisfigured by illuminated sky-signs – are simple, practical and of great dignity; the big square (Praça do Comercio) facing the Tagus is a joy for ever, and it was a stroke of real imagination of the authorities about ten years ago to pick out the spaces on the houses on two sides with a pale green to match the copper of the equestrian statue in the middle. The chief architects were Carlos Mardel, Eugénio dos Santos and Reinaldo Manuel. Some have seen in the Lisbon plan the influence of Wren's plan for London, after the Great Fire of 1666; and the brick and stone houses of only four types, the wide, straight streets with pavements, drains, street-lighting, are many of them characteristic of the plan adopted by Pombal in the reconstruction of Lisbon. But he fell before the plan could be completed.

4

Pombal's period was one of abundant legislation and economic effort through state action. It is usual to attribute to the age a definite sense of planning, a completely new sense of direction. Actually, everything remained much the same: the men in the Government and the methods employed. The country went on as before. The age called 'Pombaline' was not a break, but a continuation. Pombal was a man of his time, of the State he served, of the classes on which he depended and of the historical surroundings which bred him and directed him.[16] In 1751 the Government began with excellent prospects, on the crest of a wave of real prosperity, which had lasted since the discovery of the gold mines in Brazil fifty years before and was consolidated by the development of colonial trade which took place in that period all over Europe. By 1759, however, under the pressure of events, things had changed. The monopolist policy, the earthquake, the resignations of some politicians and long sentences passed on others, the attempt on the King's life, the economic crisis, the proscription of the Jesuits and of numerous nobles, made the political climate far less favourable.

The action of Pombal on the political and economic planes was a long struggle in the changed conditions, in an age when trade could not stand a tighter control by the Government without disastrous effects on the prosperity of many individuals and many commercial undertakings. Things which had been possible at the end of the seventeenth century were difficult in an Atlantic Portuguese world in the middle of the eighteenth.

The increase of sugar plantations abroad was immediately felt
in Portugal; though here, the Methuen treaty, the gold and
diamond mines and the slave trade, all served to increase and
extend the general prosperity. But the minority which shared to
an ever greater extent in these things, struggled with Pombal to
keep its exclusive right to the enjoyment of the profits and came
out strongly against free trade.

The problems of the State were mainly problems of the
settlement of accounts, as well as the increase in authoritarian-
ism. Pombal was not afraid to prohibit the export of gold, in an
attempt to set up an economy on a mercantilist basis. He renewed his restriction on trade, tending to limit its principal
benefits to privileged groups by creating large companies with
a monopoly in certain regions. The General Wines of the Upper
Douro Company was formed because the Upper Douro was
possibly threatened by the competition, in England, of wines
from other parts of Portugal, and the development of wine-
exports to the Portuguese colonies, especially Brazil. There was
also the problem of the excessive adulteration which was taking
place. The reasons given for founding the Company were different: there was a general crisis from 1750 to 1755, and there was
even an idea of trying to remove Douro wines from English
control. The prospectus of the Company added a religious
reason: wine-growing was the origin of a great part of the prosperity of many religious houses; yet it was declining. Protection
was therefore required against foreign shippers. They naturally
protested with some vigour when they heard of the proposals.

Following on the Methuen treaty with its assured English
market for port, came the prosperity brought by activity in the
Portuguese colonies. Portuguese wine-growing had made extraordinary progress. Earlier, Dão had been largely exported;
but the Methuen treaty, made in defence of the wines of the
Douro, reduced the importance of the others, and in fact
eliminated (in Portugal) their most dangerous competitor.
Pombal's state had intervened in defence of the traditional product against new competitors, encouraged by the Methuen
treaty and by the colonial sources of consumption.

Contrary to the opinion of many economists, Dr Macedo
finds that Pombal's legislation was not by any means a planned
economy. It was, in fact, the opposite. His legislation was nearly

always emergency legislation, without other planning than the needs of the moment, and this is also true of his legislation on the industrial problems with which he was faced. His greatness lay in the fact that he could act vigorously in a crisis. Again, the plan adopted by Pombal in the reconstruction of Lisbon was not all that he had learnt in London. His eyes were open to the practical side of the English temperament, and its beneficial results, for instance the strengthening of the power of the middle classes, which was the economic instrument he used to counter the privilege of a parasitic aristocracy.

On this point, Pombal was well understood two generations later by Almeida Garrett. When Garrett came to write his play *A Sobrinha do Marquês* (The Marquis's Niece), he took care to bring out this fundamental aspect of Pombaline policy, for experience in England had taught him to see the most significant side of the great minister in London, both in the government of a country and in his own revival of a national literature. On the other hand, the two were able to introduce into their own country uses and customs which, however frivolous they may appear, yet count for something in civilisation. Garrett taught the Portuguese the use of the word *flirtar*, and prepared them in some cases to be *desapontados* (disappointed); Pombal, on his return from his London mission, showed his compatriots a new instrument of table-manners: a fork. It was he, it appears, who for the first time used a fork at table in Portugal, where up till then, even at Court, the nobility and gentry had put their hands in their plates and eaten with their fingers.[17]

NOTES TO CHAPTER 10

[1] Sir Marcus Cheke, *Dictator of Portugal: a life of the Marquis of Pombal, 1699–1782* (1938), 13.
[2] L. Lúcio de Azevedo, *Épocas de Portugal económico*, 2 ed. (1947), 385 n.
[3] Ibid., 387.
[4] M. Gonçalves Cerejeira, t.c.
[5] Cheke, t.c. 20 ff.; V. M. Shillington and A. B. W. Chapman, t.c., 191 ff.
[6] Azevedo, t.c., gives the exact amounts.
[7] Rafael M. de Labra, 'El Marqués de Pombal'. *Bol. de la Inst. Libre de Enseñanza*, XI and XII, Madrid: 1887–1888.
[8] Shillington and Chapman say that it was carried *nem. con.*
[9] *The Wealth of Nations*, Bk. IV, c. 6.
[10] Azevedo, t.c., 433.
[11] Idem., 140.
[12] Jorge de Macedo, *A situação económica no tempo de Pombal* (Porto, 1951).

[13] António Verney, who spent nearly the whole of his life away from Portugal, published (1747) his *Verdadeiro método de estudar*, analysing education in Portugal and confronting it with the learning of his time in other countries.

Ribeiro Sanches, another educationist, wrote the *Cartas sobre a educação da mocidade* (1760). He was descended from 'New Christians', and went abroad after finishing the medical course at Coimbra. He lived in London, knew the hospitals there, and also the School of Medicine at Montpellier; in 1728 he was at Leyden. Not even Pombal dared invite him back to Portugal.

The Cavaleiro de Oliveira was a Protestant.

[14] A. Sérgio, *Hist. de Portugal* (1927).

[15] Sir Thomas Kendrick, *The Lisbon Earthquake* (1956): 'There is so much to be said against Pombal, that this one thing at least should be left indisputably to his credit, namely that his bravery and common sense rescued ruined Lisbon, inspired its citizens with the courage that resolute leadership can give, and in a large measure prevented his country from suffering an appalling economic and social disaster. . . . Nevertheless, it was really the Portuguese people who saved the situation, for the best of them behaved bravely and performed their duties calmly in the dangerous days of November 1755' (pp. 45, 47). See also C. Estorninho, 'O terramoto de 1755 e a sua repercussão nas relações luso-britânicas'. *Rev. da Fac. de Letras de Lisboa* (1955), and C. R. Boxer, 'Some contemporary reactions to the Lisbon earthquake of 1755', *ibid.* (1956).

[16] Macedo, t.c., 34 ff.

[17] Estorninho, loc. cit.

Chapter 11

The Nineteenth Century and the Twentieth

I

SPAIN HAS never recovered from the Napoleonic War; Portugal has done so through her own efforts, but the recovery took more than a century to accomplish. Before the French invasion, it was said that Portugal could live on the fabulous profits of the gold and diamonds of Brazil. The French changed all that; and though it is unnecessary to tell the story of Wellington once more – the Portuguese resistance, Buçaco and the lines of Torres Vedras – we might recall one insignificant episode: Wordsworth's spirited protest against the Convention of Sintra. It was a mere gesture by a young poet, but one worth making, like the protests of the English and French poets at the so-called 'Non-Intervention' in Spain, 130 years later.

The Portuguese royal family moved to Brazil in a British man-of-war, and in the absence of the King the country was governed by General Beresford, fresh from his inglorious expedition to the River Plate. Then Brazil was declared independent, and that overthrew the whole system on which the economy of Portugal had been based. Even Pombal had been obliged to import wheat; but now there was no more gold to pay for it, and the Portuguese people, to avoid dying of hunger, turned to the dictatorship of Mousinho da Silveira.[1] The gold mines of Brazil had been lost, and it was necessary to find another sort of mine: but where? The answer was: On the land; but the fruits of the farmer's labour should be taken out of the hands of those who exploited him. As it was, the toil of a whole year, practically the entire harvest, was taken away by the agents of landowners and clerics, leaving only a miserable remnant on which it was hardly possible for the farmer to live; and it was difficult to encourage agriculture without getting rid of tithes and other exactions. Mousinho's decrees were not political, but economic. They were not intended to be confiscatory or anti-clerical; they were, he thought, the least that could be done to save the situation, and could not be postponed; indeed, civil strife and shooting were going on while they were being drafted.

It has sometimes been suggested, as a reproach against Portuguese liberalism, that it went little further than the airy declaration of 1820; but that is hardly in accordance with the facts.[2] It was inclined perhaps to be too romantic. The new ideas only gained a hold through the urgent practical reforms proposed by Mousinho da Silveira; for just then there was a chance of making liberalism something definite in the economic structure of Portugal, and of setting the peasants free from the exactions of the Church and the landlords. But there was no financial basis, as there was later for the introduction of the welfare state in Britain; the possibilities of taxation were far from being understood, and the liberal victory of 1834 began a period of restless agitation in many parts of the country. There was also the financial drain of the overseas possessions in Africa, which had practically to be reconquered and then gradually reoccupied after the Napoleonic war.

There were several currents of popular opinion, to which political speakers gave names ending in *-ismo*. The more radical, which came to the top in 1836, was christened *setembrismo* (septemberism), and passed the Constitution of 1838. This was brought down in 1842 by Costa Cabral (*cabralismo*); *setembrismo* resisted, and led to the civil war of 1846–1847, known after a stout-hearted north-country woman concerned in it, the 'Maria de Fonte'. It was ended by foreign intervention; and the 'regeneration' which followed concentrated on public works – above all, transport – owing to the untiring efforts of Fontes Pereira de Melo,[3] the first Minister of Public Works (1852). For Mousinho, the foundations of democracy lay not in political institutions or written laws or 'isms', but in economics and education – an idea (like those of Fontes de Melo) afterwards put into practice by Dr Oliveira Salazar. Before their incorporation in the State or Constitution, the conditions of democracy had to exist in the will of the workers: their corporate feeling as a guild, a municipality or a family. A democracy was not made by politics but by economics, not by speeches of politicians but by the productive capacity of labour. But how were they to get the country to work? For years it seemed to have been a commonwealth of idleness. Mousinho asked himself this question;

and it remained the chief problem for over a century: the rock
on which broke revolts, foreign loans, bankruptcies; the problem of Herculano, trying to continue the reforms of Mousinho;
the shoal round which they were always drifting.[4] But instead
of giving the lead in economics and education, even the best-
intentioned Portuguese governments sank further and further
in the quicksands of foreign loans and political strife. Cynics
said that the one aim of politics seemed to be to draw upon the
public purse, and political parties were even described as or-
ganisations which disputed among themselves for its possession.
Foreign loans had taken the place of Brazilian gold-mines:
Portugal was living on money borrowed from abroad, or from
windfalls; not from the fruits of its own industry and savings.
Shortage of labour was made up by government subsidies, paid
out of the foreign loans; and the nation's account, embarrassed
(as already mentioned) by commitments in Africa, was settled
by exporting emigrants, a form of export which, on an average,
brought in no less than 3 million sterling annually in remittances sent home from abroad.

Some emigrants, however, were unable to send home remittances. Those were the political exiles from the constitutional
struggles in the early years of the century, who had taken refuge
in England and France. Yet three of these exiles brought home
more than money, and gave a great impulse towards the introduction of European ways of thinking into the mental and social
stagnation of Portugal: Herculano, Garrett and Mousinho. Herculano and Garrett opened a breach in the wall of isolationism,
while the separation of Brazil and then Mousinho's reforms
shook the parasitic system on which Portugal had been living.
It was perhaps the greatest revolution in Portuguese history,
and was really a condemnation of the whole of it since the time
of John II, or indeed since Henry the Navigator. Herculano
showed in his prose what the historical and social sciences might
do for Portugal; Mousinho, in his decrees, what the economic
remedies were and how there was wealth waiting for them all
at home, on their own land, if only they knew how to use it.
Thanks to Gomes de Amorim, who served as a Boswell to
Garrett in England,[5] it is possible to follow him and his wanderings in exile to the Hadleys' hospitable house at Edgbaston
and the fair Isabel Hewson; and to see that, however he might

dress from top to toe in the English fashion and adopt the tastes and the civic behaviour of the North, he returned to his own country more Portuguese than ever. It was a form of patriotism which enabled the author of *Viagens na Minha Terra* (Voyages in my Own Country) to transform a prose which had seemed almost dead into one which was very much alive, and a people of spectres into a collection of human beings with consciences, eager for truth, justice and liberty. With the example of English customs and traditions, art and literature, politics and civilisation, his prose breaks the chains of monkish restraint and clerical privilege by which Portugal had been bound before the reforms of Mousinho da Silveira.

The revolt of Antero de Quental – not an armed revolt, this time – against the classically-minded Castilho and his group, was not merely literary. Antero was right: the question was whether or not they were going to cut loose from the European spirit; but the discussions, though conducted as between friends, went right down to earth. Antero de Quental was not only a good poet but a deep thinker, whose views were constructive and pointed the way to others. Eça de Queiroz, the best Portuguese novelist of that century – or of this – has recorded how inspiring he was to pupils. It was thought that Lisbon should have an opportunity of hearing him, as well as Coimbra; but the *Conferências do Casino* (as they were called) which grew out of his University lectures were suppressed by the Government. Antero had opened with the lecture on the 'Causes of the decadence of the Peninsular peoples'.[6] He condemned, in the light of economics, both the war-mind and the spirit of conquest. The modern world, he said, depended on labour and industry; the wealth of nations came from production, not from the sterilising action of war. Under industry he included agriculture. Civilised Europe had been ennobled, and had risen to great heights, through science – as indeed Portugal had, in the time of Henry the Navigator. It was through the absence of science and the presence of civil war that the Portuguese had come down in the world; been degraded, annulled. They groaned beneath the weight of historical errors;[6] their history had always been haunted by ill-luck. Antero justly extolled the intellectual achievements of that century which had been so despised and rejected. The nineteenth century in Portugal (he said) was an age of vitality and of the impulse to awaken the most noble ambitions of the human intellect. It produced a good literature: writers of poetry and prose, historians, savants, men of character, models of loyalty, initiative and unity of purpose; travellers, explorers, soldiers, orators, politicians: the century possessed them all.[7] What it did not possess in Portugal was financial stability or a real sense of administration; and Antero's task was to extend and widen the path of Portuguese evolution in the European direction which the genius of Garrett and Herculano had pointed out.

2

The real trouble, however, was finance. Portugal had been in difficulties ever since the separation from Brazil; and after the fall of Dom Miguel and the end of the civil strife caused by his presence many European governments began to demand indemnities for losses suffered by their nationals in Portugal.[8] The September Revolution inherited these problems, and Great Britain seemed to the Portuguese to confuse the issue still further by introducing the question of slavery. The whole of Europe had at one time been deeply involved in the slave-trade, while Portugal under Pombal had at least freed all the slaves actually in the country, though slaves were still employed on the plantations in Brazil, as they were in the Southern States of America and in Mozambique. Palmela had agreed with Palmerston that slavers should be treated as pirates, liable to detention and search by ships of the Royal Navy; but the September Revolution of 1836 interrupted the negotiations, and Sá da Bandeira refused to accept Palmerston's proposals. He wished for another agreement, more in harmony with that which Great Britain had recently concluded with France, and did not admit the right of the Royal Navy to stop and search any Portuguese ship on suspicion.

In 1842 Costa Cabral signed the treaty which had been refused by Sá da Bandeira; but he was still faced by the demand for indemnities, some of which – particularly those claimed by individual British subjects – seemed, in Portuguese eyes, to be as frivolous as that of the British merchant who put in a claim for the loss of his hat and a cheese which he was carrying when caught in a riot. On the Portuguese side it was pointed out that no claim had ever been made for damage done by British troops in the Peninsular War, though it was recalled how Wellington himself, in an order of the day, had asserted that the British had caused even more damage in Portugal than the French. These recriminations were undignified on both sides, and Britain, by asserting her prestige, tended to weaken the financial position of Portugal still further and make it more difficult for her to meet her obligations. She was also in trouble with the Vatican.

It was during these negotiations that the idea arose of taking over the administration of Goa, Macao and the African colonies of Portugal as security for the debt; and these places were incidentally active centres of the slave-trade. In 1846 the British Legation in Lisbon reported a Portuguese project for the sale of Goa and Damão. In 1847 Madeira was also considered, and it was thought that Goa might be offered as security for a loan.[9] Palmerston discouraged the idea of a deal over Madeira; he did not wish, he said, 'to take advantage of the temporary distress and difficulties of an ancient ally whom the British Crown was bound by treaties to protect'; but with regard to Goa, Diu and Damão the case was different. Distance, he thought, lessened their practical value to Portugal, while they could be of some value to the East India Company. There is a world of difference between Palmerston's ideas, expressed in minutes to official dispatches, and the blatant financial pressure of sixty years later in the German designs on Angola and the Azores.

As the century wore on and the European Powers turned their eyes to Africa, they became aware that the Portuguese had been there before them. Their presence was not exactly the 'effective occupation' postulated by the Congress of Berlin in 1884; they were regarded as traders or explorers rather than colonists; but the obligation on British statesmen to defend the Portuguese overseas possessions was always admitted, in spite of the pushing imperialism of Cecil Rhodes and Joseph Chamberlain. The obligation had been once denied by Canning; but otherwise it had always been accepted, and applied to the Portuguese colonies as well as to the mainland, being firmly based on clauses of the treaties of 1642 and 1661, and expressly renewed in 1873, and later.[10]

In 1877 a Portuguese expedition under Ivens and Capelo explored the territories between Angola and Mozambique, while

Serpa Pinto separated from it and crossed Africa from the Atlantic to the Indian Ocean.[11] In 1889, however, a dispute arose with Great Britain over the railway from Lourenço Marques (Delagoa Bay); the dispute was referred to arbitration and Portugal was compelled to pay nearly £1 million to the shareholders. Further financial troubles were in store.

3

Political disturbances in Brazil, ending in the proclamation of the Brazilian Republic, led to a fall in the exchange, and this had a disastrous effect on the value of the remittances from Portuguese emigrants. Devaluation in Brazil caused indeed a financial crisis all over Europe through the loss to investments in Brazilian ports, railways and roads. This meant a difficulty in obtaining fresh advances by Portugal; and the Government, in arrears owing to lack of foreign credit, had no means of paying the interest on foreign debts. The monarchy was blamed; there was a Republican outbreak at Oporto in January 1891.

The economic crisis was aggravated by the ultimatum from Great Britain (11 January 1890) which had 'demanded and exacted' the recall of another expedition from what is now Rhodesia, led by Serpa Pinto, who was said to have attacked a British-protected tribe. The grounds on which Portugal based her claim to sovereignty, right across the continent from Angola to Mozambique, were legal and historical; but there seemed to be no 'effective occupation' to deter the adventurers encouraged by Cecil Rhodes, and Lord Salisbury was confronted by an empire-building, land-grabbing public opinion in London as powerful as the legalistic, patriotic feeling in Lisbon. Portugal, as a matter of fact, could adduce solid proofs of occupation along the banks of the Zambesi and for some distance inland, while the coastal colonies of Mozambique and Sofala stretched for 500 miles along the borders of Matabeleland. She could easily have established outposts there, but hitherto had not done so, and the aims and methods of the new expedition came as a shock to her neighbours. The ultimatum dictated, in the most humiliating fashion, the precise terms to be used in the telegram recalling Serpa Pinto; British warships stood by in the neighbourhood of Mozambique, and it was even announced that the Channel Squadron had left for the coast of Portugal.

Threatened with a rupture with Great Britain, Lisbon gave way; the dictated telegram was sent and Serpa Pinto's force withdrew. But an Anglo-Portuguese Convention, signed in August 1890, was indignantly rejected by the Côrtes, and the Portuguese Government postponed further negotiation until the excitement had died down, while the English in Matabeleland firmly established their claim to possession, and Cecil Rhodes went on with the development of his 'Chartered Company'. Lisbon thought, with some reason, that the country had been betrayed, and both the British Legation and the houses of Cabinet Ministers had their windows broken. Lord Salisbury considered that 'the balance of indiscretion' hung about even between the contending claimants; the Portuguese 'men on the spot' were neither worse nor better than their comrades of other nations.[12] He had concentrated the most powerful pieces on the chess-board in an overwhelming display of force. As the South African War approached, however, the Portuguese Government saw a good move and did not hesitate to make it. Since 1885 the post of First Secretary at the Legation in London had been held by Luiz de Soveral, whose vivacious personality had won the regard of the Prince of Wales. In 1892 he was appointed Minister, and became a prominent figure in the Prince's social circle; 'the most popular man in London', it was said, and one who filled a place that no foreign resident had held in England within living memory.[13] Some of his communications with the Foreign Office are dated from the Royal yacht. He naturally kept the Prince informed and interested in Portuguese affairs, and was able to arrange a visit of King Carlos to London, with the conferment of the Garter on him at Balmoral. In 1895 he had been recalled to Lisbon and appointed Foreign Minister; but, in 1898 he was sent back to the Legation in London with the title of Marquês de Soveral to negotiate a loan on the security of the overseas possessions in Africa, including Lourenço Marques and Delagoa Bay through which the Transvaal had its only access to the sea not under British control.

The idea of making the Portuguese possessions overseas security for a loan was not new; and since the Congress of Berlin in 1884 manœuvres had been in progress for their disposal. The German plan could not have been more cynical: it was to induce the Portuguese Government to contract a loan in order that 'when its proceeds had been extravagantly wasted' there should be a claim on the Portuguese customs. German threats moved Balfour to remark that their communications with H.M. Government were not generally of a very agreeable character; but on 22 August 1898 he and Count Hatzfeldt signed two conventions. The first laid down which territories of Portuguese Africa should be assigned to the British loan and which to the German; in case of default, the custom-houses were to be handed over, neither power to endeavour to obtain concessions except in its own sphere. The second convention was secret, and only divulged later by the Germans; it provided for the contingency of 'its unfortunately not being found possible to maintain the integrity of the African possessions of Portugal south of the Equator, as well as those in Timor'.[14]

Viscount Grey of Falloden records that the convention had been signed very reluctantly, so far as Lord Salisbury was concerned, and only in deference to German insistence – 'pressure would hardly be too strong a word'.[15] Soveral, however, knew all about the secret negotiations. With his financial connexions and his friendship with the future King Edward VII, he had known of them from the beginning and had done his best to prevent the convention from being signed. It was, he told Grey, settled at the house of Mr Alfred Rothschild (where he – and the Prince of Wales – had often dined) between Mr Chamberlain and 'Eckardstein of the German Embassy'. Soveral urged Lord Salisbury not to sign it, and he was disinclined to do so. But he went abroad, and foreign affairs were handed over temporarily to Mr. Balfour. Soveral argued against the treaty with Balfour; but the views of Chamberlain prevailed, who just then could think of nothing but the Transvaal and Delagoa Bay. On Salisbury's return, Soveral reproached him about it; it had, he said, handed over to the Germans Lobito Bay and the future control of the direct western route to Rhodesia. Lord Salisbury admitted that these considerations had not been brought before him, but was convinced that the convention could not come into execution – as indeed proved to be the case.[16] Sir Francis (afterwards Lord) Bertie, writing from Paris in 1912, was of opinion that Lord Salisbury had thought his nephew too ready to conclude the negotiations; in his latter days as Secretary of

State for Foreign Affairs, he and Arthur Balfour were not always at one, and the uncle was rather jealous of the nephew in his management of the Foreign Office during the uncle's absences.[17]

The Anglo-German Convention regarding the purchase of the Portuguese colonies never came into effect; but the Anglo-Portuguese Declaration, signed in London soon after, blocked the railway to the Transvaal and renewed the 'Ancient Treaties', in particular those of 1642 and 1661, including the guarantee to defend the Portuguese colonial possessions, which was specifically re-affirmed.[18] The Declaration was Soveral's own scheme for upsetting the Anglo-German Convention by a direct arrangement with Great Britain. He was, Salisbury wrote, 'firmly convinced that all this Transvaal question has been got up by Chamberlain, at Rhodes' and the Chartered Company's instigation', and this idea was in some measure shared by the Portuguese Government.[19] It should be remembered, however, that Salisbury's recourse to an ultimatum and its extremely brusque wording led to an outcry never sufficiently understood in England, even yet; if completely forgotten here, it is by no means forgotten in Portugal. It inspired some highly abusive prose and expressive poetry (Guerra Junqueiro), to say nothing of the original words of the Portuguese National Anthem.

Once the doctrine of 'effective occupation' had been established and the ultimatum delivered, Portugal set about saving what was left of her rule in Africa. It was still considerable: the two colonies of Angola and Mozambique (though they no longer stretched from Ocean to Ocean), Guinea, the Cape Verde Islands, Príncipe and S. Tomé. It was necessary to give the lie, by immediate action, to the idea that Portugal 'did not know the way to colonise' or had not enough military strength to occupy and administer the territory of rebellious native races. The years after 1895 in Mozambique were in fact something like a revival of the heroic age of Portuguese discovery, and produced in Mousinho de Albuquerque a fine soldier and Governor-General.[20] Cecil Rhodes had had the idea of seizing Lourenço Marques, and had armed and encouraged certain native tribes to attack the Portuguese; Lourenço Marques was only saved from surprise and capture by the alertness and courage of a few Portuguese police and marines. The tribesmen had

now European arms as well as their deadly assegais. Their chief
was Gungunhana, a leader whose raids through the bush and
massacres of Portuguese settlers had become a nightmare. After
prolonged campaigns in various parts of the country, Mousinho
received information that the chief was in hiding at a place
called Chaimite. He set out with fifty white troops and reached
the great chief's kraal on 26 December 1895. He wriggled
through a narrow opening in the palisade, drew his sword and
ran to the largest hut. There were native guards armed with
rifles, but they were too astonished to fire. 'Gungunhana!
Gungunhana!' A gigantic African appeared; but Mousinho
ordered two soldiers who had followed him through the palisade
to bind the chief's hands behind his back and make him sit on
the ground, in sign of ridicule. He was brought in handcuffs to
Lourenço Marques. These actions in Mozambique were followed by others in Angola and Guinea and also in Timor; they
inspired the plain words of Mousinho's letter to the Crown
Prince: 'Your Royal Highness should remember that the few
brilliant and consoling pages which there are in the history of
contemporary Portugal were written by us soldiers in the wilds
of Africa.'

Mousinho de Albuquerque, after his return from Mozambique, committed suicide; but, to superficial observers, life in
Portugal seemed to go on with its usual 'unconscious spon-
taneity', until the shock of the assassination of King Carlos and
the Crown Prince in 1908. Regicide appears to have been un-
premeditated. The assassins had determined to put an end to
the unpopular dictator Franco (not to be confused with his
namesake in Spain); but the minister may have been warned
and failed to appear, and on the spur of the moment the
assassins changed their minds and fired on the royal carriage.
The friendly bibliophile, Manuel II, reigned for two years
(until 1910), and was then picked up by a British destroyer near
Peniche; the long-desired Republic had come at last.

4

The 'Liberal Republic' has been described – even by the
Manchester Guardian [21] – as an execrated period of Portuguese
history. Politically and economically it started with so severe a
handicap that it never had a chance. Nor had it the support of

the intellectual movement, the *Renascença Portuguesa*, though that included most of the real brains in the country, but now, after nearly fifty years, shows signs of awakening fresh interest in its ideas.

The Republic had been in power only four years when Portugal became involved in the 1914 war. Public opinion was certainly moved by idealism; but the Government could not be blind to the fact that, in the event of an allied victory, Portugal would find her position greatly strengthened in Africa, though the country was quite unprepared for war, both in a military sense and a financial one. The army, however, possessed some excellent field artillery which Kitchener needed; and Portugal was persuaded to enter the war.[22]

The fine behaviour of the Portuguese troops at Armentières and in Africa, has never had due recognition, though several officers received high British decorations; but it caused a revolution in Portugal, and solved none of the country's outstanding problems. The Republic, in spite of high hopes and much good will, had had no time to do what it meant to do; it left political enemies in key positions and was powerless to restore order or cope with the financial crisis, though Afonso Costa and Marques Guedes presented balanced budgets. There were successive *coups d'état*, monarchist insurrections well supplied with funds, and abortive popular risings leading to the ruin of all attempts to achieve sound finance. There were good and talented men among those Republicans who went into politics, but none of them were administrators; none of them knew how to run the country, and few were up-to-date economists. Further loans were impossible without inspection of the public finances by the League of Nations, and that was indignantly refused. In 1926 a military dictatorship seized power, banished the politicians, and defeated an attempt to overthrow it in the following year. As usual, finance was the difficulty, and in 1928 the soldiers at last persuaded the Professor of Economics at Coimbra to accept the Ministry of Finance. He hesitated, declined, then demanded full control over the spending departments, eventually becoming President of the Council (i.e. Prime Minister).

Dr Oliveira Salazar is a man who has rejected liberalism and parliamentary democracy, and also the party spirit as he had

known it in Portugal, though as a student he had supported the
Catholic party on social and political matters. He was a man of
vehement but practical patriotism, 'obsessed with ways and
means of regenerating his country', which (he saw) could only
be saved by the fearless study and ruthless application of the
teachings of contemporary economics. 'The truth is I am profoundly anti-parliamentary,' he declared; [23] and, he is, of course,
profoundly anti-marxist.

During the 1939 war he was for a time Foreign Minister as
well. Though the country was officially neutral, and the
Foreign and Prime Minister had to see that neutrality was
strictly observed,[24] public opinion was firmly, though not exclusively, on the side of the Allies, and became more so as time
went on. Yet to be *anglófilo* or *francófilo* in 1940 needed intellectual courage; and the individuals who had it were never
made to feel afterwards that their devotion to an apparently lost
cause had been appreciated. They felt, after the war was over,
that the official representatives of Britain were paying more attention to the impenitent fascists than to their own faithful and
tried supporters. The only really neutral people in the country
were those who had wolfram to sell. There were 'mad foreigners' who wanted this brown earth and were prepared to pay
fantastic prices for it; to the dealers it was all one whether their
customers were British or German. Gradually, however, even
the Government began to come round. Before D-day Portugal
had stopped all supplies of wolfram to Germany; and then, by
prompt action, permitted the seizure of German documents in
Portugal. She also contributed to the successful outcome of
the Battle of the Atlantic by allowing Britain, from 1943 onwards, to use the Azores as a base.[25]

Contrary to what most people imagine, not many University
professors would accept a task like that of Dr Oliveira Salazar,
giving up their life's work of teaching and research for a post in
the full glare of publicity, where they would receive little but
abuse and hostility. Few would believe that a professor could
accept so onerous a charge for purely patriotic reasons; yet that
seems to have been so in Portugal. Dr Oliveira Salazar has
never been a public figure, never been in the limelight; he might
(for all the press and public knew) still have been at Coimbra,
or his little native town on the Dão, or in the old fort where he

sometimes stayed by the sea. And yet for thirty years he has been constantly involved in administration and presiding at meetings of the Council of Ministers. For most professors this would be an extremely unattractive prospect. Lecture audiences and pupils can reasonably be expected to have some degree of intelligence, or they would not have been admitted to the University; and they must have some knowledge of or interest in the subject, or they would never have attended the lectures. A cabinet minister's colleagues need have neither of these qualifications, nor need a political audience. Further, University lectures are not reported or misrepresented in the press. Dr Oliveira Salazar has stayed in the Government, not only because he wished to use his own specialist knowledge for the good of his country, but because he showed that he could run it; he turned out to be not only a first-rate economist but a born administrator. He has been accused, with good reason, of dictatorial methods, above all in the censorship which (as even *The Times* admits) is almost 'McCarthy-like in its hysteria and absurdity' against all new writing, and can be turned on at any moment and used to suppress any views which the secret police may find unhelpful or inconvenient. It was instructive to read what appeared in the press when, in 1950, the censorship was temporarily lifted.

University professors are probably somewhat dictatorial by nature, more dictatorial on their Faculty Boards and in their laboratories than most people imagine. They do not suffer fools gladly, because they are unaccustomed to them. A University may be supposed to have skimmed the cream, in making appointments to its teaching staff; it believes that some, at least, of the students will, in due time, become the cream too, and fools (though always liable to be present) are not encouraged. Salazar showed that he could teach economics even to a military dictatorship. His methods were draconian; but they were methods which the soldiers understood – like deportation to a remote island. One group, however, has some real ground for complaint against Dr Salazar: that of the University professors like himself, whom he treated drastically, unfairly and severely, if he thought that they were not toeing the line which he had laid down for them. The result is that some of the best men, with world-wide reputations in their subjects, have been dismissed from their chairs and replaced by lesser men, while even the University Press of Coimbra was closed down. But in choosing or suggesting the names of men to serve on the Council as his colleagues in the Cabinet, he has often shown great judgement, and on the whole has been admirably served, though his associates have not always possessed his own high standards of rectitude. The system gives scope for toadying and trying at all costs to please, in the lower grades of the Government service and the 'Youth Movement'; scope also to the secret denunciations of informers, and to those whose idea of the 'New State' is by no means as lofty as those of its founder.

For Dr Oliveira Salazar was not merely a practical economist of the most modern type, and a man with a flair for administration; he had a theory of the State (*Cristianismo Social*) [26] which he proceeded to put into practice. It was a professor's theory, and in danger of falling into discredit or even ridicule, in view of what was happening in Italy. It was to be a New Order, based on a wide conception of society and of the State regarded as composed essentially of the family and the 'corporation'. That is to say, it gives political importance to the natural groupings of men and women: the family, united by bonds of relationship; the municipality, united by the fact that the inhabitants are neighbours; and the trade, occupation or employment, with bonds that are essentially economic. The New State, therefore, considers the individual not in himself but in the group to which he belongs. This is the system in broad outline; but one would hesitate to enter into the theory in detail, to deduce what the implications of the system are and how it works out in practice. Although decreed in 1938, the bill embodying its basic principles was only sent to the National Assembly in 1956, and it has generally happened that foreign observers describing it turn out a piece of mere propaganda, aimed at their own country or intended to justify a particular way of thinking, rather than the understanding of contemporary Portugal.

The President of the Republic is elected by direct suffrage for a period of seven years, and may be re-elected indefinitely; there has occasionally been an 'opposition' candidate (though there is no Opposition as we understand it); but the rival has generally been advised to withdraw before the election. The National

Assembly consists of 120 members elected by direct suffrage; the 'Corporative Chamber' is composed of 'procurators' of the economic and cultural corporations. It lies with the National Assembly to initiate legislation, though the Government (i.e. the Council of Ministers) may submit bills to the Assembly after the Corporative Chamber has given its technical advice. The government of the country is carried on by the Council: a President and 14 ministers who are chosen by the President of the Republic and to whom they are responsible. No doubt the names are suggested to the President by the Prime Minister; but in this he has often shown good judgement. Labour is grouped by trades or occupations in national *sindicatos* (unions) and *gremios* (guilds). Wages are fixed by collective bargaining between these two; differences between workers and employers are settled by Labour tribunals.

Church and State are separate. 'Liberty of cults' is, in theory, absolute; but religions, other than the Roman Catholic, may not hold services outside the edifice reserved for them, nor after sunset. In fact, most churches seem to be closed in the evening (except at Fátima), and no priest walks abroad (again except at Fátima) in ecclesiastical costume. A Portuguese priest is no more conspicuous than an English parson, and as well-washed; indeed no difference between Spain and Portugal is greater and more striking than this; the filthy priest in his greasy, sweaty cassock is not seen in Portugal. Monasteries and convents have, in theory, been closed; but they certainly exist, and the Dominican Order has been revived at Fátima with recruits from Canada.[27] It is laid down that the liberty to believe what you like, and practice what religion you choose, is absolute. No one may be deprived of his legal rights because of his beliefs, or be disqualified from any civil employment; but to be a regular church-goer and a practising Catholic seem essential for anyone in a Government office or official appointment. Nor is anyone obliged to answer a question on what religion he professes, except in filling up a census-paper. About 5 per cent of the population – 8,441,312 at the census of 1950 – registered themselves 'atheist', a percentage not far short of that of Roman Catholics in England.

Everything said so far about religion is in accordance with the official view; but that applies only to the larger towns. The real religion of Portugal, the religion of the country, is (Unamuno said) like the religion of Galicia: to be looked for beneath the regular forms of official religion. The comely fish-wives of Nazaré pray passionately, in the little tiled seventeenth-century chapel up on the Sitio, to the Virgin, who saved Fuas Roupinho from riding over the edge of the cliff; but if anything goes wrong with their men, or the fish, they will abuse the Holy Virgin roundly . . . in the language of a fishwife. Beneath the official forms there still lives and throbs a nature-worship which has much of paganism and not a little of pantheism. DEUS SIVE NATURA . . . Spinoza must have been thinking in Portuguese when he wrote that. 'The Spanish Christ', the poet Guerra Junqueiro once said to Unamuno, by way of comparing the attitude to religion in their two countries, 'was born in Tangier. He is an African Christ, and never comes down from the cross but hangs there bleeding. The Portuguese Christ plays in the fields with the country-people, has his lunch with them, and only at certain times has to be on duty and hang himself on the cross again'. 'But is there then', Unamuno asked, 'no sense of religion and of sorrow in this Portuguese pantheism?' There is, and even more than in the stern asceticism of Castille. Sorrow is the note which sounds most often in the best of their poetry: for Portuguese philosophy, such as it is, must be sought for in the poets: in the rustic lyric, erotic elegiac, and dreaming naturalism.[28] That is their true religion: it cannot be deduced from propaganda figures or census papers. 'Of course country people go to church,' a friend said to me, as he finished a first-aid dressing for a ragged urchin. 'And they will go a long distance. They like to see one another.' The truth about Portugal often escapes the logic of statistics.

Few country people can read or write. Primary education is now compulsory, though illiterates still number some 36 per cent of the population. There is still a shortage of schools, to say nothing of teachers; and in secondary schools there is bitter competition for places. The greatest attention, however, is being paid to technical high schools.

5

All this may sound, to the down-to-earth politician and trade-unionist, a typical 'professor's theory'; but the fact remains, that, in a way, it works. There is, as already stated, no open opposition; but dissent occasionally makes itself heard [29] and it is possible to meet men in good positions said to have served sentences of imprisonment for their failure to toe the line. The system has behind it an efficient administration, a thing which Portugal has not always known. The men and women in their jobs are capable and well-trained. Further, after twenty-five years, Portugal enjoys an apparent prosperity, though individuals sometimes tell a different story, comparing their wages with the rising cost of living, and workers on the land – possibly because they are believed to be immune from communism – are still miserably underpaid and generally uncared for, though they form about 60 per cent of the population.[30] In spite of everything the Portuguese labourer can only pay his way at the cost of not having enough to eat.

External events, and the economic difficulties of other countries, may have helped Portugal; but that is only because Dr Oliveira Salazar has been able to steer the country – firmly and sometimes ruthlessly – between the clashing rocks, and keep off the siren shoals on which other countries have run. He has never broken with Spain, of course, nor yet been too familiar. General Franco, before 'non-intervention' won his war for him, was allowed a 'Black Embassy' at a well-known Lisbon Hotel; and Spanish Republican refugees in Portugal were rounded up and sent back to Spain, to be drafted into forced labour camps or summarily shot.[31] Totalitarian regimes have done the same; but this, if correctly reported, is a blot on the new Portugal. The Spanish refugees were not 'reds', but reputable citizens who had in many cases been promised visas by the Mexican Embassy; and Mexico since then has had cause to know what good and loyal citizens Spanish Republican exiles can make. Apart from this, Dr Salazar has not fallen into the brutalities and absurdities of that flamboyant regime of totalitarianism over the border. Here again the contrast with conditions in Spain is most striking. If Portugal to-day is outwardly prosperous, that is largely due to the excellence of her scientists and technicians and to the sagacity and alertness of her business men; also possibly to the fact that taxation on private incomes is low, and that there is no supertax. It is a 'quiet phenomenon',[32] 'held in position by a stiff differentiation of classes',[33] in terms of bank balances; a state of law and order by decree, to which spiritually they are having to sacrifice a great deal, though economically, at least, and as a people, they are better off than would have seemed possible.[34] Coloured shirts with political significance have given place to well-washed white ones; but the official history books prescribed for use in schools still contain laudatory notices and flattering photographs of Hitler and Mussolini – or did so until lately.

'The Portuguese is intelligent,' Oliveira Martins wrote. 'What is sometimes lacking is a strong steel spring in his inmost being.' In his time there were the extenuating circumstances and the natural complications of old age: 'the brain in vassallage to the traditions of many centuries, the memories of things happening as if by the merciful dispensation of providence under an absolutist regime, the musty odour of the sacristy to pervert the sense of smell, and the vice of waiting for a miracle so that all action could be delayed'. They were demoralised by deception, bent beneath the weight of a past which had left them in a moth-infected wardrobe of historical costumes, 'because they had lost the ancient vice of thrusting forward and the simple energy of those nations which were affirming their indestructible will to exist'.[35]

That is over. The Portugal which once provided Europe with technicians and organisers, practical scientists and master mariners with a scientific turn, has been re-born with a new generation of scientists, concerned above all with agriculture (agronomics), forestry, plant-pathology and tropical medicine. In the eighteenth and nineteenth centuries the Portuguese élites were continually running on the rocks; they were adventurers and dreamers, men who acted mainly on intuition; and that was not at all like the men of the fifteenth century, the princes, pilots, captains and merchants who were not tenacious from mere instinct or sentiment, but were methodical organisers, prudent diplomats; sensible pupils who had learnt from experience and been hardened by their contact with the world, joining the study of scientific detail with exact performance. We may say of the leaders of Portuguese intellect to-day what was said by the chronicler João Afonso: that it was the clarity of their understanding which was the first efficient cause of their stupendous success.[36]

G

NOTES TO CHAPTER 11

[1] Damião Peres, in *História de Portugal* (Barcelos, 1935), VII, 625 ff. The *relatorio* introducing his reforming decrees is printed on p. 631 (note).

[2] José d'Arriaga, *História da Revolução de Setembro* (Lisbon, n.d.), I, cap. I.

[3] Damião Peres, VII, 649 ff.

[4] A. Sérgio, *Considerações* . . . (1915).

[5] Carlos Estorninho, 'Garrett e a Inglaterra', *Rev. de Fac. de Letras*; Simões, in *Diario de Noticias*, Lisbon, 20 Sept. 1956.

[6] Antero de Quental, *Prosas* (Coimbra, 1926), III, 92–140; A. Sérgio, *O problema da cultura e o isolamento dos povos peninsulares* (1924).

[7] Joaquim de Carvalho, *Estudos sobre a cultura portuguesa do século XIX* (Coimbra, 1955).

[8] José d'Arriaga, t.c., III, 561.

[9] G. P. Gooch and H. W. V. Temperly, *British Documents on the Origin of the War* (1927), VIII, 725.

[10] Idem, I, 51–52, 94 n., and App. 328–330.

[11] Marques Guedes, in *História de Portugal* (Barcelos, 1935), VII, 413. Serpa Pinto's own very readable account of his great journey was published in London (in Portuguese and English) in 1881.

[12] Gooch and Temperley, op. cit., I, 44 n. Lady Gwendolen Cecil, *Life of Robert, Marquis of Salisbury*, IV (1932), 257–273. See also Marques Guedes, 'Os últimos Tempos da Monarquia', 1890–1910, in *História de Portugal*, VII, 412 ff., and Lopes de Almeida, 'Domínio portugués na Africa: A ocupação efectiva', ibid. VII, 593 ff. The Ultimatum has given rise to a considerable literature.

[13] Sir Sidney Lee, *King Edward VII* (1927), I, 635–638, and particularly, II, 59. The Portuguese study by W. Archer de Lima, *O Marquês de Soveral e o seu tempo* (Oporto, 1923) had not the advantage of the documents afterwards published by Gooch and Temperley, which shew Soveral to have been a clever and well-informed diplomat and a faithful servant of his country. The German memories of Hermann Freiherr von Eckardstein, *Persönliche Erinnerungen an König Eduard* (Dresden, 1927) 35, 40 are characteristic: the writer seems to have regarded Serpa Pinto as a colonial myth.

[14] Gooch and Temperley, I, 329–330. See also B. E. C. Dugdale, *Arthur James Balfour* (1936), 264–272.

[15] *Twenty-five years* (1925), I, 42, 45.

[16] Gooch and Temperley, X(2), 427.

[17] Idem, X(2), 425.

[18] Temperley and Penson, *Foundations of British Foreign Policy* (Cambridge, 1938), 513.

[19] Gooch and Temperley, I, 90.

[20] Marques Guedes, loc. cit., Lopes de Almeida, loc. cit., and various publications in connexion with the centenary of Mousinho de Albuquerque, e.g., O. Rodrigues de Campos, 'Presença de Mousinho', in *Rev. Portugal em Africa*, no. 72 (1955); 'No tempo de Mousinho', in *Independencia*, XIV e XV (1955) and the articles in the same number by J. Oscar Ribeiro Pereira.

[21] 27 October 1955.

[22] *Twenty-five years* (1925), II, 226–227.

[23] *The Times*, Supplement on Portugal, 25 October 1955.

[24] Lord Templewood, *Ambassador on Special Mission* (1946), 125.

[25] Sir Ronald Campbell (formerly British Ambassador at Lisbon) in *The Times*, 17 November 1953.

[26] Based on the Papal encyclicals *Quadragesimo anno* and *Rerum novarum*.

[27] *Manchester Guardian*, 27 October 1955.

[28] M. de Unamuno, *Por tierras de Portugal y de España*.

[29] In July 1956, fifty well-known liberals, including three former premiers and one of the leaders of the revolution which brought Dr Salazar to power, signed a petition in favour of a certain mitigation of the regime. The document (which the censorship passed for publication in three of the Lisbon evening papers) requested a political amnesty, the strict observance of constitutional guarantees, in particular those relating to freedom of speech and public meeting, and the removal of the censorship, *Le Monde* (Paris), 13 July 1956.

[30] 'Even apologists of the *Estado Novo* wince at the standard of living prevailing in many parts of Portugal to-day. . . . In 1953 it was officially estimated that a farm worker earned the equivalent of about 5/-, a day, a miner rather more than 10/-, a worker in a glass-factory . . . about 15/-.' *The Times*, Supplement on Portugal, 25 October 1955.

[31] Claude Bowers, *My Mission to Spain* (1954), 308. The American Ambassador describes 'the horrible slaughter at Badajoz . . . when large numbers escaped to Portugal, they were driven back to their death', at the hands of Franco's Moors. See also *Documents on German Foreign Policy*, Series D, vol. III : 'Germany and the Spanish Civil War' (H.M. Stationery Office, 1951), 53–55, 61. The Portuguese Government, it is alleged, 'gave every assistance in the moving of matériel for Spain which arrived in Lisbon on German ships, and despite British pressure, gave the Spanish rebels full support. A munitions shipment of the (Franco) revolutionaries en route from Seville to Burgos was allowed to pass through Portuguese territory'.

[32] *The Economist*, 17 April 1954.

[33] *The Manchester Guardian*, 27 October 1955.

[34] *The Times*, 25 October 1955.

[35] Oliveira Martins, *Portugal nos mares*.

[36] A. Sérgio, *Ensaios I*, 279–305.

Chapter 12

The Language

I

T is sometimes said that Portuguese is not a beautiful language. The Portuguese themselves, with that courteous deference which they are accustomed to show – outwardly – to the opinion of foreigners, will admit that some of the sounds are hard and rough; and one of the earlier editions of the *Guide Bleu* went so far as to state that, with the exception of certain districts of Minho and Beira Litoral, 'where the accent has something of the harmony and sweetness of Italian', the sounds of Portuguese in ordinary speech are disagreeable, bare and nasal, without 'the full endings, the open vowels, the vivacious movement, the energy and sonorous éclat of Spanish'.

Since this indictment is partly based on the evidence of Italian, perhaps an Italian [1] may also be called as witness for the defence; and the first question that might be put to him would run something like this: 'You say that Portuguese is not "beautiful"; what qualities do you require for beauty in a language? What tests can be applied to it?' It is not enough to declare that a language is beautiful or ugly, pleasing or displeasing. We must distinguish between the language of poetry read aloud, and the language of every day shouted in the street. Yet spoken language is always music, and contains the possibilities of many musical sounds and the germ of all form and rhythm.

The melodic elements of a language are the vowels, either pure or enriched by the influence of neighbouring consonants, which confer on them the mysterious power of expressing sensations, images and ideas. Musical notes (in concert-music) are vowels exaggerated into a shout or a lament; they are united in longer musical phrases to form a tune; and finally, when the word is left behind, they go on existing as pure sound. But the vowels, in order to live, need rhythm as well as pitch; and the rhythm of music and of language is much the same. The

196

rhythms of poetry, speech, music and dancing, all exist in spoken language. Does each language possess its own rhythm, or are the same rhythms found in all?

Since it is the vowels which constitute the melodic substance of a language, it is evident that, the greater the number of vowel-sounds a language has, the greater the number of melodic and expressive possibilities will be available to the speaker; while the 'purer' the vowels, the simpler the melody.[2] The Spanish vowels can almost be counted on the fingers of one hand; Italian distinguishes clearly between the open and closed E and O; but that is all, leaving the possibility of few melodies, even if very beautiful, and a richness of sound giving a great range of expression.

Portuguese has 13 vowels: 2 U's, 3 O's, 3 A's, 3 E's and 2 I's, together with 5 nasal vowels; and there are at least 27 diph-thongs [2] of which 7 are nasal. The diphthongs are not merely the union of a vowel with another vowel or a semi-vowel like I or U, but also a combination of sounds from which a new sound has been created. Portuguese, then, is one of the richest of the neo-Latin languages, in variety of sounds of the most delicate shades, and any number of new effects are possible; the 3 A's, for instance, may all be heard in one name: that of the pleasant place across the Tagus opposite Lisbon, called Almada.

There are also something like 24 consonants, including four different *s*'s: as in *so* (s), *goes* (z), *she* (sh) and *pleasure* (zh). The name of the province, Tras-os-montes, has three of them (all except the first), while Camoens brought all four into the first line of his great epic 'of arms and of great men': *As* (z) *armas* (z) *e os* (zh) *baroes* (z) *as* – (s) – *sinalados* (sh).

The Portuguese did not simply inherit, like other neo-Latin peoples, the vowels of Vulgar Latin; they enriched them with diphthongs and narrowed them to effects which they specially preferred, blending them with qualities of tone strange to Vul-gar Latin. They invented new sounds altogether, with the finer shades which are entirely their own. The phonetic values of the vowels are new; they depend on a peculiar feeling for sound which has remained permanently in the ears of the Portuguese people.[3]

The dilemma, then, whether Portuguese is or is not a beauti-ful language, becomes the dilemma of the foreigner growing accustomed to it and understanding its musical qualities. What do our foreign ears make of it? And how much of it can we make our own sound-apparatus reproduce?

The languages which many Europeans speak are composed of sounds pitched far apart, at wide musical intervals, or at least as far apart as tones and semitones. Such are Italian and Spanish. Portuguese is more subtle, with 'quarter-tones', vowels sliding into one another. People who dislike (or think that they dislike) the sound of Portuguese are thinking 'diatonically' (in the usual tones and semitones) – thinking of Italian as a foreigner thinks of it when he says that he likes opera in Italian, though he can hardly understand a word of it, and still protests that he likes it, even when the singers are not Italians themselves and cannot really produce the sounds of the words for which the composer wrote.

Foreigners do not generally hear the true musical qualities of Portuguese speech at all, except in an approximate and incomplete manner, deformed by their own special phonetic and auditive constitution: by their particular way of hearing. As an Englishman deeply sensitive to music, I am ashamed to think that I can only make these sounds imperfectly; for, after all, English has far more sounds than Spanish or Italian, over forty, in fact – and English speakers, again, have many sounds which glide into one another.[4]

Words can only be understood and felt when they have pitch and rhythm. If you lose the pitch or destroy the rhythm, it is as if the words were not there at all; for if you want to be understood, and understand what others are saying, you have to acquire the rhythm and pitch of the words. Portuguese has two features, in virtue of which it acquires – in rhythm as well as in pitch and tone-quality – a music which is peculiar to it. Its distinguishing character in sound is that, along with the gliding, indistinct quality of its simple vowels, there is the clear distinction between the widely separated sounds of its nasals. The first produces a persistent cross-rhythm; the second, a continuous undulation, a tremor of sound, which goes from one phrase to another; Spinelli, our Italian witness, compares it to the effect of a light breeze passing over a wheat-field. Portuguese, he says, is not sung like Italian, declaimed like Spanish, or danced like French. Portuguese is spoken. There is a play of

light over the language, full of delicate shades and without
violent contrasts, and with an appeal of modesty and reserve,
accentuated by the special shape of the phrases.

The discovery of the Portuguese language and its unequalled
power of expression in the field of sentiment, produced two
centuries of medieval lyric spread over the entire Peninsula;
then came the lyrics of Camoens, and after that the Coimbra
revival of 100 years ago, the force of which is not yet spent.

2

Examples of foreign influence do not affect the fundamental
originality of the Portuguese language. Historically conserva-
tive, Portuguese has remained at an earlier stage than Spanish.
'The spell which that language produces on us Spaniards',
Unamuno said,[5] 'comes partly because we can believe that we
are hearing the fresh, infant stammerings of our own – not that
I mean to suggest that Portuguese has not progressed also. But,
for us, there is something youthful about it; it produces an
effect like that of our primitive poets: Berceo, the Archpriest of
Hita, Don Juan Manuel; and it has words which caress our
ears and our imagination.' Valery Larbaud and other men of
letters who were not Portuguese have noticed the 'sweetness and
grace' of some Portuguese words. *Só*, alone, '*quelle solitude, quel
abandon*'! In the diminutive *sòzinho* the suffix seems to give the
attitude of a spirit 'folded back upon itself in solitude': while
rapariga, girl, compared with its equivalents in Spanish and
Italian, *rapaza*, *muchacha*, and *ragazza*, is a gay clatter of girl-
students as they come out into the street; but a Portuguese
rapariga would make more noise than any.[6]

All those learning a new language receive subjective impressions of this kind; the sense of the unaccustomed word com-
bines with the image created by the sound to give the impression of a special meaning. Writers are particularly liable to
these illusions. They have a tendency to consider the word as
a thing in itself, freed from the fetters of the phrase to which it
belongs; and the meaning, for them, will always be affected by
their power of imagination. *Coitado*, for instance, so representative of the Portuguese and so expressive of their gentle manner,
alludes nowadays to someone who is poor and unhappy, someone for whom life is not going too well. Yet in its origin, at the

time of the troubadours, the word was applied to the lover sighing for his lady; though it is little use thinking of this to-day, when a friend sees a beggar in rags and says, as he gives him something, '*Coitado, tome lá!*' [7]

Portuguese can, at any rate, be described as the way Latin is spoken now, on the western edge of the Peninsula, and Camoens – certainly one of the world's great poets – thought it very like Latin; in the *Lusíadas* he makes Venus tell a meeting of the gods that the Portuguese are civilised people because the language they speak is, with a few corruptions, almost Latin. Camoens, besides being the greatest master of the Portuguese language who has ever lived, had a classical education and read the Latin poets in the original. Indeed, in the sixteenth century – and right down to reforms in modern spelling – it was still possible to write sentences which might be read either in Latin or Portuguese; and when, in 1947, the Duke of Palmela, the Portuguese Ambassador, received an honorary degree at Cambridge where he had been an undergraduate, the Public Orator quoted a sentence which made sense in both languages. [8]

Formerly, it was believed that the differences which distinguish Portuguese from other Romance languages were to be explained by the different languages which the inhabitants had spoken before they learnt Latin. This theory fitted in with the experience of people who have struggled to learn various languages: it is not vocabulary or grammar but the musical rhythm and sense of pitch (intonation) which are most difficult to acquire, and always (or almost always) there remain reminiscences of our mother tongue in the pronunciation of a language which we learn later. Some investigators, however, deny the relationship between ethnology and phonetics, and attribute the characteristic changes which divide the Neo-Latin languages to the action of the Germanic peoples who imposed themselves on the Romanised inhabitants. The phonetic changes, they say, are late; and, if really due to ethnic causes, would have shown themselves earlier: would have become apparent immediately in the first Latinised generation and not centuries later. The truth probably lies somewhere between the two extremes. There are certainly vestiges of the accent or intonation of the Pre-Roman peoples; but, by what-

ever means the Germanic peoples may have exerted their influence, it was precisely during their domination that the Romance languages first began to develop. The Germans gradually adopted Latin themselves, or as near as they could get to
it.⁹

The Latin spoken in the western strip of the Peninsula under
the Roman Empire, before the arrival of the Germanic invaders, was that of a remote country district. The evidence
comes from inscriptions. An inscription is a document which has
the advantage of being an autograph, protected from the altera-
tions consciously or unconsciously produced by later copyists
and belonging to a definite place and date: official formulæ,
honorific titles, stereotyped military phrases; proper names
which do not vary very much and epithets which are almost
always the same. Yet, in so remote and rustic a part of the Empire as Lusitania, inscriptions were often cut by men of little
education and faults crept in which give a curious indication of
how the stone-cutter really spoke. *Domeno*, for instance, instead
of DOMINO; *felex* for FELIX; E instead of I when another vowel
follows it, e.g. *terteo* for TERTIO, while EI used instead of I gives
a superficially Portuguese appearance to the Christian names
ALICIA and PONTIA spelt *Alleicia* and *Ponceia*. A difficult word
like MAUSOLEUM becomes *misolio*; MONUMENTUM is confused with
MUNIMENTUM, while *hic munumentus* appears instead of the usual
neuter. Final -M drops off in spelling as it had already in pronunciation; N in the middle of a word falls out, giving *mes* for
MENSES, *cosul* for CONSUL. T is changing into D: *imudavit* for
IMMUTAVIT, *adque* for ATQUE. In an inscription beginning *Dibus
M*, the gods below, DIS MANIBUS, have been confused with the
days of the week, DIEBUS, or even with the late form DEABUS, 'to
the goddesses'.

Such vagaries are not exclusively Lusitanian, but they show
the direction which spoken Latin was taking, even while the
Empire was still there. A few diminutives – it need hardly be
said how characteristic diminutives are of Portuguese and
Spanish – have only been found in Lusitania; while Latin
speakers, in Lusitania and elsewhere, often preferred a diminutive to the ordinary word: AURICULA, for instance, for 'ear'.
In Lusitania, in Roman times, this had already become *oricla*
which is half way to the modern Portuguese *orelha*.

In the Portuguese vocabulary almost all the usual words come from Latin. Words of Celtic origin also came in through Latin, and had generally reached other languages first, before they underwent the phonetic changes characteristic of Portuguese.[10] Some of these changes are, at first sight, extremely puzzling, e.g. *cheio*, full, derived – quite regularly – from the Latin PLENU(M), though after passing through many intermediate stages.[11] The most thoroughly acclimatised do not come from the polished Latin employed by the writers of Imperial Rome, but from the plebeian language of taverns and such places, spoken by soldiers, land-workers and small tradesmen. These were the elements of the Roman population which introduced their language into the Hispanic Peninsula at times of invasion and conquest. It was the language of the conquerors; but it gradually became that of the conquered, because it brought with it the prestige of a great civilisation.

Portuguese, like all other Romance languages, had a humble origin. This popular Latin was the language which eventually, through numerous transformations of various kinds, became Portuguese. It was, like every plebeian language, a means of communication which was at first clumsy, short-winded and down to earth. It had a vocabulary in many ways distinct from literary Latin: for 'mouth' it said BUCCA (cf. English 'mug'), not the classical OS, ORIS; for 'horse' CABALLUS, not EQUUS; for 'house' CASA, not DOMUS; for 'great' GRANDIS, not MAGNUS. How important this was for the future is obvious; and the choice made by the speakers of Vulgar Latin is still valid today. Speaking unpretentiously, the Portuguese still say *bôca, cavalo, casa, grande*; though for derivatives of these words they use the old Latin literary terms *oral, eqüestre, doméstico, magnitude*. The Romans, by means of their schools, had spread through the territory occupied by them a knowledge of Latin culture and its great writers, to whom these words were familiar; so that soon there took place in Portugal something which has happened in all countries: the Lusitanians began to use two languages, one for speaking and another for writing.

Then came the attacks by the Germanic tribes. The Peninsula was once more invaded and devastated. But the Germanic civilization was inferior to the Roman; their fighting men dominated by force of arms only and left the older culture intact, with certain modifications in the realm of law. The language continued as before, with the addition of a few new words connected with Germanic habits: war, noisy feasting, garlands, gloves, pride, race, robbery, and military terms like scaling a wall.

After the arrival of the Arabic-speaking Moslems, the Portuguese words show the direction which Moslem influence took: new techniques in agriculture, industry, science and art, games, trade and administration. Arabic enriched the vocabulary of practical occupations and of the earthly joys of life.

Later, other influences came, above all from France. The first leader of Portugal in the struggle for independence was a French noble, Henry of Burgundy. Men from France and Norman England came to fight in Portugal, and afterwards settled; gallicisms of speech have been there ever since and plays upon words. The first grammarian of the Portuguese language, Fernão de Oliveira, observed in 1536 that archaisms made people want to laugh; indeed, the archaic meaning of a word has often a comic effect, especially when used as a joke and even Camoens indulged in plays upon words. There is still a considerable difference between the spoken language and the written, and the pompous, formal style can be laughable in conversation and effective on the comic stage.

3

Our language, Wittgenstein said, can be seen as an ancient city, a maze of little streets and squares, of old and new houses with additions from various periods; and this, surrounded by a multitude of new boroughs with straight, regular streets and uniform houses. By selecting from what still exists, and imagining what does so no longer, we can excavate the old language and follow the development of the new, studying the present features by pointing out some of the alternative possibilities, which were not adopted.

Portuguese is said to be rich in synonyms. But Professor Rodrigues Lapa asks whether there really are such things. If we mean words which have a similar meaning, it is evident that they exist; but if we think, with the old-fashioned grammars, that synonyms are words which may be substituted for one another because they have much the same sense, we shall soon be convinced that this is impossible. One and the same idea, one act, one object, may have different names; but these names are not, cannot be, exactly equivalent.

It might be objected that there are names of plants, utensils, various products, with different names in different parts of the country. Pine-needles, *agulhas do pinheiro*, have half a dozen different names in different districts, every place and every region adopting one in preference to the others which are generally unknown there.[12] A visit to the Folk-Art Museum at Lisbon will show thirteen different types of basket, each with its proper use and place and word.[13] There are many kinds of pot, at least four different kinds of sickle and hoe, five different rakes, various sieves, seven different tools used in salt-pans, a number of threshing implements, and a small vocabulary concerned with spinning and weaving. One of the largest parts of the Portuguese dictionary comes from the sea; and that is only to be expected, considering that the country's history is mainly maritime.

The wide geographical distribution of Portuguese has further increased its vocabulary. The language has not only borrowed a number of words from Indian and Eastern languages but has contributed to their vocabularies as well.[14] Portuguese has also contributed to English. To mention only words connected with discovery and exploration, there are coolie and curry from India; banana, negro and piccaninny from Africa, and also coconut.[15] Brazilian Portuguese, again, is full of picturesque and expressive words taken over from the Tupi- and Guarani-speaking Indians.

4

It is enlightening to observe the treatment given by the language to forms which are 'divergent'. These are words which have arisen from the same Latin root, but have become differentiated in meaning, e.g. *areia*, sand, and *arena*, a sandy place used for a circus.[16] These may once have been synonyms, but are so no longer; some now belong to more cultured surroundings than the rest, while others have changed their meaning completely. *Cheio* and *pleno* still mean full, and both are derived from the same Latin word; but one is used in ordinary, current speech, while the other belongs to the literary language and would sound absurd in ordinary conversation. The maximum difference of meaning is seen in *traição* and *tradição*, treason and tradition; it is almost incredible that one Latin word should have generated two such diverse interpretations.

Like English, Portuguese has words which serve many purposes, comparable with our do, go, get. One of these is *deixar*, which can be used for to leave, to give leave, to leave off, to put off, to give way, to leave out. *Ter* (to have or to hold) means also to have a care, have nothing to do with; while *ir ter com* . . . (literally to-go to-have with . . .) signifies to go to a place in order to have a meeting with another person. It is a considerable achievement for a language to be able to express so complicated an idea in three words, each of one syllable. Examination of this and other stereotyped phrases leads to a curious conclusion: there is no doubt that, in Portuguese, as in some other languages, people say and write things which often seem illogical when we try to think out the grammatical construction. What is important, however, is not to attend to the words separately but to listen to the whole phrase. The speaker did not invent it; he found it ready-made to express certain true and common ideas, and used it because it saved him from having to invent something for himself.

5

Another important side of the Portuguese language is that of prefixes and suffixes. A syllable prefixed to a word generally adds a qualifying idea, like our vision and prevision (*visão e previsão*), or *lembrar*, remember, and *relembrar* remind. With the addition of a suffix, the meaning is conveyed with greater energy, and feelings of love, aversion or ridicule, are reflected perfectly in some of the Portuguese suffixes. *Comboio* (cf. our 'convoy') is a train, but *comboizinho* is not necessarily a little train, as the diminutive suffix might lead us to expect, but rather a train we know and like. *Homenzinho* is a little man; but the suffix gives a rather contemptuous tone, implying moral or intellectual littleness as well. Sr. Rodrigues Lapa takes the word *livro* book, and shows how suffixes can alter what we think of it. *Livrinho* is not necessarily a little book, but a favourite one; *livrito* is a little book, but of light reading ; *livreco* is a bad book, disliked or despised; *livrório*, a big book, but ugly and of little value. The word *livralhada* contains three units of meaning:

book *plus* bad book *plus* many books, i.e. a heap of books of
little value. *Livresco* is bookish, as *fradesco* is monkish. There are
many other Portuguese suffixes, for those who are born to the
language.

Among the grammatical pecularities of Portuguese [17] is the
future with a pronoun in the middle (*far-lo-ei*, 'to do it I have'
for 'I shall do it'), and the infinitive with a personal pronoun
added to it, as a suffix, in the Spanish manner. The breaking
up of the future tense is a survival from past times, from a
condition formerly common in Spanish, Catalan and Provençal.
But although they say *ver-me-ia*, 'I should see myself', with a
negative at the beginning they would say *nao me vería*, 'Not myself should I see'. Unlike Spanish, Portuguese cannot begin a
sentence with an unaccented pronoun. Spanish says *lo veo* for
'I see it', Portuguese *vejo-o*; but with a negative in front, 'I do
not see it' is *Não o vejo* (Not it do-I-see). In sentences beginning
with a personal pronoun there is some hesitation between 'I am
reading them', *eu lhos leio*, and 'She thinks she is happy' *ela
julgar-se-ha feliz* (She to-judge-herself-has happy). This should
be compared with 'You will do it' *tu o farás*, and 'I shall find
them' *eu as acharei*. In popular and country language there is
something very like it: 'You will take yourself off?' *Tu irás-te
embora*? for 'Are you going?' or 'Must you go?'

The 'personal' or 'inflected' infinitive has given rise to much
discussion. One idea is that it is the Latin imperfect subjunctive,
which, though not preserved as such in any neo-Latin language,
except Sardinian, is found in the barbarous lawyers' Latin of
medieval scribes. It is used in legal documents of 1004 and 1018
in much the same way as the modern Portuguese personal infinitive; and in modern speech this is used instinctively and correctly by quite unlettered persons. There is something like it in
Hungarian – an 'agglutinative' language, unrelated either to
Portuguese or Latin – where the infinitive, like any other sub-
stantive, can be inflected according to the person, and the
'vowel-harmony', in the suffix must repeat and echo a vowel
in the word itself. But the subject is complicated and would
need a great many carefully chosen examples for illustration:
all that can be said here is that it enables Portuguese to express
delicate shades of meaning, only possible in other languages
with much circumlocution.

None of the oversea varieties of Portuguese has attained the development and importance of that which is spoken in Brazil, with its population of 53 millions (according to the 1952 census) for whom Portuguese is the official language, whether they all actually speak it or not. Brazil is the largest country on the American continent and represents wider interests (particularly in commerce) than Portugal in Europe, and also has a considerable literature, with excellent novels and original modern poetry. Brazilian Portuguese seems less startling in Portugal than 'rich, twanging American' (Hemingway called it) to some ears in Europe; but it has its differences in pronunciation and shades of meaning, and an enormous vocabulary such that many Brazilians think it should be called *lingua brasileira*, and not *lingua portuguesa do Brasil*. Its morphology, however, remains the same, though it has types of syntax and word-order unknown in Portugal; while other peculiarities are descended from those of the late medieval language spoken by the first colonists.

In Portugal itself there are four clearly-marked provincial varieties of pronunciation and usage: Minhoto (Minho), Transmontana (Tras-os-Montes), Alentejano and Algarvio. There is also Portuguese, with local peculiarities, in Ceylon and Macau; Java, Timor, Malacca and Singapore. In India, Goa has developed special peculiarities; Portuguese is the official 'second language', the predominant speech being Konkani. In Damão, Portuguese has been influenced by the surrounding Gujerati. The islands of Madeira and the Azores, have special pronunciations. On landing on the latter, the traveller is sometimes asked an ancient and childish riddle: What is the animal which has four paws and a half? *Qual e o animale que taim quatro patas e meia?* It's the cat. *É o gato.* And why? *É por que?* Because the cat has four paws, and mews. *Porque o gato taim quatro patas, e mia.* The point is that an accented I in that position is pronounced in the Azores EI.

In gender, one of the characteristics of the Portuguese vocabulary which most clearly distinguish it from other languages is the constant preoccupation with sex. It is natural that animated beings should be divided according to sex, e.g. *cão* dog, *cadela* bitch, with the necessary morphological distinction. But what is more curious is that the same tendency should be seen in objects with no sex. Along with the masculine, Portuguese has

created feminine forms for a large number of familiar words,
e.g. *saco* and *saca*, bag; *poço* and *poça*, well; *barco* and *barca*, boat;
cesto and *cesta*, basket. Comparing these parallel forms, Rodrigues Lapa finds that as a general rule the masculine represents
something bigger or longer, the feminine something broader.
The Portuguese, he says, are inclined to see things in the images
of men and women; the man, stronger, taller and slimmer, the
woman shorter and broader, with more curves and round-
nesses. In this comparison between male and female, reflected
in their own affairs, it is possible to read one of the fundamental
characters of Portuguese civilisation which depends, both in the
house and working on the land, on the joint effort of both men
and women.

The main factor in the development of Portuguese was
neither Celtic nor Germanic, but the Latin language itself: not
Ciceronian, artificially rhetorical Latin, but the familiar Latin
which is sometimes found even in the letters of Cicero, and
went on being spoken in daily conversation all through the
classical period. From this language, which was alive and came
naturally to anyone who spoke it, Roman culture created the
artistic, literary language that seems to us now as if it had been
chiselled and carved in stone. During all the centuries which
the Roman Empire lasted, the language preserved an apparent
fixity. But though sometimes partly visible, its evolution went
on: the immobility of its outward form concealed a radical
change in its internal structure; and when the ruin of the Empire came and its civilisation fell, the results were soon apparent
in the language. If we add to this the consideration that Gallæcia and Lusitania were remote rural districts, we shall be on
the way to discovering how the change took place.

It has been urged that Portuguese is a 'countrified' language,
because it has preserved primitive forms and keeps close to
things of the earth. But so, too, was Latin: a countrified language. The classical Latin vocabulary is full of country words;
and the Romans themselves knew it. Cicero explained that
PECUNIA, 'money', came from flocks and herds. Pliny said that
to 'prevaricate' meant originally to plough a crooked furrow.
Words which afterwards came to have a general sense appear
at an ancient date with a specialised meaning to do with cultivation or pasture. AGER was a ploughed field before it meant

territory; AGERE was originally to lead a flock, FERRE was to 'bear' in the sense that a tree bears fruit; it was connected with 'fer-tile'. A good crop was said to be 'glad' LAETUS, but the word was thought to be connected with LAETAMEN, 'manure'; PULCHER, 'beautiful' referred originally to *l'embonpoint de l'animal*: fat stock. The tribulations of life were called so from the blows of the flail (TRIBULUM) in threshing. Rivalries were the contests of peasants living on the river-banks (RIVALES) of the same irrigating stream (RIVUS). A FORUM was originally the back yard of a house or even a lean-to shed. Even the words to do with the practice of writing are of country origin. Not only the words and phrases, but the look and sound of the language are evidence of primitive, peasant mentality.

One of the signs of the country mind, though it can distinguish between things precisely enough, is a certain slowness in giving expression to different shades of thought. The calm, monotonous existence in which few things happen unexpectedly, the rarity of new impressions or meetings with fresh people, the habit of only talking to people interested in the same things and understanding the thing half said and the sentence half-finished; all this leads a man to spare effort in his search for the right word to express his thought and to pronounce it clearly when he has found it. It has been called AGRESTIS VERBORUM IMPERITIA: a country slowness with words; but the very phrase betrays the verbal facility of a town-dweller, conscious of the tradition of his language. The moderation and economy of classical expression were largely the peasant tradition.[18] Neither of Portuguese nor of Spanish could it be said that they suffered from PATRII SERMONIS EGESTAS: the poverty of native speech; but while Spanish had from the beginning a dramatic, ringing quality and an IMPERATORIA BREVITAS to which the verbal facility of town-dwellers added a quantity of expressions generated by centuries of oratory, Portuguese, with its allusiveness, its unclear articulation and its infinitely subtle shades, has inherited more of the peasant tradition of Ancient Rome.

NOTES TO CHAPTER 12

[1] Vincenzo Spinelli, *A língua portuguesa nos seus aspectos melódico e rítmico* (1946).

[2] A Swedish scholar claims the number of Portuguese diphthongs to be even higher; Styrbjörn Lindstrand, 'Os 86 ditongos do português culto', in *Rev. de Portugal*, Sér. A, II, 145 (1943).

[3] F. da Silveira Bueno, *A Formação Histórica da Língua Portuguesa* (Rio de Janeiro, 1955). The influence of the Celtic substratum during the Romanization of Lusitania may also be responsible for the transformation of the diphthongs AI and AU into EI and OU. These are important for the characteristic tone-colour which they give to Portuguese; and it may be due to these phonetic influences from Celtic that Portuguese approximates to French and is separated from Spanish and Catalan (pp. 24–25).

[4] Henry Sweet, 'Spoken Portuguese', in *Transactions of the Philological Society*, 1882–1884, p. 220, found the intonation of Portuguese to be more marked even than that of English. *Coração* (heart) has a falling tone. This, when the word is isolated, begins on the first syllable, the voice gliding evenly down through all three. An English ear, accustomed to a fresh rise or fall on the emphatic syllable of a word, is apt to imagine that such a word as *coração* is stressed on the first syllable, whereas the first syllable is not stressed but spoken at a higher pitch.

[5] M. de Unamuno, *Por tierras de Portugal y de España*: *saudade* longing, *soturno* saturnine, *luar* moonlight, *nevoeiro* mist, *magos* pain, *noivado* betrothal . . . 'words the soul of which is untranslatable'.

[6] Valery Larbaud, 'Divertissement philologique', *Œuvres complètes*, I, 273–301 (1950).

[7] M. Rodrigues Lapa, *Estilística da língua portuguesa* (1945).

[8] *Canta tuas palmas, famosos canta triumphos*, the first verse of eleven quoted by Duarte Nunes de Leão (d. 1608), *Origem da Língua Portuguesa*, cap. XXV.

[9] C. M. Vasconcellos, *Lições de Filologia Portuguesa* (1946), 222.

[10] Such are *camisa* shirt, *saio* and *saia* skirt, *cabana* hut, *cerveja* beer, *légua* league, *carro* cart or waggon, *carpinteiro* carpenter, *brio* liveliness, *vassalo* vassal, *parra* trellis, *camino* road, *gato* cat, *calandra* lark, *lança* lance.

[11] Others are: *chão* (level) PLANU(M), *chaga* (wound) PLAGA, *chegar* (arrive) PLICARE, *chopo* (poplar) plopu- POPULU(M), *chorar* (weep) PLORARE, *chumbo* (lead) PLUMBU(M), *chuva* (rain) PLUVIA; and also *chama* (flame) FLAMMA, *cheiro* (smell) FLAGRARE, *achar* (find) AFFLARE, *inchar* (swell) INFLARE. *Chave* (key) is the Latin CLAVI(s), but *Chaves* – the place in the far north where there is a Roman bridge – is the last two syllables of AQUAE FLAVIAE.

[12] *Caruma, sama, branza, bicos, picos* . . .

[13] *açafate, açafatinho, alcofa* (Arabic); *cabaz* (for fruit), *cabazada* basketful, *cesto, cesta* (for olives, sardines, seeds or for marketing), *cestinho* (eggs), *cacifo*, *canastra* (fish or bread) *canastrinha* (bread), *roca* (fruit), *teiga* (with lid), *zote* (for river-fish).

[14] S. R. Dalgado, *Portuguese Vocables in Asiatic Languages*. Translated . . . with notes, additions and comments by A. X. Soares (Baroda, 1936).

[15] *History in English words*. 2 ed. (1954), 68.

[16] *Cadeira* chair, and *cátedra* professorial chair; *solteiro* bachelor, and *solitario* solitary; *meigo* affectionate, and *mágico* magic.

[17] Holgar Sten, *Les particularités de la langue portugaise* (Copenhagen, 1944). A clear and up-to-date account.

[18] J. Marouzeau, *Quelques aspects de la formation du Latin littéraire* (1949), 8 ff.

PORTUGAL

0 50 100
Miles

◎Corunna

Santiago
de Compostela

Cape Finisterre

GALICIA

◎Astorga

Vigo◎

Tuy◎ *R. Minho*

Valença◎

R. Lima

Chaves◎ Braganza◎

Braga◎ **TRAS OS MONTES**

R. Tamega Miranda◎

Guimarães◎

OPORTO◎

R. Douro

Ciudad
Rodrigo◎

Aveiro◎ *R. Vouga*

Guarda◎

Bussaco◎ *R. Mondego*

B E I R A

Figueira da Foz◎ Coimbra◎

R. Zezere

Leiria◎

Batalha◎ Tomar◎ Alcántara◎

Alcobaça◎ Cáceres◎

R. Tagus

Torres Vedras◎ Santarem◎

Mérida◎

Elvas◎

Cintra◎ **LISBON**◎ Badajoz◎

Cascais◎ Évora◎ Olivença◎

Almada◎

Setubal◎ Alcácer
do Sal◎

A L E N T E J O

R. Guadiana

Moura◎

Beja◎ Serpa◎

Sines◎

Aljustrel◎

Mértola◎

SEVILLE◎

ALGARVE

Huelva◎

Cape St.Vincent◎ Lagos◎

Sagres◎ Faro◎

A T L A N T I C   O C E A N

E S T R E M A D U R A

M I N H O

S   P   A   I   N

37° *Latitude North*

9° *Longitude West of Greenwich* 7°

The Drawing Office ~ St.Albans.

Index

Abdu'r-Rahmán III, 47
Abrabanel, Isaac, 155
Admiral, 102, 103
adscripti glebae, 37, 63
Æneid, The, 140
Afonso Henriques, ix, 58, 62, 67, 81, 86, 95, 104, 105, 118
Afonso II, 49, 92, 100
Afonso III, 64, 92, 100, 101, 114
Afonso IV, 118, 130
Afonso V, 114, 126, 127
Alans, 23, 24
Albuquerque, x, 137, 138
Alcázar Quibir, 153, 154, 158
Alcobaça, 80 ff., 89, 91, 94, 106, 114
Alentejo, 17, 35, 64, 69, 77, 121, 148, 207
Alfaiates, 71–74
Alfama, 51
Alfonso III (Castille), 57
Alfonso VI, 58, 63
Alfonso X, el Sabio, 32
Alfonso XI, 119
Alfred, Laws of King, 33, 40
Algarve, 17, 64, 90, 92, 148, 153, 207
Al-Himyárí, 48, 49
Aljubarrota, xi, 122–124, 126, 127, 152
Alliance, The English, 116 (*see also* Treaty)
Almada, 51, 58, 89, 197
Al-Maqqarí, 54
Almeida, Francisco de, 136, 137
Almeida Garrett, 140, 173, 177, 178, 179
Almohades, 59
Almorávides, 59, 72
Alorna, Marquês de, 170

Amsterdam, 148
'Ancient Treaties', The, 184
Andeiro, Conde de, 120 ff.
Anglo-German Convention, 183, 184
Anglo-Portuguese Declaration, 184
Angola, 180, 181, 184
Antwerp, 132, 135, 145
Appian, 18
Arabs, 42, 43, 203 (*see also* Moslems)
Aragon, 119, 128, 155
Arala Pinto, A., 22, 112, 113
Arian heresy, 26, 29, 31
Arrábida, 51
Arras, 85
Astorga, 19, 20, 25
Asturias, 24, 44, 45, 55, 65, 66, 81
Atouguia, 94; Conde de, 169
Augustus, Era of, 25
Aveiro, Duque de, 159
Avila, 68
Avis, House of, 128; Master of (*see also* John I)
Azamor (Morocco), 153
Azeitão, 51
Azevedo, Lúcio de, 156, 157, 168
Azores, 133, 180, 187, 207
Azurara, 131

Baetica, 25, 30
Balfour, Arthur, 183, 184
Ballads, 140, 141
Balsemão, Visigothic Church at, 37
Bandarra, 155
Barcelona, 99, 108

Barros, João de, 150
barristas, 54
Batalha, 151, 152
Batista i Roca, J. M., 39
Baynes, Norman, 39, 40
Beckford, William, 81, 84
Behaim, Martin, 133
Belém, 40, 55, 151, 153
Bell, A. F. G., 151
Benedictine Order, 82
Berbers, 42, 82
Beresford, General, 175
Berlin, Congress of, 180, 182
Bernard, St., 87
Bertie, Sir Francis (Lord), 183
Bishop, penalties permitted to a, 37
Biscay (Basque Provinces), 14, 88
Black Death, 114, 125
Bojador, Cape, 133
Bombay, 164
Bormanicus (god), 16
Bosch Gimpera, P., 22
Boxer, C. R., 136, 139, 174
Braccari, 19
Braga, 19, 20, 25–27, 66
Braganza, Catharine of, 164 (see also John IV, V)
Braudel, F., 144, 148, 157
Brazil, 135, 141, 161, 162, 169, 171, 175, 177, 179, 181, 207
Briteiros, Castro de, 16
Brotero, 170
Bruges, 89, 95, 132, 142
Buçaco (Bussaco), 108, 175
Byron, 105
Byzantine, 31, 33, 42 (see also Greek)

Cabral, Pedro Alvarez, 135, 136
Cáceres, 19
Calicut, 87, 136, 137
Callaecia, see Gallaecia
Cambridge, 200
Caminha, 93
Camoens, x, xi, 55, 111, 118, 137, 148, 151, 199
Canary Islands, 131

Canning, 180
Cape Verde Islands, 133
Capelas Imperfeitas, 152, 153
Capelo, 180
Carlos I, 182, 185
Caro Baroja, J., 22, 55
Carthaginians, 37
Carvalho, J. de, 22, 194
Castel Bom, 71, 73, 74
Castel Melhor, 71
Castel Rodrigo, 71
Castilian Plain, 14
Castilians, Castille, 14, 21, 88, 102, 103, 118, 119, 122, 126, 127, 159
Castro, Américo, 56, 59, 74, 76
Castro, Eugénio de, 118
Castro, Inêz de, 118
Castro Daire, 16, 107
Castro Marim, 20
Castro de Sabroso, 16
Castros, 15, 16, 17, 28, 50, 64
Catalans, Catalonia, 14, 29, 128, 130, 159, 160, 206
Celtic peoples, 17, 18, 155, 202
Centaurs, 14
Ceuta, 94, 131, 133
Ceylon, 207
Chaimite, 185
Chamberlain, Joseph, 180, 183, 184
Charles II (Stewart), 164
Chaves, 21, 27
Cheke, Sir Marcus, 165, 173
Childe, V. Gordon, 22
Christ, Order of, 102, 152
Cid, The, 63
Cintra, see Sintra
Cistercians, 82, 85
Citânia de Briteiros, 16
Citânias, 15
Chronica Pacensis, 45
Cleynaerts (Clenardo), 147
Cochin, 136
Coimbra, 16, 20, 23, 27, 28, 50, 51, 57, 62, 67, 69, 74, 85, 89, 91, 95, 99, 150, 151, 169, 170, 178, 187, 199

Columbus, 136
Communal ownership, 79
Concubinage, 34
Condeixa-a-Velha, 20
Conferências do Casino, 178
Conimbriga, 6, 23
Congo, River, 133
Convention of Sintra, 175
Conventûs, 20
Copts, 42
Córdoba, 32, 43, 55
Côrtes, 101, 114, 182
Cortesão, Jaime, 22, 88, 93, 96, 112, 131, 136, 142
Costa, Afonso, 186
Costa, João da, 151
Costa Cabral, 176, 179
Counter-Reformation, 148
Cresques (Crescas), 133
Cristianismo Social, 189
Cromwell, 163
Cunha, Anastasio da, 169, 170

Damão, 180, 207
Dão, River, 166, 187
David, Pierre, 39, 41, 75
Delagoa Bay, see also Lourenço Marques
Denis (Dinis), King, 79, 83, 90, 94, 98 ff., 114
Desonci, 19
Despoblado, 65
Dias, Bartolomeu, 133, 135
Diu, 137, 180
Dionysius Exiguus, 25
Divorce, recognition of, 34
Dominican Order, 190
Douro, passim
Duarte, 128
Durbedicus (god), 16
Dutch, The, 158

Earthquake, Lisbon, 170
Eça de Queiroz, J. M., 178
Eckardstein, H., Frh. von, 183
Edward I (England), 101
Edward II, 102
Edward III, 117

Edward VII, 182, 183
'Effective Occupation', 180, 184
Egica, 27
Encoberto, El, 155
Endovelicus (god), 16
Entre-Douro-e-Minho, 101
Era, The Spanish, 25
Erasmus, 150, 151
Eulogius, 46
Euric, 29, 32, 35, 36
Evora, 21, 48, 68, 69, 72, 86

Fairs, 85 ff.
Familia Ecclesiae, 37
Faro, 24, 64
Fátima, 190
Ferdinand (Aragon), 126, 127
Ferdinand I (Castille), 48, 89
Ferdinand I (Portugal), 103, 117
Ferdinand III (Castille), 32
Ferdinand, El príncipe constante, 135
Fernão Lopes, 113, 118, 124
Ferreira, António, 118
Ferreira do Castro, 113
Finisterre (Galicia), 88
Fisheries, 87 ff.
Flanders, 58, 71, 85–88, 90, 92, 102–104, 144, 146
Folk-right, 31
Fontes Pereira de Melo, 176
Foral, 66 ff.
Foro, 31, 33, 66, 68, 71 ff.
Forum Judicum, 32, 33
Francis of Assisi, St., 141, 142
Franks, 35
Fructuoso, St., 37
Fuero, 31
Fuero Juzgo, 32
Fugger, House of, 132

Gago Coutinho, Admiral, x
Gaia (Vila Nova de), 28, 29
Galba, 19
Galicia, 20, 24, 43, 51, 55, 59, 86
Gallaecia, 20, 24, 25, 27, 29
Galleys, 102

Gama, Vasco da, 104, 144, 135, 137, 143, 144, 148
Gama Barros, 63, 65, 74, 97, 122, 128, 129
Ganshof, François-L., 132
Garrett, see Almeida Garrett
Gaunt, John of, ix, 119, 122, 125, 128
Genoa, 130, 132
Goa, x, 138, 139, 145, 180, 207
God, Judgment of, 35
Goes, Damião de, 145, 147, 151
Gonçalves, Nuno, 87
González de Clavijo, 131
Good Hope, Cape of, 133, 135
Gouveia, Andre de, 151
Granada, 43, 48, 49, 86, 119
Greek, 26, 29, 30, 31
Grey of Falloden, Viscount, 183
Guadiana (river), 14, 17, 19, 21, 65
Guarda, 86
Guedes, Marques, 186, 194
Guerra Junqueiro, 107, 113, 184, 191
Guimarães, 16, 85, 86, 116, 122, 128
Guinea, 144, 184
Guizot, 32
Gujerati, 207
Gungunhana, 185

Hannibal, 17
Hapsburgs, 13
Hatzfeldt, Count, 183
Hebreo, León, 155
Henriques, Afonso, see also Afonso Henriques
Henry of Burgundy, 58, 203
Henry the Navigator, x, 102, 128, 132, 135, 177, 178
Henry of Trastamara, 118, 119, 122
Henry IV (Castille), 126
Herculano, 43, 45, 75, 177, 179
História Trágico-Marítima, 139–141, 148
Holanda, Francisco de, 151

Homer, 150, 151
Homicide, penalty for, 69
Honorius, Emperor, 24, 25
Horse-shoe arch, 55
Huguenots, 148
Hydatius (Idacio), 24, 25, 27

Iberians, 17
Iceland, 34
Idacio, see Hydatius
Idanha, 27, 28
Idrísí, 48–51, 53, 93, 94
Ilha Encoberta, A, 156, 157
Ilurbeda (god), 16
Ine, Laws of King, 33, 40
Inquirições, 100, 101
Inquisition, 147, 151, 157, 162, 168, 169
Isabel of Castille, 'La Católica', 126
Isabel, St., 'a Raihna Santa', 90, 98
Isidore of Beja, 44
Ivens, 180

James, M. R., 38
Java, 207
Jerome, St., 25
Jerónimos (Belém), 151
Jews, 30, 31, 40, 42, 43, 45, 59, 84, 86, 95, 101, 102, 135, 147, 148, 160, 162, 169
João das Regras, 120
John I, 25, 101, 117, 119 ff., 128, 144, 159 see also Avis, Master of
John II, 114, 133, 150, 157
John III, 144, 147, 151
John IV, 158 ff., 164
John V, 158, 169
José I, 158
Juan I (Castille), 119, 120 ff.
Juan II, 126
Juana, 'La Beltraneja', 127
Julius Caesar, 23, 24

Kendrick, Sir Thomas, 174
King's College Chapel, 153

King's Law, 32
Kitchener, Lord, 186
Konkani, 139, 207

Labra, Rafael, 165
Lamego, 27, 85, 86, 107
Lapithae, 14
Larache, 154
La Rochelle, 90, 103
Las Siete Partidas, 32
Lauridosa, 60
League of Nations, 186
Leiria, 89, 94, 104, 105, 108
León, 21, 24, 58, 59, 67, 87
León, Luis de, 54, 55
Leonor Teles, 117, 120 ff.
Lethe, 19
Levantines, 43
Lex Romana Visigothorum, 32, 33
Liber Forum Judicum, 32
Lille, 85
Limia (River), 19
Lis (River), 65
Lisbon, passim
Livermore, H. V., x
Livy, 19
Lopes, Vieira, Afonso, 110, 111
Lorvão, 53, 63
Los Atoleiros, 122
Louis XIV, 64
Lourenço Marques, 181, 182, 184
Lucretius, 150
Lugo, 20, 65
Lusíadas, Os, 140, 148, 150, 200
Lusitania, 18, 20, 21, 24, 25, 29, 42, 43, 140, 201
Lusitanians, 17–19, 27, 201

Macau, 180, 207
Macedo, Jorge de, 168, 172
Magalhães, Sebastian de, 65
Malacca, 87, 138, 207
Malagrida, P., 168
malagueta, 135, 144
Malakite Law, 45
Mansilha, Fr. João de, 166
Manuel I, 94, 106

Manuel II, 185
Manuel, Reinaldo, 171
Manueline architecture, 151–153
Mar Tenebroso, 141
maravedís, 72, 73
Marco Polo, 142
Maria I, 158
Maria da Fonte, 176
Marine insurance, 103
Mariner's compass, 134
Martin of Braga, St., 26
Masséna, 109, 122
Matabeleland, 181, 182
Maynard, Mr., 163, 174, 167
Melgaço, 70, 71, 86
Melinde, 137
Mendez Pinto, 138, 140
Mérida, 19, 20, 27, 30, 37
Mértola, 19, 31, 36, 49, 55
Meseta, 77
Messianism, 155–157
Methuen Treaty, 164 ff., 172
Miguel, Dom, 179
Minho (river), 14, 51, 55, 70, 86, 93, 196; (province), 79
'Miramolin', 82
Miranda do Douro, 85
Mombasa, 137
Mondego (river), 51, 57, 95
Montemôr-Novo, 122
Montemôr-o-Velho, 51, 95
Montesquieu, 32, 40
'Moors', 49, 65, 86, 109, 135, 154
Morabitinos, see maravedís
Moriscos, 148, 162
Morocco, x, 42, 59, 82, 86, 131
Moslems, 31–33, 42 ff., 55, 59 ff., 64, 65, 84, 87, 88, 101, 102, 105, 130, 203
Moura, 100
Mousinho de Albuquerque, x, 184, 185
Mousinho da Silveira, 175–178
Mozambique, x, 179–181, 184
Mozárabes, 42, 44 ff., 57, 59 ff., 77, 86, 95
Mozárabic bishop, 58

Mozárabic liturgy, 41
Mudéjares, 77
Músá ibn Nusair, 53
Mutilation, 37

Nacimento, see Presépio
Napoleonic War, *see* Peninsular War
National Anthem, 184
Nau Catrineta, 141
Nazaré, 28, 94
'New Christians', 155, 174
Newman, Cardinal, 30
nora, 55
Norway, 14, 34
Nova, João de, 135
Nowell, C. E., x
Nun'Alvares Pereira, The Constable, 120 ff., 160
Nunes (Nonnius), Pedro, 151

Óbidos, 94
Olivares, x, 158, 161
Oliveira, Cavaleiro de, 168, 174
Oliveira, Fernão, 203
Oliveira Martins, J. P., 57, 74, 87, 96, 125, 144, 155, 193, 195
Oliveira Salazar, Dr., 186 ff.
Oporto, *passim*
Ordeal by fire and water, 33, 34, 41
Ordenações Alfonsinas, 73
Orense, 58
Ormuz, 137, 138
Orosius, 18
Osbern, 49, 58
Ourique, 105

Padrón, 51
Pais, Alvaro, 117, 120 ff., 125
Palencia, 71
Palmela, Duques de, 58, 179
Palmerston, 167, 179, 180
Paternity, disputed, 34
Peçanha, Manuel, 103
Pedro I, 118
Peniche, 94, 185
Peninsular War, 175, 176

Pepys, 164
Pereira, Duarte Pacheco, 136
Pericot, L., 22
Persians, 42
Peter the Cruel (Castille), 117, 119
Philip II (Spain), x, 13, 127, 154, 155, 158, 160
Philip III, 93, 127, 148, 158
Philip IV, 93, 127, 158
Philippa of Lancaster, ix, x, 119, 128
Phoenicians, 17
Pinhal do Rei, O, 98 ff.
Place-names, 51, 52
Pliny, 23
Politian, 150
Pombal, x, 84, 147, 156, 163, 165, 167 ff., 175
Ponte de Lima, 85, 93
Praça do Comércio, 170
Presépios, 54, 56, 108
Prester John, 133
Presúria, 78
Priests, illegitimate children of, 34
Príncipe (Island), 184
Pronunciamento, 30
Pseudo-Isidore, 44
Punic traders, 17; wars, 17

Rabelais, 91
Rape, penalty for, 69
Rau, Virgínia, 96, 97, 128
Ravenna, 105
Republic, 185 ff.
Reccared, 31
Reccesvinth, 27
Rechiar, 25
Renan, 141
Renascença Portuguesa, 186
Resende, Andrea de, 151
Residencia de Estudiantes, 55
Restelo, Old Man of, 148–149
Rhodes, Cecil, 180–182, 184
Rhodesia, 181, 183
'Ribeirinha, La' (Maria Pais Ribeiro), 99

Richard II (England), 120, 125
Rio de Oro, 133
Ripuarian Laws, 32, 33
Rodrigues Lapa, M., 117, 129, 203, 210
Roman Law, 32
Roman Provinces, 20, 21
Roman Roads, 19, 20
Romans, 13, 17, 18, 49
Rothschild, Alfred, 183
Runaway slaves, 33
Rupert, Prince, as pirate, 163
Russell, P. E., 37, 103, 117, 123

Sá de Bandeira, 179
Sá de Miranda, 150, 151
Sacadura Cabral, x
Sado (river), 15, 51, 90
Safi, 153
Sagres, 133
St. Vincent, Cape, 53, 75, 133
Salé, 48
Salic Laws, 32, 33
Salisbury, Marquis of, 181–184
Salt, 87, 90
Samorim, The, 136
Sanches, Ribeiro, 168, 174
Sancho I, 48, 88, 94, 99
Sancho II, 49, 86
S. Martinho, 94
S. Pedro de Moel, 110
S. Tomé, 184
Santiago de Compostela, 51, 95
Santiago do Cacém, 51
Santos, Eugénio dos, 171
Santos, Reynaldo dos, 152, 157
Sarum, Use of, 41
Schulten, A., 22
Sebastian, King, x, 146, 153, 159
Sebastianismo, 155–157
Seduction, Law of, 34
Segovia, 71, 86
Selir, 90, 94
Seneca, 26
Serfs, 37, 63
Sérgio, António, 87, 125, 128, 131, 133, 155, 174, 194

Serpa, 100
Serpa Pinto, x, 181, 182, 194
Serra da Estrêla, 108
Sertorius, 21
Setúbal, 89, 90, 92, 152
Seville, 19, 43, 90, 103
Shelley, 105, 110
Silius Italicus, 18
Silves, 43, 51, 59
Simonet, F. J., 56
Sinbad the Sailor, 42
Sines, 104
Singapore, 207
Sintra, 58, 108, 175
Slaves, 61, 62, 64, 86, 134, 135, 162, 169, 179, 180
Soares de Taveiros, 99
Soldevila, F., 22
Sortes Gothicae, 30
Soure, 51
Southampton, 92
Soveral, Marquês de, 182–184, 194
Spanish Succession, War of the, 154
Spices, 143 ff.
Spinoza, 148
Stevens, Thomas, 139
Stockholm, 92
Strabo, 17
Strayed animals, 36
Studium Generale, 99
Stukeley, Sir Thomas, 154
Sudan, 130
Suevi, 23 ff., 49
Sulla, 21
Sweden, 14, 29
Syrians, 30, 42

Tagus (Tejo), passim
Talavera, 21
Támega (river), 80
Tameobrigo (god), 16
Tangier, 154, 164
Távora, Marquês de, 169
Teive, Diogo de, 151
Teixeira, João, 150
Teles, Leonor (Queen), 117

Templars, 102, 152
Teresa (Tareja), Countess (afterwards Queen) 58, 86
Teresa Lourenço (mother of John I), 119
Tetuan, 131
Theotonio, St., 62
Theudemirus, 27
Timor, 183, 185, 207
Toledo, 29, 30, 35, 43, 49, 127
Tomar, 152
Tongoenabicus (god), 16
Toro, 127
Torres Vedras, 122
Trancoso, 108
Transvaal, 182, 184
Trás-os-Montes, 79, 80, 207
Trastamara dynasty (Castille), 13, 117, 119, 126; *and see* Henry of
Treaties, the 'Ancient': Windsor, 116; of 1642, 163, 184; of 1654, 164; of 1661, 184
Trees, protection of, 36, 72
Trevelyan, G. M., 116
Tridiavi, 19
Tunis, 88
Tuy, 20, 51, 58

Ultimatum, 181
Ulysses, 13
Ulyssipona, 13, 19
Unamuno, 191
University, 99, 150, 151, 169, 170, 187–189 (*see also* Coimbra and Studium Generale)

Vaccei, 19
Valença do Minho, 93
Valencia (Spain), 63, 65
Valladolid, 127
Valle-Inclán, 38

Vandals, 23, 34
Van Gogh, 110
Vasconcelos, C. M. de, 74, 140
Vélez de Guevara, 118
Verney, António, 163, 174
Viana do Castelo, 93
Viana, Prince of, 126
Viareggio, 110
Vicente, Gil, 150
Vieira Natividade, J., 84, 96
Vigo, 87
Vikings, 50, 61, 75, 134
Vila do Conde, 94
Vila Formosa, 22
Vila Mendo, 86
Virgil, 18, 54, 55, 71, 96, 153
Viriathus, 18, 19
Viseu, 27, 65, 107
Visigothic architecture, 37; coinage, 39; laws, 29, 30, 31 ff.
Visigoths, 13, 23 ff., 66
Vitae sanctorum patrum emeritensium, 39
Vives, J., 39, 40
Vouga (river), 16, 44, 94
Vouzela, 85
Vulgar Latin, 197

Wales, Prince of, *see* Edward VII
Wallia, 24
Wellington, 175
Wills, 6
Windsor, Treaty of, 116
Wiseman, E. J., 22
Witiza, 31
Wolfram, 187
Wordsworth, 175

Xavier, St. Francis, 138

Zambesi, (river), 181
Zézere, (river), 19

THIS BOOK IS SET
IN ELEVEN POINT BASKERVILLE TYPE
AND PRINTED IN GREAT BRITAIN BY
RICHARD CLAY & COMPANY LIMITED
AT THE CHAUCER PRESS
BUNGAY · SUFFOLK